English Literature in History
1730–80

An Equal, Wide Survey

John Barrell

Hutchinson
London   Melbourne   Sydney   Auckland   Johannesburg

Hutchinson & Co. (Publishers) Ltd

An imprint of the Hutchinson Publishing Group

17–21 Conway Street, London WIP 6JD

Hutchinson Group (Australia) Pty Ltd
30–32 Cremorne Street, Richmond South, Victoria 3121
PO Box 151, Broadway, New South Wales 2007

Hutchinson Group (NZ) Ltd
32–34 View Road, PO Box 40–086, Glenfield, Auckland 10

Hutchinson Group (SA) (Pty) Ltd
PO Box 337, Bergvlei 2012, South Africa

First published 1983

Set in Times by TJB Photosetting Limited
South Witham
Lincolnshire

Printed in Great Britain by The Anchor Press Ltd
and bound by Wm Brendon & Son Ltd
both of Tiptree, Essex

British Library Cataloguing in Publication Data

Barrell, John
English literature in history 1730–80.
   1. English literature – History and criticism
   I. Title
   820'.9   PR83

ISBN 0 09 149820 1 cased
      0 09 149821 X paper

For Harriet

Contents

Editor's introduction

'Literature' and 'history' are common names for two obviously related but apparently distinct bodies of human activity. By 'literature' we commonly mean certain kinds of writing, though at different times, and on different occasions, we often use the term variably, over a range from all printed writing, through printed writing of a certain quality, to the important specialized sense of a body of 'imaginative' writing. Further, because of this last sense, we often extend the term 'literature' to include 'imaginative' composition which was not primarily written to be printed but to be spoken or in some other immediate way performed. Thus 'literature' in the important but narrow sense of printed imaginative writing of a certain quality belongs, in fact, to a specific historical period, after the invention of printing, after further specializations, and before the invention of modern media of delivery and performance (especially radio and sound recording). At the same time, however, our thinking about literature, from the experience of that specific period, is commonly extended before and after it, to other related forms of composition.

These shifting meanings of 'literature' bear closely on the question of its actual and presumed relations with 'history'. Moreover, 'history' itself has a significant range of reference. At its broadest it indicates the sum and detail of all human actions. When this is so it must be held that it already includes the making of literature. In practice, however, 'history' is most commonly used to indicate general and specific accounts of such actions, grouped by period and by place. That is 'history' as an account, a narrative, and the writing of history, in this sense, is often reasonably seen as a form of 'literature'. Regularly, however, this element of account or narrative is overridden by the sense that the actions really occurred, at a level independent from their narration. Historical inquiry is often a continuous and detailed comparison of the received accounts or narratives and what can be shown, from other forms of evidence and record, to have actually taken place. Literature, in some respects, seems different from this process of historical inquiry, in that its works appear to have a relatively fixed form.

Any inquiry into the relations between 'literature' and 'history' has at some point, if it is to be adequate, to recognize these variable and shifting senses of the primary indicative terms. In recent years there has been widespread recognition of the inherent complexities of reference and evidence which these considerations emphasize. This is why there has been a move away from previous methods of inquiry, even when many of their results have been noted and respected. What is now felt as most difficult is the simple assumption that there is, on the one hand, a relatively unproblematic body of 'literature', with its own inherent and autonomous qualities, and on the other hand, a body of general and summary knowledge which is, correspondingly, 'history'. For if these two bodies existed, in simple ways, the study of 'literature and history' would be a matter of tracing and illustrating evident connections between them, in ways that illuminated both but altered neither. That assumption produced a good deal of interesting work, of two kinds. The possessors of 'history' illustrated aspects of their material from the literature of the time, going naturally to those works in which the connections were evident, and feeling no need to deal with those works in which such connections seemed to be absent. Meanwhile the possessors of 'literature' looked to history as a 'background', against which, in a foregrounded emphasis, works of literature occurred. It was then mainly when 'background' and 'foreground' evidently connected, in discoverable and explicable ways, that history – parts of the history – became relevant.

Each of these methods was fundamentally selective and partial, and was at its best when this was recognized to be so. Yet paradoxically the confidence of the initial assumptions – the assumed possession of the bodies of 'literature' and 'history' – tended in practice to produce effects of completeness. The 'background' showed all the history that was relevant. The illustrative literature was all the writing of historical significance. Confident accounts of whole periods, extending in secondary work to fully reasoned catalogues of 'a period and its literature' or 'the literature of a period', had an intended and often achieved effect of completeness.

It is of course easier to criticize these conventional methods than to find better practical ways. Yet one result of this new sense of inherent difficulty has been a widespread retreat from the problems. This has been notably assisted by theoretical developments in which the significance of 'history' has been widely questioned and even denied. In some formalist and structuralist tendencies in literary studies the whole effort at correlation has been declared to be *a priori* irrelevant, and much has been made of the undoubted errors of externality and reduction which could be found in previous studies. Yet these errors cannot reasonably be used to justify the much more fundamental error of declaring an arbitrary distance between the acts of writing and other kinds of human action. It has been useful to define actual and variable distances, but to expand and stabilize them as an *a priori* refusal of relationships is merely evasive. However, it is in this more qualified and sceptical environment that new inquiries into such relationships have in practice to be undertaken.

The aim of the present series is to provide a place for essays of an open investigative kind, which do not have from the outset to be committed, or to pretend to be committed, to explanatory completeness. Its emphasis is on literature *in* history: the study of actual works, practices and conditions, in a particular place and period: some 'literary', some 'historical', but never assumed to belong, by definition, to pre-formed bodies of 'literature' and 'history'. Its authors were invited to choose a period of English life, typically but not exclusively of some fifty years, and then within that period (though looking before and after if it was necessary to clarify or complete an argument) to select two or three themes, in which the relations between actual writing and actual historical events and conditions seemed interesting and important. No author was asked to represent these themes as a whole account of the chosen period, though it is obvious that in choosing their themes authors have taken what they believe to be significant elements of that time. The method of inquiry and presentation then adopted has been the author's own choice of a method appropriate to the actual theme or themes.

It is hoped that as the series develops there will be a broad range of such themes and essays, over the whole run of English writing. It is possible that in particular periods there will be more than one book, representing different selections of themes. Moreover, several authors will have seen each other's work, and there will be cross-reference and discussion. A definite area and style of work may in these ways be expected to develop, but it is intended to be distinct from the pre-planned 'coverage' which is the more expected form of such a series. It follows further from this emphasis that the authors are not writing to any brief or line, and that disagreements and reservations may be expected within the series. I believe this to be a condition of serious work of this kind in present circumstances. It may also in any case be its own form of acknowledgement of the genuine diversities of literature in history.

Raymond Williams

Jesus College
Cambridge
1981

Preface

The sage Historic Muse
Should next conduct us thro' the Deeps of Time:
Shew us how Empire grew, declin'd, and fell,
In scatter'd States.

JAMES THOMSON, 'Winter', *The Seasons*, ll. 587–90

Of the various books that might be written in response to an
invitation to discuss the literature and history of the mid eighteenth
century, I have chosen to attempt one which may not, at first sight,
seem appropriate to that invitation at all. I have not focused, for
example, on the history of the economic expansion of Britain, on
the development of agriculture, manufactures, trade and banking,
on related changes in economic and social relations, and on how
these topics are directly represented in poetry, the novel, the
drama and the periodical essay, as those forms of writing began to
engage an expanding audience. I do not have any quarrel with
such an approach, but when I set out to write this book it was with
a different problem in mind, one which defines history in terms
rather different, perhaps, from those set out in the general
introduction to this series. Instead of attempting to write a summary
of one or more aspects of the history of the period as it can be
reconstructed from the late twentieth century, and then attempting
to compare that construction with what we can learn from the
literature, I have tried to ask how some writers of the period
themselves attempted to construct an understanding of contemporary social changes. What was it that most struck *them* about what
was happening in their society, and in what ways did they try to
comprehend what was happening as an historical process ? What
sorts of knowledge did that effort require of them, and from what
perspective, and in what language, could social change be
described?

To the first of these questions, of course, a host of answers
suggests itself – the writers of the mid eighteenth century were
'struck' by, for example, the growth of the population of Britain, by
pauperism, by the rising poor-rates and urban crime, by 'rebellion',
by agricultural depression and innovation, by the ascendancy of
Britain as a mercantile power, and so on. But if such instances of
social, economic, and political change were understood, not simply
as 'change', but as 'history', it was because they were understood,
this book suggests, in terms of a notion of the 'Historic Muse', by
which her primary function was to teach us 'how Empire grew,

declin'd, and fell' – and the answer most often returned to that
question was that Empire grew in states which exhibited a high
degree of internal political unity, and declined in those which fell
prey to internal political division; and that such 'changes' as those
listed above were to be understood, in historical terms, as the
evidence or the result of the political unity or division whose
progress was the primary object of historical inquiry.

Between 1730 and 1780, the unity of Britain was threatened, or
called into question, by two historical events in particular, the
'rebellion' of 1745, and the War of American Independence, both
of which were understood as civil wars by those most anxious to
assert that Scotland and the 'United States' were integral parts of
the commonwealth of Britain. It is not, however, to those events
that I have addressed my attention, though I have sometimes
referred to both of them; and this is not simply because I have
accepted the invitation of the general editor of this series to be
selective, but because a concentration on the challenge to the
unity of Britain offered by those particular events would have been
at the expense of what is a more general issue in the writing of the
period, one which was present to the consciousness and conscience
of writers throughout the century. This issue concerns the increasing
belief that British society was becoming highly differentiated in
terms, particularly, of occupation, and that those whose living
depends on their success in the specific occupation they practise
will tend to place their own interests, or those of that occupation,
before those of Britain as a whole. In terms of this concern, the
most important questions for an historical understanding of change
became these: how could inherited notions of political unity be
adapted so as to represent what seemed to be the increasingly
differentiated society of Britain as a still unified one, and by whom
could its unity be grasped?

In my introduction I have, rather baldly, outlined the various
questions I have raised in this preface and some answers to them,
by reference partly to writers in the various genres of social
philosophy, partly to writers in one of the genres of polite literature,
the periodical essay; and in this my aim has been to indicate a
community of concern among writers we normally study as
'literature', and those we assign to the history of ideas. But that
done, I have been content to remain within the boundaries of
literary studies, and have pursued my theme in some poems, a
couple of novels, and in works on the English language. Here again
I have accepted the invitation to be selective in my choice of the

works I discuss, and have quite deliberately turned my attention from those authors and works which are, in my experience, most popular with, or at least most read by, students of English literature, and for which a good deal of critical literature already exists. Such considerations have led me to refer only occasionally to Swift (all of whose major works had in any case been written by 1730), to Pope and to Fielding, and hardly if at all to Richardson, Sterne, Goldsmith, Sheridan, or to the poems and literary criticism of Johnson. I have preferred to take the opportunity of writing about some works which seem to be of enormous interest, and quite central to an understanding of the theme of this book, but which are not much read by those who do not make a living by studying the literature of the eighteenth century; and I have preferred to write at length about a few such works, rather than more briefly about a larger number.

I would like to thank a number of my colleagues in this college – Norman Bryson, Harriet Guest, Keith Snell, and Tony Tanner – who read the manuscript of this book and commented most helpfully upon it, and Miss Guest in particular for drafting a few paragraphs for me when my argument got stuck; and here too I should acknowledge the valuable advice of the anonymous scholar who wrote a report on the manuscript for Hutchinson, and who pointed out in particular where I seemed to be too single-minded in the pursuit of my theme, and my thanks to Claire L'Enfant for performing the same service. I must thank also Stephen Copley of University College Cardiff, John Higgins of the University of Geneva, Colin MacCabe of the University of Strathclyde, and David Simpson of North Western University, with whom I discussed at length various topics in this book before it was written. Of the influence of those I know only through their writings, I must particularly acknowledge that of J. G. A. Pocock, whose work – as may be already apparent to those who know *The Machiavellian Moment* – was especially valuable to me in helping me to understand how such issues as I discuss in this book were to be approached in terms of an idea of history. Thanks, finally, to Alex Wood, for typing the manuscript, and Les Boyd for helping with the proofs and the index.

John Barrell

King's College,
Cambridge
1982

Introduction: artificers and gentlemen

The division of trades In 1804, Patrick Colquhoun published a table which attempted 'to exhibit a GENERAL VIEW of SOCIETY, and to estimate the NATIONAL INCOME, applicable to each Class of the Community', and with it the table made by Gregory King in 1696, described as 'a Scheme of the INCOME, and EXPENCE, of the several FAMILIES of England; calculated for the Year 1688'.[1]* If they are roughly accurate, a comparison of the tables suggests that in 110 years or so the population of England and Wales increased from about 5.5 million to something near 9.5 million, and the 'national income' had increased from over £43 million to nearly £222 million per annum. But it is not the accuracy of the figures, nor even the remarkable increases they exhibit, that I want to call attention to, though we shall need to bear the latter in mind, but the remarkably much greater fullness of Colquhoun's table when compared with King's 'scheme'. Both classify families according to the rank or occupation of their heads, from 'temporal peers' and 'spiritual lords' down to 'cottagers', 'paupers' and 'vagrants'. In King's scheme the space between is filled by about twenty or so ranks and occupations, and in some of these he seems to make no distinction, for example, between employers of labour and those they employ, or between labourers in agriculture and in the various branches of what we now call 'industry'. Colquhoun begins by basing his table on King's classifications, which however he continually amplifies in order to specify more clearly the variety of the occupations they include, and to these he appends a 'Description of Persons not included in Mr Gregory King's estimate' – manufacturers, for example, 'employing capitals in all branches, wool, cotton, flax, hemp, silk', persons 'engaged in the education of youth', 'in theatrical pursuits', and so on. The number of King's classifications is more than doubled, and many of them greatly

---

* Superior figures refer to the Notes and references on pages 211–24

amplified: the principals in the clothing industry, for example, appear in one classification, but are described as 'persons employing capital as tailors, mantua-makers, milliners, &c. in the manufacture of stuffs into wearing apparel and dresses, including army clothiers'.

But though Colquhoun is much more detailed in his specifications of occupation, in the 'remarks' which accompany his table he still acknowledges its inadequacies: some families cannot easily be listed under one source of income rather than another, for they may have several, and some classifications still remain far too general:

All persons who employ capital in fabricating or finishing for sale or consumption any article *whatever*, are here ranked as *manufacturers*. – Others, who are employed in these various businesses, and must receive wages, are classed as working *artisans, handicrafts, mechanics*, or labourers.

The possible divisions of society, in short, that might be made on the basis of rank, occupation, or source of income, are much more minute than the table can possibly record, for there must be a limit to its detail if it is to reveal at once the diversity of society and of the sources of the national income, and the categories which will enable us to grasp that diversity in terms of a system, a 'general view'. For in addition to presenting, to the 'statesman, the political economist, and the public in general' a view of the 'numerous and intricate ramifications' of society, and thus 'the different sources from whence the national income is derived', Colquhoun is also anxious to make the point that those sources can all be grasped under five '*branches of industry*', '*Land, Manufactures, Fisheries, Foreign Commerce, and Colonial and East India Remittances*':[2] and of these, following his metaphor, all specific occupations are minor branches and twigs. The income of many persons is not immediately derived from those sources, of course, but mediately or immediately, the income of everyone in society, whatever they do, must be. The concept of 'national income' is thus one by which the diversity of English society can be confirmed, and understood in terms of a unifying order.

No doubt among the reasons for the greater specificity of Colquhoun's table is that some of the occupations he lists were pursued by too few people in 1688 to have been worth recording then in a separate classification, but had since grown in importance with the increase in population and of national wealth, and that the tasks to which some individual 'labourers' applied themselves were less various by 1800 than they had been a century before; but such considerations will not be very influential on our understanding of the differences between the two tables when we notice the relative size of the occupational groups listed by King and Colquhoun. The smallest occupational group listed by King, 'merchants and traders by sea', numbers 2000 heads of families, and only two other groups – officers in the army and navy – number less than 10,000; Colquhoun's smallest occupational group is of 'persons keeping houses for lunatics' – only forty heads of household – and another five groups number less than 1000. Clearly, if King was not less aware of the variety of occupations in England and Wales than was Colquhoun, he was less concerned to represent that variety in his table, and this asks to be explained, not least, for our purposes, because it corresponds with what I hope to establish as one of the most salient features of the imaginative literature of the period covered by this book, that much of it is concerned to represent the diversity of English society more fully, perhaps, even than had Chaucer, or Langland, or Jacobean comedy, or indeed than any literature produced before 1700.

This concern, as we shall see, necessitated the introduction of literary genres new to England, among them, the periodical essay, the georgic poem, and the picaresque or comic epic novel offering a 'panoramic' view of society. The explicit aim of many of the periodicals of the early and mid eighteenth century is to represent as wide an 'expanse of life' as possible. *The Spectator* (1711–14), for example, is partly organized around the meetings and conversation of a club comprising the Spectator himself who is a gentleman born to a small hereditary estate, the rents of which enable him to live in London; a country gentleman of the minor aristocracy; a member of the Inner Temple, more interested in literature than in the law; a merchant of the city of London; a retired soldier; a man about town; and a clergyman; and the idea of the club is that its members collectively will have a far wider experience of contemporary English society than could be represented in a periodical imagined as the record of the experience of one man only.[3] Or, to take examples from the works discussed in this book, *The Fleece* (1757), by John Dyer, offers an account of the production of raw wool, its distribution to factories, the various processes by which the finished cloth is produced, and its marketing abroad; *Roderick Random* (1748) by Tobias Smollett, names or represents well over 100 practitioners of different occupations, far more, probably, than any earlier work of imaginative literature in English.

This new concern to represent the diversity of English society in terms of diversity of occupation is shared, of course, by other newly developed genres of writing we do not usually think of as 'literary'. 'What a Bustle', writes Mandeville, in 'A search into the Nature of Society' (1723),

is there to be made in several Parts of the World, before a Fine Scarlet or Crimson Cloth can be produced, what multiplicity of Trades and Artificers must be employ'd! Not only such as are Obvious, as Woolcombers, Spinners, the Weaver, the Clothworker, the Scowrer, the Dier, the Setter, the Drawer and the Packer; but others that are remote and might seem Foreign to it; as the Millwright, the Pewterer and the Chymist, which yet are all necessary as well as a great number of other Handicrafts to have the Tools, Utensils and other Implements belonging to the Trades already Named.

'But', he continues, 'all these things are done at Home'; the dyes must be fetched from abroad – and he goes on to list the variety of voyages necessary to their acquisition.[4] Or, to give a famous example, the first chapter of Adam Smith's treatise on political economy, *The Wealth of Nations* (1776), describes how 'the important business of making a pin is . . . divided into about eighteen distinct operations, which, in some manufactories, are all performed by distinct hands', and in the rhapsodic manner of much of Mandeville, or of Dyer's poem, a page or so later, exclaims,

How many different trades are employed in each branch of the linen and woollen manufactures, from the growers of the flax and the wool, to the bleachers and smoothers of the linen, or to the dyers and dressers of the cloth! . . . The woollen coat, for example, which covers the day-labourer, as coarse and rough as it may appear, is the produce of the joint labour of a great multitude of workmen. The shepherd, the sorter of the wool, the wool-comber or carder, the dyer, the scribbler, the spinner, the weaver, the fuller, the dresser, with many others, must all join their different arts in order to complete even this homely production.

The 'many others' turn out to include merchants, carriers, ship-builders, sailors, sail-makers, rope-makers, the miner, the furnace-builder, timber-seller, brick-maker, bricklayer, millwright, forger and smith.[5]

Changing ideas of social unity The occasion of this concern with the diversity of occupations in society, is complex, not easily discussed in terms of cause and effect, and can anyway be discussed here only in the most general terms. Clearly it has to be understood in the context of the increasing aggregate wealth of Britain, the 'national' income, the extension of trade, the development of more, and of more sophisticated, manufactured goods and means of manufacture and communication, and of a greater efficiency in agriculture. It is related also to changes in the reading-public in the eighteenth century, themselves related to the increasing wealth of the nation – not simply the extension of that public, but its willingness to conceive of English literary culture as a national culture, or as capable of contributing to a supranational, a European culture without necessarily ignoring what was specific about English experience in favour of a delocalized notion of what was universally true about human nature, at all times and everywhere. This conception of English culture as itself a source of national pride was of course related to the increasing awareness of, and pride in, the economic power of the nation, which therefore becomes regarded – though the notion was frequently contested – as a proper topic for representation in writing. Thus there is evidence, throughout the period, of a progressive relaxation of the embarrassment at writing or reading about objects, occupations and people regarded at the start of the century as too 'low', 'minute' or 'mean' to be worthy of literary attention: an embarrassment which is still apparent, for example, in Smith's ironically defensive description of pin-making as an 'important business', but which does not prevent him from writing about it. We can produce relations, too, between all these factors and the general sense by which Britain is understood, in the eighteenth century, to be a democracy, a form of polity which enables and demands consideration of the whole of society, even of its unrepresented, or 'virtually' represented members, if only by way of justifying their exclusion from the franchise.

To such factors as these, however, we should add also a change in the conceptions of how the organization of society could be described – how the various elements that compose a society could be identified, and how they could be represented as sharing a common concern for the unity and stability of that society. By the various traditions of political thought inherited from the seventeenth century, the unity of society was often understood as requiring to be produced out of, and in spite of, the conflict of the various particular interests within it, and in such a conception of politics, the different passions, the different goals, the different interests of men were perceived as evidence of the instability of human nature and thus as a threat to a unified and stable society capable of enduring through time. The art of government was therefore to be entrusted to those who could claim the public virtue of disinterestedness – who they were, we shall see later; and their task was to regulate or subdue that variety of contrary passions and interests. If, in such conceptions of social organization, particular interests were acknowledged, it was because they could not be ignored if the state was to survive; and to survive it must regulate them as best it could, by a strong central authority, by the persuasive example of men of public virtue, or by a form of constitution which allowed for the representation of competing interests primarily as they might be harnessed in such a way as to limit each others' influence.

This conception of the state never disappears in the eighteenth century; but upon it is grafted another notion of social coherence by which the passions, the interests, the competing elements that compose a society could be understood also in a more positive way. We can think of this as an economic idea of society, in which its health is measured largely by its aggregate wealth: the appetite for luxury provides employment to artisans, merchants and labourers, and so increases the wealth of the nation, whose health is seen as endangered now by economic decline rather than by the corruption of an enervating luxury. The most striking exponent of this argument is Mandeville, in whose writings the 'private vices' of avarice, vanity, envy, prodigality, are represented as 'public benefits', by which the wealth of developed mercantile nations has been so advanced that the poor now live better than the rich could have done in the golden age before the eruption of these vices and passions. In this view, the individual, who is motivated entirely by self-interest, imagines that he works only for himself, but can be represented also as working, unconsciously, or in spite of himself, for the 'common good'.[6] The more thriving is the economy of a nation – the more 'unreal' wants are created, and the more trades they support – the more, paradoxically, can the nation be represented as unified, for the more specialized an individual becomes in what he produces, the more dependent he becomes on the products of others. Thus, if government has anything to do with the regulation of the economy – though such a view of society is likely to give rise to a policy of *laissez-faire* – it should be to encourage the self-interest of the governed, in all its apparently centrifugal variety, not to attempt to persuade them to sacrifice their immediate interests to those of the nation as a whole. For to encourage self-interest is at once to foster the growth of the aggregate wealth of the nation, and to enable the creation of a nation so complex and interdependent that it must develop an indissoluble economic, and therefore also political, unity.

This idea of social coherence does not become especially respectable, even in more cautious versions of it than Mandeville's, until the mid century, for it required that self-interest, and not simply self-preservation, be now approved as necessary to the well-being of a society whose survival had earlier seemed dependent on its success in subduing self-interest to a sense of the interest of the whole. Mandeville offered instead to identify self-interest with the public interest, and not by distinguishing between the 'true' interests of men, which *were* those of society as a whole, and what they mistakenly perceive to be their immediate interest, the gratification of their desires; but by announcing that it was their immediate material interests themselves that served the interests of society at large. This challenge to traditional ideas of virtue, where it is influential on writers after Mandeville, seems to become so only by being reattached by one means or another to the virtues of disinterestedness and stability from which Mandeville had so deliberately exonerated modern society. Thus in Pope's *Essay on Man* (1733–4), for example, we can see a version of an economic account of society at once departing from and being recovered by the political virtues that Mandeville had challenged: 'each individual' is represented by Pope as impelled by his 'ruling passion' to seek 'a sev'ral goal'; the different 'ruling passions' are distributed 'to all *Orders* of men' by a Providence whose concern is with the 'plenitude' of the universe – specifically, here, with the maximum variety of interests necessary to the performance of the world's work – and also with the production of virtue out of happy frailties. Thus though each individual, each order of men, pursues a different, a private interest,

Heav'n forming each on other to depend,
A master, or a servant, or a friend,

Bids each on other for assistance call,
'Till one Man's weakness grows the strength of all.
Wants, frailties, passions, closer still ally
The common int'rest, or endear the tie . . . .

The self-love. of the ruling passion is claimed to become, by the
need of each man to gratify his desires by the co-operation of
others, a 'social' love, and disinterested virtue is built on interested
vanity. And there is still room in the poem for a more reassuringly
traditional notion of social affiliation, whereby the pursuit of true
happiness is perceived only as inimical to the 'blind' pursuit of
material riches, so that while in one passage this pursuit is the
foundation of the unity of society, in another it can only endanger
it.[7] In the essay that follows this introduction, we will see James
Thomson, in *The Seasons*, similarly attracted to aspects of an
economic idea of social coherence, and similarly unwilling to
accept the threat it seems to represent to a notion of 'public virtue'
as properly disinterested, concerned with the good of the whole as
something necessarily opposed to, not built upon, the immediate
apparent good of the individual.

The rehabilitation of self-interest, by the argument, as it is stated
for example by Pope, that it is, by necessity if not by nature, not
merely *co-operative* but *benevolent*, was confirmed by representing it also as *industrious*. For as the pride in and preoccupation
with the growing wealth of Britain increased, so did a sense of the
virtues necessary to support and to continue that power, of which
the most important was recognized as industriousness, to be
enjoined as warmly as possible on the artisan and labourer, and to
be attributed (if possible), as we shall see in the next essay, to the
consumers as well as to the producers of Britain's wealth. It thus
became possible to understand the virtue of industry as necessary
to the pursuit of self-interest, and to represent industry as redemptive,
therefore, of the self-interest by which it was motivated; and
industriousness was thus understood as a stable virtue, which by
stabilizing the volatility of the interested passions could offer, to a
society defined in economic terms, a stability similar to that which
the virtue of disinterestedness had offered to a society where self-
interest had seemed primarily a force for political dissolution. An
economic account, or vindication, of contemporary society was
thus produced, by which public and private virtues could be
identified, and the various members of society could gratify a
private and the public interest in the same act.

A healthy society is now perceived as based on the competing but fundamentally co-operative industry, the 'joint labour', in Smith's phrase, of its members; and by this notion it is the various professional and occupational groups that are cast in the role of separate and opposed interests, while each still pursue different ends yet contribute to the well-being of a nation by contributing to its increasing wealth. There may still sometimes be dispute, of course, about whether all trades can be regarded, by this account, as useful, or whether some – most obviously agriculture – should be approved as necessary, and others disapproved as catering only to the appetite for luxury, and thus as evidence of the corruption of society. But by the end of the century, the awareness of the impossibility of separating, in a complex economy, the 'good' trades from the bad, and the increasingly urgent need to recommend the virtue of a peaceable industriousness to artisans and labourers, to the near exclusion of a consideration of what their industry should be employed upon – such factors as these limit the idea of a society in which good trades only would be admitted, to a concern only of those who are regarded by the pragmatic centre as utopian radicals.

This economic idea of social unity is therefore one by which it becomes increasingly possible to acknowledge and inspect the variety of elements that compose a society, by representing them in the form of occupational variety, and by understanding them therefore as no longer necessarily, or no longer simply, disruptive of social coherence, but capable also of confirming it. Such an economic idea of society is already to be glimpsed in Gregory King's scheme, which is methodized, as far as it is at all, by the computations King makes at the foot of his table, of those who increase and those who diminish the wealth of the nation – though what is intended by those notions is not at all clear: but the more intricate 'ramifications' of Colquhoun's scheme, is an evidence of the greater explanatory power that has accrued to the idea in the course of the period covered by this book.

The invisibility of the social structure More will be said in the next essay about these competing notions of social unity: I want now to point out a more general feature of social philosophy in the period of this book, that the unity it is capable of discovering among apparently opposed individuals or occupational groups is wholly or partly invisible to those individuals or groups themselves. This is the case, for example, in the society described by

Mandeville, in which the vice of luxury is privately pursued by individuals unaware of the result that the employment they mutually create for each other, in their attempts to gratify that vice, produces a coherent and a progressively wealthy society, and unable to see that the avarice they at once practise, and condemn in others, is the basis of all 'public benefits'. The essay by Mandeville I quoted from earlier is directed against Shaftesbury's insistence that the world is governed not, or not primarily, by interest, but by 'natural affection', 'sociableness', a benevolent spirit which enables the members at least of free nations to grasp the common good. But these affections seem to be felt, to a degree sufficient to counterbalance self-interest, only by men 'of thorough good-breeding': the 'mere vulgar of mankind', writes Shaftesbury, 'often stand in need of such a rectifying object as the gallows before their eyes',[8] if they are to be persuaded to sacrifice their private interests to those of the public; so that the gallows they *can* see is for them the embodiment of a public interest invisible to them.

Hume was no less anxious than Shaftesbury to argue against the notion that society is composed of men with 'little regard to any thing beyond themselves': if doctrines such as Mandeville's become generally accepted, 'a free constitution of government must become a scheme perfectly impracticable among mankind, and must degenerate into one universal system of fraud and corruption'.[9] In his *Treatise of Human Nature* (1739–40), he proposes instead 'sympathy' – the 'propensity . . . to sympathize with others, and to receive by communication their inclinations and sentiments' – as a basis of morality and of social unity;[10] but it is not easily determinable, either in the *Treatise* or in Hume's later writings, to what degree sympathy or benevolence is recognized by the majority of men as governing their actions, and not simply *discovered*, by the philosopher himself, to be an influence on their behaviour and on the language in which they describe the behaviour of others; and the same is true of the *Essay on Man*, where the interdependence that Pope represents as 'social love' seems certainly not to be perceived as that by the individual members of the society he describes.

Nor, in Hume's *Treatise*, is it clear that sympathy, whether perceived or not, is adequate to unify the extended and ramified society of a whole nation: it seems rather to explain the nature of 'society' understood in terms of fellowship, immediate acquaintance, a society of friends.[11] The unification of society in the wider sense of the word seems to be treated by Hume as a different problem, to be understood in terms of an account of the nature of government more than of the affections; for though sympathy or generosity may cause men, on occasions, to place the interest of their friends before their own, it does not seem sufficient to persuade them to prefer an abstract notion of the public interest to their immediate private interests, which in an extended society are much more apparent to them. Their selfishness, indeed, which prefers contiguous to remote objects, does lead them also to protect themselves against that infirmity, by appointing magistrates who will oblige them to observe the laws of justice towards each other, and so to prefer their true to their immediate interest. In this way, men can make the observance of the law their present, its violation their remote interest, though they cannot change the 'narrowness of soul, which makes them prefer the present to the remote'. Their magistrates will be similarly infirm, and so must be chosen from those who, 'satisfied with their present condition, and with their part in society, have an immediate interest in every execution of justice, which is so necessary to the upholding of society'; so that it seems that all men in society, the governors and the governed, are left by Hume to pursue their own immediate interest. But for the governed, this will be to observe the law when necessary, to free themselves from its obligations when they can do so with impunity; and for this reason it is 'very difficult, and indeed impossible, that a thousand persons shou'd agree' in 'so complicated a design' as, for example, the draining of an area of wet land; more difficult still for them to combine and execute it, 'while each seeks a pretext to free himself of the trouble and expence, and wou'd lay the whole burden on others.' But

political society easily remedies both these inconveniences. Magistrates find an immediate interest in the interest of any considerable part of their subjects. They need consult [take into consideration] nobody but themselves to form any scheme for the promoting of that interest .... Thus, bridges are built; harbours open'd, ramparts rais'd, canals form'd, fleets equip'd, and armies disciplin'd; every where, by the care of government ....[12]

The magistrates are evidently able to see the value of such 'complicated designs' more clearly than those whose view of the world is more confined, and can arrange the execution of such designs; but they can comprehend more of the organization of society than those whose view is occluded by private interests, only because the interests of the magistrates coincide, whether they recognise it or not, with the interests of society as a whole.

As the organizing principles of the polity are, through the century, increasingly understood as being economic as well as abstractly political, the invisibility of those principles to the majority of its members is particularly emphasized in what becomes an increasingly dominant model of the social structure, notably in the writings of Scottish political economists and social philosophers, the division of labour, understood as a principle operating not simply within specific processes of manufacture but in society as a whole, as the different tasks of producing, processing and distributing consumer goods are divided, in the interest of greater efficiency, among the various members of that society. The economic progress of society is understood as a process of the progressive sub-division of tasks among its members: 'who could anticipate', asks Adam Ferguson in his *Essay on the History of Civil Society* (1767),

or even enumerate, the separate occupations and professions by which the members of any commercial state are distinguished; the variety of devices which are practised in separate cells, and which the artist, attentive to his own affair, has invented, to abridge or to facilitate his separate task? In coming to this mighty end, every generation, compared to its predecessors, may have appeared to be ingenious; compared to its followers, may have appeared to be dull.[13]

Thus, from an original moment of unity in the real or notional past, when each man could himself adequately perform all the tasks necessary to his survival, those tasks, and the abilities necessary to their performance, have become increasingly the separate concern of separate individuals and groups. In 'barbarous societies', writes Smith, the 'varied occupations of every man oblige every man to exert his capacity and to invent expedients for removing difficulties which are continually occurring'; and 'the mind is not suffered to fall into that drowsy stupidity which, in a civilised society, seems to benumb the understanding of almost all the inferior ranks of people'. In such societies every man is a warrior and, 'in some measure', also a 'statesman', who 'can form a tolerable judgment concerning the interest of the society, and the conduct of those who govern it';

In such a society, indeed, no man can well require that improved and refined understanding, which a few men sometimes possess in a more civilised state. Though in a rude society there is a good deal of variety in the occupations of every individual, there is not a great deal in those of the whole society. Every man does, or is capable of doing, almost every thing which any other man does, or is capable of doing. Every man has a considerable degree of knowledge, ingenuity, and invention; but scarce any man has a great degree .... In a civilised state, on the contrary, though there is little variety in the occupations of the greater part of individuals, there is an almost infinite variety in those of the whole society. These varied occupations present an almost infinite variety of objects to the contemplation of those few, who, being attached to no particular occupation themselves, have leisure and inclination to examine the occupations of other people. The contemplation of so great a variety of objects necessarily exercises their minds in endless comparisons and combinations, and renders their understandings, in an extraordinary degree, both acute and comprehensive .... Notwithstanding the great abilities of those few, all the nobler parts of the human character may be, in a great measure, obliterated and extinguished in the great body of the people.[14]

As society itself becomes more various, and as the abilities of the individuals who compose it become proportionately more limited, the ability of each link in a productive chain (whose employment is 'confined to a few very simple operations; frequently to one or two') to see, to *comprehend* the range and organization of activities necessary to its survival and progress, is impaired, and this is perceived as a political problem, as a threat to social coherence, and one which is proposed to be solved either by the provision of compensatory education, or by its deliberate non-provision, according to whether it appears to the proposer that social unity is best guaranteed by an attempt to teach an understanding of its principles, or to conceal them. It may seem that by education 'the great body of the people' can be taught to 'see through' the 'interested complaints of faction and sedition' and so to arrive at a view of the balance of interests by which the unity of a modern state is necessarily composed;[15] or, on the other hand, it may appear that to teach the ability to read, and especially to write, is to facilitate the communication of such 'interested complaints', as well as to relax the habit of industry necessary to economic progress, which is produced by the habit of attending to one task only, as surely as, in the opinion of most commentators,

the ability to comprehend many is now available only to men of
leisure. 'Ignorance', writes Ferguson, 'is the mother of industry as
well as of superstition.' Reflection and fancy are subject to err; but

a habit of moving the hand, or the foot, is independent of either.
Manufactures, accordingly, prosper most, where the mind is least consulted,
and where the workshop may, without any great effort of imagination, be
considered as an engine, the parts of which are men.[16]

The image of the workshop, and of society at large, as a
machine, is used elsewhere by Ferguson, when writing of the
minor functionaries of government who

are made like the parts of an engine, to concur to a purpose, without any
concert of their own: and, equally blind with the trader to any general
combination, they unite with him, in furnishing to the state its resources,
its conduct, and its force.[17]

It is an image, like that of the 'chain of production', perhaps
derived originally from attempts to describe the position of Man
within a universe whose organization and harmony he cannot
understand – both of them familiar from Pope's account, for
example, in the *Essay on Man*, of the great chain of being, the
chain of love, and of man as a moving part in the machine of the
universe, his function perhaps to 'touch some wheel' which is
invisible to him.[18] But the image of the machine develops in the
eighteenth century a considerable explanatory power as a description of society as a unity of interests and of occupations which,
from a disinterested point of view, can be seen as 'concurring to a
purpose', but which in an interested perspective appear to be in no
relation with each other. The image is attributed by Hume,
ambiguously, to 'the stoic' in an essay of that name:

Like many subordinate artists, employed to form the several wheels and
springs of a machine, such are those who excel in all the particular arts of
life. *He* is the master workman who puts those several parts together,
moves them according to just harmony and proportion, and produces true
felicity as the result of their conspiring order.[19]

For Hume, the process of 'refinement in the arts', as it increased
the wealth of the subordinate workman, brought also a 'new
vigour' to the mind, an enlargement of its powers and faculties –

and to the mind of the workman as well, and not only, as Ferguson
and Smith were to argue, to those outside the machine. This
'enlargement', however, was not thought by Hume so considerable
as to do away with the need 'to govern men' by animating them
with 'the spirit of avarice', to possess more than the mere necessities
of life, and thus to pursue the interests of society as a whole by
apparently pursuing only their own, as do Ferguson's bureaucrats
and traders.[20] And it seems to have been with Hume particularly in
mind that in the 1820s Hazlitt wrote, of the Scottish school of
social philosophy,

This is their *idea of a perfect commonwealth*: where each member
performs his part in the machine, taking care of himself, and no more
concerned about his neighbours, than the iron and wood-work, the pegs
and nails in a spinning-jenny. Good screw! good wedge! good ten-penny
nail![21]

The image, then, of society as a machine, which occurs also in
writers as diverse as Shaftesbury and Mandeville,[22] is one by which
the various members of the incalculable numbers of different
occupational groups are 'equally blind' to any 'general combination', and the same is true of what will appear in this book as
another frequent eighteenth-century image of social organization
– also originally employed in attempts to describe the order of the
universe – of society as landscape, as painting, or as landscape
painting, in which the various objects in the view, in which light
and shade, may appear in one perspective to be in no relation or
even to be in conflict with one another, but can, from the correct
viewpoint, be seen in 'just harmony and proportion'. If we cannot
grasp the design of the landscape, that is because we are a part of it
– we are the trees, the hills, the light, the shade. To discover its
proportion and unity, we must occupy, as it were, a position
outside the landscape, in the same way as the 'master workman' is
outside the machine. From what viewpoint, then, is the composition
of the landscape, the working of the machine, the structure of civil
society, visible? To whom is it visible? And what qualifications are
necessary to those who wish to discover the coherence of the
whole?

The qualifications, character and viewpoint of the gentleman The
answers to these questions were given by the way the questions

were framed. If the attempt to understand the organization of society was to be undertaken from within traditions of political thought which saw the unity of society as requiring to be composed out of the conflict of particular interests, then interest itself was what distorted or occluded a perspective on the processes by which those opposing interests were, or could be made to be, harmonious. If it was to be undertaken for a society whose unity was defined as being produced out of the competing but co-operative labours of different occupational groups, then to be a member of such a group was to have only a partial view of the organization of society as a whole. In either case, to grasp the relations among opposed or apparently opposed individual or group interests, an indispensable, though not necessarily a sufficient qualification was to be disinterested. Who, then, was disinterested? Ideally, the magistrate to whom the task of reconciling opposed interests was assigned; the statesman who is qualified for office by virtue of having no interest other than that of the state as a whole, or of demonstrating the ability to prefer the common interest to his own. But to those who, in the period of this book, preoccupied themselves with the question, that answer was inadequate for various reasons, of which perhaps the most important was that, in the democratic or mixed constitution of a free country, the electorate exercised a responsibility not only for choosing who should govern, but also for deciding who should be allowed to participate in the election. An answer was required which could demonstrate that those who had the power to vote were qualified by their own disinterestedness to do so, and that those who did not have it were not. I am not suggesting that, especially at the start of the period covered by this book, the question of who should have the vote was, at all times, a burning issue to all men who wrote about politics. If and when it was not, this was because, among such men, there was a substantial consensus, on the question of who could be regarded as disinterested, that finds expression in definitions of the 'disinterested man'.

By the tradition of republican thought in which democratic political theory was framed, and by the constitution of England, the right to vote was based on the qualification of owning property in land; for by his possession of 'permanent', heritable property, a man was or could be assumed to have a concern for the permanence of the polity, and to be above the temptation to sacrifice that concern to the consideration of immediate, local, or private interests. In theory, if not in practice, the property qualification

was pitched high enough to ensure that the owner of property in land who was also enfranchised, would not need to cultivate his lands himself, but would have the leisure to devote himself to a consideration and comprehension of the public interest as well as his own – which could be defined, as we have seen, as anyway identical. Thus the gentleman of landed property had a two-fold qualification to be regarded as disinterested: his permanent stake in the stability of the nation, and his freedom from engaging in any specific profession, trade, or occupation which might occlude his view of society as a whole.

The gentleman, it was often believed, having no need to follow any determinate occupation, had the potential to comprehend them all, if not in their specific detail – for that would have been a degree of knowledge at once unbecoming, and liable to disturb his comprehensive view – at least in their relation to the interests of the whole. Professional men, tradesmen, merchants, and (when they were considered) artisans and labourers did not have that potential, for the practitioners of any particular occupation were assumed to be concerned solely or largely with the immediate ends of that occupation. A 'scholastick education' or 'a trade', argues Defoe, in his manuscript work *The Compleat English Gentleman* (*c*. 1728), may 'so fix a man in a particular way, that he is not fit to judge of any thing that lyes out of his way, and so his larning becomes a clog to his natural parts'.[23] The gentleman was thus able to exhibit a form of virtue unavailable to those of lower rank: the merchant might be honest in his transactions, frugal in his personal expenses, prudent in his calculation of an adventure; the labourer might be patient, resigned, or industrious; but even if these private virtues could be argued, by an account of social relations as economic relations, to be public virtues also – in that they served at once the interests of their practitioners and those of society as a whole – they remain private virtues to those who practise them; who, because unable to see society as a whole or to judge of its interests, have no thought for the public in their pursuit of private ends. It is only by the comprehensive observer that such private virtues can be described also as public. The virtues of the gentleman, on the other hand, were defined not by his occupation but by the fact that to be 'bred a gentleman' was, as Fielding remarked, to be 'bred up to do nothing':[24] 'the wisdom of the learned man cometh by opportunity of leisure: and he that hath little business shall become wise'.

Also by virtue of his lack of occupation, the gentleman, as w

shall see in a later essay, was believed to be the only member of society who spoke a language universally intelligible: his usage was 'common', in the sense of being neither a local dialect nor infected by the terms of any particular art. If the whole of society was able to be not only understood, but described, it could not be by the professional man, the merchant, or the artisan: 'as any action or posture', writes Johnson, 'long continued, will distort and disfigure the limbs; so the mind likewise is crippled and contracted by perpetual application to the same set of ideas ... [so] there are few among men of the more liberal professions, whose minds do not carry the brand of their calling, or whose conversation does not quickly discover to what class of the community they belong'. Every occupation has its own 'uncouth dialect', a 'cast of talk' peculiar to itself, a particular 'cant' or 'jargon' which indicates that its members, 'have fixed their attention on the same events' so long and to such a degree that they cannot easily understand whatever is out of the way of their own line of business:[25] 'how can he get wisdom, that holdeth the plough ... and whose talk is of bullocks?' It must be open, then, only to those who perform no regular, determinate task to comprehend and describe the relations between such tasks.

The authority of the language of the gentleman, if it was threatened later in the century by the perception that he was less and less in a position to grasp the unity of society – defined as produced less by the resolution of conflicting interests than by the co-operation of specialized occupations – easily survived the threat; and perhaps for two main reasons. There was in eighteenth-century England, as we shall see, a tradition by which the language of the polite had been invested with something analogous to the force of law; and just as a society whose order was no longer validated by being perceived by the gentleman could still be understood as regulated by the law, by the collective wisdom of men – or of gentlemen – in general, so the language of society could still be represented as regulated by a deference to the collective customs of a class, no *individual* member of which had the right to announce his own linguistic usage as correct. Whatever threat was offered to the language of the polite towards the end of the century, it was not offered on the grounds that the languages of various occupations had a right to be understood as contributions to the language of the nation as a whole; and, on the contrary, the need to discover a lingua franca, by which men of

different areas and occupations could communicate with each other, was one by which also the value of the apparently placeless language of the gentleman, uninfluenced by the 'dialect' of any occupation, was reinforced. Thus, in spite of the Royal Society's preference for 'the language of Artizans, Countrymen, and Merchants',[26] it was largely by teaching the polite language that the attempt was made in the eighteenth century to establish a national, a 'common' standard of grammar and vocabulary.

In the figure of the landed gentleman the disinterested viewpoint was, in the first half of the century at least, actualized in such a way as to legitimate the limited form of democracy practised in England, by dividing men into those qualified to observe and those qualified only to be the objects of others' observation. It is to the comprehensive view of the gentleman that the poet James Thomson ascribes the possibility of seeing the common good: it was the happy man as country gentleman who, having retired from the conflicts of the world, could 'see' the relations among those still blindly engaged in conflict. When the 'Spectator' describes himself in the first number of the periodical of that name (1 March 1711), it is as one

born to a small Hereditary Estate, which, according to the Tradition of the Village where it lies, was bounded by the same Hedges and Ditches in *William* the Conqueror's Time that it is at present, and has been delivered down from Father to Son whole and entire, without the Loss or Acquisition of a single Field or Meadow, during the Space of six hundred Years.

But, however small, this estate, this exaggeratedly 'fixed' property, was large enough to support him in the leisure which enabled him to be a 'spectator' on the range of conditions of men represented in the periodical, and which the genre was, to an extent, invented in order to represent. If, in the *Essay on Man*, we are puzzled by the question, from what point of view can Pope manage to see the whole of society to which other men are blind, one answer is offered by the poem's opening lines:

  Awake, my ST.JOHN! leave all meaner things
To low ambition and the pride of Kings.
Let us (since Life can little more supply
Than just to look about us and to die)
Expatiate free o'er all this scene of Man;
A mighty maze! but not without a plan ....

Together let us beat this ample field,
Try what the open, what the covert yield;
The latent tracts, the giddy heights explore
Of all who blindly creep, or sightless soar;
Eye Nature's walks, shoot Folly as it flies,
And catch the Manners living as they rise . . . .

It is as a man of landed property that Bolingbroke, an adherent to the country party to which the disinterested virtues of the country gentleman were particularly apparent, can 'expatiate free' (and with him, by association, Pope) 'o'er all this scene of Man' – can grasp the 'plan', the design of the landscape. His freedom from interest enables him to *see* what is invisible to those who, situated in one partial position or another, 'latent tract' or 'giddy height', can only 'blindly' creep, or 'sightless' soar. And it is thoroughly appropriate that, as Bolingbroke and Pope range freely over the landscape, they do so as sportsmen: they 'beat' the field, and 'catch the Manners' they thus put up: only the lords of manors, or those possessed of an annual income of £100 from a freehold estate, were permitted to shoot game.

It was probably not any part of Pope's intention to argue that only a gentleman so specifically defined could appreciate the composition of the social prospect – at the end of the poem this privilege is assigned to the 'happy man' who is defined by his virtues rather than by his status. The point is rather that the claim that the 'scene of Man' is a maze, although with a plan, pre-supposes in Pope himself some ability to grasp that plan, and that to make such a claim he must first negotiate a positon for himself from which it can be made. The image of the sporting gentleman offered him such a rhetorical position, but it is not one that, in the body of his argument, he chooses to represent as the one from which a comprehensive view is available, nor perhaps could he have done, by the 1730s, without severe qualification. For well before that time it is clear that, though the gentleman may survive as the ideal of a comprehensive observer, he is no longer easily identifiable with any very considerable body of men within the society of England. In the Augustan periodical essay there are a number of attempts to define the 'true' gentleman in such a way as to distinguish him from his embarrassing literary stereotypes, the foxhunter and the modish fop; and these redefinitions disclose the problems of identifying the 'true' gentleman with anyone it might have been possible to meet in London or the shires.

'By a Fine Gentleman', writes Steele, 'I mean a Man compleatly qualify'd as well for the Service and Good, as for the Ornament and Delight, of Society' – but his definition is worth quoting at length:

When I consider the Frame of Mind peculiar to a Gentleman, I suppose it graced with all the Dignity and Elevation of Spirit that Human Nature is capable of: To this I would have joined a clear Understanding, a Reason free from Prejudice, a steady Judgment, and an extensive Knowledge. When I think of the Heart of a Gentleman, I imagine it firm and intrepid, void of all inordinate Passions, and full of Tenderness, Compassion, and Benevolence. When I view the fine Gentleman with regard to his Manners, methinks I see him modest without Bashfulness, frank and affable without Impertinence, obliging and complaisant without Servility, chearful and in good Humour without Noise. These amiable Qualities are not easily obtained; neither are there many Men, that have a Genius to excel this Way. A finished Gentleman is perhaps the most uncommon of all the great Characters in Life. Besides the natural Endowments with which this distinguished Man is to be born, he must run through a long Series of Education. Before he makes his Appearance and shines in the World, he must be principled in Religion, instructed in all the moral Virtues, and led through the whole Course of the polite Arts and Sciences. He should be no Stranger to Courts and to Camps; he must travel to open his Mind, to enlarge his Views, to learn the Policies and Interests of foreign States, as well as to fashion and polish himself, and to get clear of National Prejudices; of which every Country has its Share. To all these more essential Improvements, he must not forget to add the fashionable Ornaments of Life, such as are the Languages and bodily Exercises most in vogue: Neither would I have him think even Dress itself beneath his Notice.[27]

That this creature is more easily described than discovered – that he is indeed 'the most uncommon of all the great Characters in Life' – is evident from much of the language of Steele's definition: 'I imagine', 'methinks I see him', and so on. For together with the natural propensities of this gentleman that enable him to exhibit the 'Reason free from Prejudice', the 'steady Judgment', the open-mindedness of the disinterested man, he must develop his comprehensive view through 'a long Series of Education': he must be acquainted with all the polite arts and sciences, he must be, in some manner, both courtier and soldier, and so equal to the occasions of peace and war, and he must be well travelled.

However, equally striking as this blend of natural and acquired virtues, is what Steele omits from his definition: the gentleman is not defined as a man of landed property – evidently he must be very comfortably off but the source of his income is not specified – and, secondly, though his character is formed not only for the 'Delight and Ornament' of society, but also for its 'Service and Good', it seems no part of the definition that the gentleman must put his qualities and accomplishments to use. The end of his education appears to be, simply, to 'appear', to 'shine': he 'polishes' himself so that he may 'shine in the world'. The same is true of the more ironic description of the universal man given by Mandeville, the source of whose 'tollerable Fortune' is not stated, and the comprehensiveness of whose knowledge seems to have fitted him primarily for 'Conversation'. 'Most People of any Taste' would much enjoy conversation with him, and would 'justly prefer it to being alone, when they knew not how to spend their time; but if they could employ themselves in something from which they expected either a more solid or a more lasting Satisfaction, they would deny themselves this Pleasure, and follow what was of greater consequence to 'em.'[28]

These features of Steele's and Mandeville's gentlemen must be understood in the context of problems which seem always to have been inherent in notions of the perfect courtier, but which became particularly salient in the last years of the seventeenth century and the early years of the eighteenth, when the renaissance ideal of the courtier was being transformed in England into that of the gentleman of civic virtue, but when that transformation was being hindered just because the gentleman was still required to carry around with him so much of his old courtly baggage. If the gentleman is described as a man of no determinate occupation, it must seem that any degree of participation on his part in the affairs of society must compromise him, must oblige him to descend from the elevated viewpoint his status and leisure define for him; and particularly from the perspective which understood the proliferation of occupations as evidence of the corruption of the state by luxury and interest, for the gentleman to do anything would be for him to participate in that corruption. But if he does nothing, he can learn nothing: his ownership of land will give him at best a potential to grasp the relations in a complex society, but one which can never be fulfilled: such gentlemen, writes Defoe, are 'useless in their generacion, retreated from the State, because uncapable to serv it'.[29] Steele, Defoe, and Mandeville put him to work, therefore, to study 'the polite arts and sciences' – but not to practise them; he can work to develop his potential to understand the world, but he cannot put that understanding to work.

All three writers, of course, had reasons, which will appear in the next paragraph, for wishing to detach the gentleman from the freeholder; but in attempting to broaden the definition to one which did not necessarily demand a property qualification, they were not thereby enabled to find a social function for those who might now be included within the expanded definition, for they cannot imagine a disinterested position which is not also an entirely detached one. All three were aware of the problem, and Mandeville delighted in it: the boasted virtues of Shaftesbury, he writes, 'are good for nothing but to breed Drones'.[30] Where, on the other hand, Steele attempts to argue that 'the Appellation of a Gentleman is never to be affixed to a Man's Circumstances', and that therefore 'that Tradesman who deals with me in a Commodity which I do not understand, with Uprightness, has much more Right to that Character, than the Courtier that gives me false Hopes, or the Scholar who laughs at my Ignorance', he is offering the character to one who practises only the virtues particular to his particular calling, and thus he excludes not only land, but the comprehensiveness of vision that went with it from his new definition.[31]

Steele's refusal to confine the title of gentleman to men of landed property, and the fact that Mandeville, who had no great esteem for the title, and Defoe, who esteemed it only as it could be made to apply to 'bred gentlemen', whether or not they were also 'born gentlemen', would not thus confine it, are to be understood in terms partly political and partly economic, though the two are not easily separable. It is partly a response, no doubt, to the attempt of the country party to annex the virtue of disinterested- ness exclusively to the interest they represented; it arises partly from the awareness that more and more landed estates were kept whole only by infusions of money from the City – Defoe gives a long list of nobles who had formed alliances by marriage with families whose wealth was derived from commerce and banking; and it is partly a result of the perception, difficult to ignore from any viewpoint, that the ownership of land was for that reason among others also an *interest*: a political interest, of course, and an economic one, implicated in the economic interest it opposed. For to own land was no longer a convincing guarantee that one's interests were identical with the permanent interests of the state, because the ownership of land was inevitably and increasingly involved in an economy of credit, where values and virtues were unstable, and where a man was estimated not by an 'objective' standard, but in terms of an opinion of his credit worthiness which was liable to fluctuate whatever the source of his income.[32] If the gentleman is no longer the repository of public virtues, then his title may as well be put up for auction, and attributed, as it was by Steele, to the merchant exercising the private virtue of fair-dealing.

But if no man was now truly disinterested, and there is therefore no disinterested position from which the common good can be discovered, there is no comprehensive view: society is no longer capable of being understood; and if Allworthy is far closer to the ideal of a gentleman than Squire Western, he is not perhaps much less at sea in the society represented by *Tom Jones*. It was still possible, still usual, indeed, to assert that the gentleman, in one form or another, was still adequate to the social purposes for which he had been defined – in a later essay we shall find that assertion being made, in remarkably different ways, by Smollett and by Chesterfield; and even Hume offers to argue 'the middle station of life' as a more plausible condition of gentlemanly independence, a position from which to exercise a comprehensive intellectual and sympathetic understanding of society – a claim he perhaps makes more insistently in view of his having put in question, in the first part of his *Treatise*, the possibility of our acquiring any coherent knowledge at all.[33] But the perception that society is no longer open to comprehensive inspection, recognized by some writers and denied by others, seems by the mid century to be at least implicit in the work of a range of writers, of a variety of political persuasions, who seek to negotiate for themselves a position from which they would describe, or argue for, the unity of a society apparently separated by the separation of trades and professions.

Some problems of knowledge In Johnson's periodical essays, we discover a wide range of responses to the perception that society and social knowledge are now so complex that it has become impossible for any individual to understand them as a whole. A complete knowledge of any individual art is, for Johnson, certainly still possible, at least to one prepared to exercise the ungentlemanlike virtue of industriousness in assiduous inquiry:

Among the productions of mechanic art, many are of a form so different from that of their first materials, and many consist of parts so numerous and so nicely adapted to each other, that it is not possible to view them without amazement. But when we enter the shops of artificers, observe the various tools by which every operation is facilitated, and trace the progress of a manufacture through the different hands that, in succession to each other, contribute to its perfection, we soon discover that every single man has an easy task, and that the extremes, however remote, of natural rudeness and artificial elegance, are joined by a regular concatenation of effects, of which every one is introduced by that which precedes it, and equally introduces that which is to follow.

The same is the state of intellectual and manual performances .... Complication is a species of confederacy, which, while it continues united, bids defiance to the most active and vigorous intellect; but of which every member is separately weak, and which therefore may be quickly subdued if it can once be broken.[34]

But, as Johnson perceives, the more diligently we learn to understand the principles of any individual art, the harder it becomes for us to relate our knowledge of it to that of any other. By an image to which he repeatedly returns, life and knowledge are a maze, through which each inquirer picks his way ignorant of the routes taken by his fellows. It is of the nature of study itself that what we already know so influences what we can come to know that 'as we proceed further, and wider prospects open to our view, every eye fixes upon a different scene; we divide into various paths, and, as we move forward, are still at a greater distance from each other'.[35] The image of the landscape will no longer serve to represent social knowledge as coherent; for if we want to study the landscape, we must descend from our elevated viewpoint, and disperse ourselves by different routes throughout the prospect. How then can a writer – and one particularly of polite essays, a genre which committed its author to represent and reflect upon the whole range of social experience – negotiate for himself a viewpoint from which he can claim to have the comprehensive understanding necessary to his task?

The titles of Johnson's periodicals – the *Idler*, the *Rambler* – suggest something of the rhetorical irony by which Johnson can at once avow and cope with the loss of a general view. To be an 'idler' 'where all other beings are busy', where 'innumerable multitudes' are passing by, where 'every face' seems 'settled in the contemplation of some important purpose', is not perhaps, to be in a position to impart much useful general knowledge, but shares the advantage of leisure enjoyed by the gentleman, unattached to any determinate business, and is therefore a state which seems to offer the potential, destined always to remain unfulfilled, of understanding the relation between the innumerable multitudes and the purposes they pursue. To be a 'rambler', to be one who has followed the Goddess Curiosity through 'the maze of life with invariable fidelity', who has 'turned to every new call', and quitted, at the nod of the goddess, 'one pursuit for another', is to claim some acquaintance, though it may be an unhelpfully brief one, with all the callings of life, and thus again to have the potential for an understanding of their relations – but not, of course, the overview necessary to its fulfilment.[36]

But these are rhetorical identities only: knowledge worth having is not to be won in idleness, or by attributing the 'invariable fidelity' with which each man may follow one purpose to the man who flits casually from one to another. They are identities which, as they pretend to legitimize the claim to a comprehensive view, avow that, by these means, it cannot be attained. And the irony seems to suggest that, if that claim is to be legitimized, it must be by a course of meticulous, diligent, and persevering inquiry into the 'maze' of life – only thus can we hope to discover whether or not it has a plan. By the practice of steady intellectual virtues we can substitute for the permanent public virtues of the universal man a private firmness of purpose: we can avoid being misled by 'the meteors of fashion', 'temporary curiosity', the 'topick of the day'. But we must not expect from the objects of our inquiry the steadiness that, in observing them, we demand of ourselves, for society and social knowledge are in a continual state of change, and we must find our way through 'fluctuations of uncertainty' and 'conflicts of contradiction'. Fashion itself, indeed, is to be investigated; for 'by the observation of these trifles it is, that the ranks of mankind are kept in order, that the address of one to another is regulated, and the general business of the world carried on with facility and method.'[37] We must thus pursue a general knowledge with the same firmness of purpose by which a scholar pursues his particular inquiry, but to the scholar or to the practitioner of any determinate occupation that general knowledge is not available, for, by the nature of their tasks, their view of the world is confined.

It is available, perhaps, to the man 'of powerful genius', except that the universal curiosity by which he is characterized may also be his downfall: 'he makes sudden irruptions into the regions of knowledge, and sees all obstacles give way before him; but he never stays long enough to compleat his conquest, to establish laws, or bring away the spoils'.

There seems to be some souls suited to great, and others to little employments; some formed to soar aloft, and take in wide views, and others to grovel on the ground, and confine their regard to a narrow sphere. Of these the one is always in danger of becoming useless by a daring negligence, the other by a scrupulous solicitude; the one collects many ideas, but confused and indistinct; the other is busied in minute accuracy, but without compass and without dignity.

The general error of those who possess powerful and elevated understandings, is, that they form schemes of too great extent, and flatter themselves too hastily with success .... Every design in which the connexion is regularly traced from the first motion to the last, must be formed and executed by calm intrepidity, and requires not only courage which danger cannot turn aside, but constancy which fatigues cannot weary, and contrivance which impediments cannot exhaust.[38]

We can understand Johnson's own career in terms of the attempt to combine the taking of 'wide views' with the 'steadiness and perseverance always necessary in the conduct of a complicated scheme, where many interests are to be connected, many movements to be adjusted' – one thinks of his heroic effort to become a polymath, his determination to become competent in, or at least well acquainted with, more than the merely polite arts and sciences, an effort sometimes thrown off, however, by the retreat into an assertion that the mechanic arts are too mean, and too fluctuating, to be a proper object of investigation, or that 'a whole life cannot be spent upon syntax and etymology, and that even a whole life would not be sufficient'. That last realization sums up the impossibility of combining a comprehensive knowledge of what is now perceived to be an increasingly complex and ramified world, and the steadiness which perceives that a thorough investigation of any one of its parts may not easily be completed within a single life. And that realization seems to lead to another: that if the tasks of study are becoming progressively divided, the task of achieving a general knowledge must be shared among many. It is only by a general co-operation that knowledge can be advanced, and the attempt of any individual to discover a general view must be attended by two considerations: that it will be an attempt only, but one that must be made if society is not to degenerate into an atomized multitude of men each pursuing a separate objective.[39]

To attempt to comprehend the range of what other men know, we need to cultivate a sympathetic interest in the interests they pursue, and must recognize that if an overview of the whole is denied to any individual, we become, at once, the observers and the observed, and must become vigilant spectators on ourselves. The pronoun 'we' takes on a double duty, to be at once the subject and object of any inquiry whose results must always be provisional, never complete, for 'we' as subject fluctuate ourselves, and have no advantage of knowledge over 'we' as object, beyond the 'vigilance of attention' we can hope to attain by the exercise of firmness and steadiness of purpose, or beyond the extensive sympathy by which we ensure that those qualities are not exercised in the pursuit of confined or merely personal ends. However, firmness, steadiness, resolution, and diligence are personal virtues: no man acquires them by *virtue* of what he is, as the gentleman acquired a perception of the public good by virtue of his ownership of land. They must be enjoined on men who cannot be guaranteed to listen, and the same, for Johnson, is true of sympathy. It is not something we discover in the hearts of men whether they know they feel it or not, but must be cultivated. It is not enough, for Johnson, to assert that the 'philosopher' and the 'artificer' are mutually dependent on each other for the gratification of their interests, and that 'without mechanical performances, refined speculation is an empty dream, and . . . that, without theoretical reasoning, dexterity is little more than a brute instinct'; for if each does not *recognize* that fact, he will simply 'endeavour at eminence . . . by pulling others down'.[40] A society held together not by virtues which men *do*, but which they *may* practise, and one which no individual can be guaranteed to comprehend fully enough to ensure its regulation, is far more fragile than any we have encountered so far: and the separation of trades and occupations, the condition for the awareness of which, I have suggested, was the belief in the existence of a viewpoint from which they could be understood as the basis of social coherence, instead ensures the impossibility of attaining that viewpoint, for no one is not implicated in the process of separation.

This consideration of Johnson's periodical writing may have put us in a position to understand more clearly the process by which the gentleman became displaced from his position of comprehensive knowledge, as well as the difficulty in finding any other candidate to fill the position he had vacated. As long as the various occupations of men could be understood, in the terms of political theory, simply as various interests requiring to be adjusted to each other, the disinterested man could be represented as the only person adequate to that task. But as the basis of social affiliation was increasingly understood in economic terms, the definition of occupations as *interests* became evidently inadequate. They are understood, instead, as activities: they produce goods, or perform services, which they bring to the market and offer for exchange, and thus demand a complex knowledge of their processes and principles if they are to be improved and if we are to be able to decide whether their relations can be, or need to be, regulated. Such knowledge was, as Defoe scornfully put it, 'below a gentleman', beneath his notice – it was the knowledge of objects too 'mean', not plausibly to be represented as within the grasp of one whose viewpoint is so elevated, and whose claim to a comprehensive understanding is based on his entire detachment from the system of exchange.[41] A new kind of knowledge was required, and a new kind of knower; but if detachment from the market did not favour the acquisition of that knowledge, how could engagement, which seemed to favour only a confined knowledge derived from the production or performance of the goods or services specific to one's own occupation?

This question becomes a particularly crucial one to those writers of the Scottish school who particularly develop the models of 'the separation of the arts and professions', 'the division of labour', as those by which the history, whether as progress or decline, of civil society can be understood. Their answers, whether explicit or implicit, show themselves to be caught, often knowingly, in the contradiction that while they claim to have discovered a mode of historical explanation by which the history and structure of modern society can be thoroughly understood, they find great difficulty in negotiating for themselves a position from which that explanation can proceed. The contradiction is particularly salient in Ferguson's *Essay* which is, by and large, committed to showing that, if the separation of arts and professions can bring societies to great prosperity, it may also eventually bring them to decline. It is a repeated theme of Ferguson that in proportion as national security is made the object of government, especially in nations of any considerable size, and the occupations of men are developed and subdivided, 'the public becomes an object too extensive' for the conceptions of men:

If nations pursue the plan of enlargement and pacification, till their members can no longer apprehend the common ties of society, nor be engaged by affection in the cause of their country, they must err on the opposite side, and by leaving too little to agitate the spirits of men, bring on ages of langour, if not of decay.

'Under the distinction', he argues, 'of callings ... society is made to consist of parts, of which none is animated with the spirit of society itself', and 'men cease to be citizens'. For 'how can he who has confined his views to his own subsistence or preservation, be intrusted with the conduct of nations?'[42]

This separation may, in fact, be conducive to a greater liberty than an organization of society by which men of the highest class, 'bound to no task', are entrusted with the government of others; for their elevation is achieved at the cost of the enslavement of the rest of society, by which the dignity of the rulers themselves is diminished. By this structure of society, 'we make a nation of helots, and have no free citizens'; but while men 'pursue in society different objects, or separate views', they 'procure a wide distribution of power, and by a species of chance, arrive at a posture for civil engagements, more favourable to human nature than what human wisdom could ever calmly devise'.[43] But it is the price of this liberty that the ability to understand the public good, by comprehending the aims of the whole of society, is entirely destroyed: and it is not at all clear whether Ferguson thought the price worth paying, or whether indeed he thought the forces he was describing were so inevitably determined by the course of history that it was to no purpose having an opinion on the matter.

He considers the possibility we have already encountered in Adam Smith, that if the separation of callings tends 'to contract and limit the mind' of those engaged in them, there may be others who escape this effect, and who, in proportion as the intellectual scope of the inferior orders of men is confined, are led to general reflections, and to enlargement of thought:

Even in manufacture, the genius of the master, perhaps, is cultivated, while that of the inferior workman lies waste. The statesman may have a wide comprehension of human affairs, while the tools he employs are ignorant of the system in which they are themselves combined. The general officer may be a great proficient in the knowledge of war, while the soldier is confined to a few motions of the hand and the foot. The former may have gained, what the latter has lost . . . .

However, the provisional tone of this writing, 'perhaps' . . . 'may', seems to put this possibility in doubt, for it is not clear to Ferguson either that, in the modern society he is describing, anyone escapes implication in the process of the separation of callings, or that, if they do, and in societies in which most certainly they did, any substantial knowledge is to be derived from the position of detachment and of leisure, which may anyway be regarded itself as a *determinate* position, a calling in itself: in modern societies, 'reason itself becomes a profession'.[44]

It is, Ferguson argues, 'the most glaring of all other deceptions, to look for the accomplishments of a human character in the mere attainments of speculation'. 'Men at a distance from the objects of useful knowledge, untouched by motives that animate an active and a vigorous mind, could produce only the jargon of a technical language, and accumulate the impertinence of academical forms'. But if this is true – if to contribute usefully to social knowledge it is necessary to abandon our distant viewpoint and write not in a spirit of remote speculation but from direct experience of that portion of life which most immediately discloses itself to us, and if therefore writing may become a trade, and 'thinking itself, in this age of separations, may become a peculiar craft', from what position can the *Essay on the History of Civil Society* be written?[45]

Only, it seems, from an entirely provisional and ironic one. Thus Ferguson is prepared to invent a rhetorical spectator, like Johnson's Idler or Rambler, who may appear to have a comprehensive view, but the value of whose opinions is doubtful precisely because they derive from that view. 'The practitioner', he writes for example, 'of every art and profession may afford matter of general speculation to the man of science'; but it is not at all clear who this comprehensive 'man of science' can be, or what authority we can attribute to his 'general speculation' when, a few pages before, we have been told that to estimate the value of a man to society on the basis of 'the mere attainments of speculation' is a 'glaring deception'. Or, again like Johnson, Ferguson repeatedly reminds us that what we conclude on any issue is a function of the particular perspective we have on it, and that we can find no absolute by which to compare the value and relation of different perspectives – if we view a problem 'on this side', our conclusions will be such and such, if on another, they will be different, and we can find no absolute by which to compare the value and relation of different perspectives. These thoroughly typical sentences, for example, begin and conclude the last paragraph of Ferguson's second chapter on 'the Manners of Polished and Commercial Nations':

But whatever was the origin of notions, often so lofty and so ridiculous, we cannot doubt of their lasting effects on our manners . . . . And if our rule in measuring degrees of politeness and civilization is to be taken from . . . the advancement of commercial arts, we shall be found to have greatly excelled any of the celebrated nations of antiquity.[46]

In the second of these sentences, 'we' as the objects of investigation are judged by a rule that 'we' as investigators have established, and if the judgment made by the application of that rule is a flattering one, that is evidently because the two 'we's are the same. A disinterested history therefore requires the production of an additional investigator, to comment on the partial view of the 'we' who have established the rule; but that additional investigator appears, in the first sentence, also as 'we', so that what 'we cannot doubt' might certainly, it seems, be doubted, if it were not impossible to find the position from which this infinite regression of investigators and of partial knowledge could be halted.

A glance at almost any page of Ferguson's essay underlines the inescapably provisional and ironic status of the knowledge 'we' and he can have of society: not only the repeated use of the subjunctive 'may', that we have already noted, occurring again and again in such phrases as 'we may consider', 'we may presume', 'it may be thought', 'it may be doubted', but, again and again, 'perhaps', 'it is probable', and so on. It seems likely, indeed, that a detailed comparison of the modes by which Ferguson describes ancient and modern societies would reveal him as employing a tone of much greater certainty as he looks back on states in which the separation of arts and sciences was not much, or not at all advanced, than he can manage when, from the provisional and partial position assigned him by the fact of 'thinking itself' having become 'a peculiar craft', he attempts to understand the society before his eyes.[47]

A similar problem, though less explicitly recognized, seems to emerge from the *Wealth of Nations*. On the one hand, there is the passage, already quoted, which in a far from provisional mode suggests that, by the separation of arts and professions, the understandings of those few who remain 'attached to no particular occupation' are rendered 'in an extraordinary degree, both acute and comprehensive' – and thus, in a position, as it were, to write the treatise in which these words appear. On the other hand, it has been argued earlier in the treatise that the practice of philosophy itself, 'not to do any thing, but to observe every thing', is itself a 'trade',[48] and, like other trades, minutely subdivided and implicated in the mesh of exchange and interest – and thus, one might have imagined, incapable of producing such a philosopher as Smith himself, apparently able to grasp from the perspective of one determinate occupation, the relations between all others.

This narrative could be continued, of course, far beyond 1780, the end of the period to be studied in this book. The perception that, in a complex modern society, the possibility of a comprehensive understanding has disappeared, is perhaps the crucial issue between Burke and Paine, as Burke argues that no one man is in a position to grasp, by speculation, the proper order of government and the function of established institutions, and so to demand that they be changed – and particularly not men 'confined to professional and faculty habits ... rather disabled than qualified for whatever depends on the knowledge of mankind, on experience in mixed affairs, on a comprehensive connected view of ... various complicated external and internal interests'.[49] The same perception may inform the personal, ironic mode of authority deployed in Wordsworth's poetry, and Coleridge's attempts to become competent in a yet wider range of knowledge than even Johnson had attempted. But the division of labour among the writers of this series of books has spared me the effort of making my account of the issue I am discussing much more comprehensive, and I want now, instead, to indicate briefly what the remaining essays of this book contain.

In the essays that follow I concentrate on the final versions of James Thomson's poem *The Seasons* and on his *Castle of Indolence*, on John Dyer's poem *The Fleece*, on Johnson's *Dictionary*, and on *Roderick Random* by Tobias Smollett. In all of these works we will discover a concern with the problems outlined in this introduction, for all of them, I shall argue, have this in common; they are attempting to represent a wide range of social knowledge and experience, and thus to exhibit society as a various and complex organization, while at the same time they can be seen as still concerned to suggest that the gentleman, in one form or another, is still adequate to the task of comprehending that organization. It is as if the condition of representing that complexity and variety is that it be still capable of being understood as a unity, and of being understood by men who thereby justify the privileges and the authority they claim as members of the ruling class. The first essay, which is mainly about the idea of the gentleman in poetry, as a man of wide, comprehensive vision, and the third, which is about the process by which a gentleman might be imagined as developing that vision, have this question in common: at a time when the structure of society was coming to be understood in the economic terms of separate but co-operative labours – terms which I have tried to show must inevitably have challenged the claim of the gentleman to understand that structure – how could the gentleman be defined, how represented, in such a way as to appear still to be in intellectual control of a society which he could still to a large extent control *in fact* – on a national level, by the limitation of the franchise, and locally, by personal influence and authority? The central essay, which is an abridgement of a more ambitious work in progress, is concerned with a rather different version of this problem: how the authority of the gentleman, and of the ruling class, was reinforced at the level of language; how, that is, a 'correct' English was defined in such a way as to represent it as the natural possession of the gentleman, and to confirm that possession, too, as a source of his political authority.

1 An unerring gaze: the prospect of society in the poetry of James Thomson and John Dyer

James Thomson: vision and virtue In 1737 the Lord Chancellor, the Right Honourable the Lord Talbot, died, and James Thomson, whose patron Talbot had been, wrote a poem to his memory. Over nearly 400 lines, this poem sets out to define Talbot as the ideal of the patriot and statesman: a man of 'wide Knowledge', of 'Insight deep into BRITANNIA'S Weal', of reason 'steady, calm, diffusive, deep and clear'. Indeed, asks Thomson,

What grand, what comely, and what tender Sense,
What Talent, and what Virtue was not His?
All that can render Man or great, or good,
Give useful Worth, or amiable Grace?

Disdainful of 'low Views Of sneaking Int'rest or luxurious Vice', Talbot had been concerned instead with 'the Good of all', animated by those 'high Joys that teach the truly Great To live for Others, and for Others die'. If he had not perhaps been able to see, to comprehend the *totality* of knowledge, for even at the height of Thomson's hyperbole he must reserve that ability to 'ETERNAL WISDOM', still no one had ever been vouchsafed a 'larger Portion' of heaven's 'directing Light', and, at least in the comprehension of civil society, it is not clear from the poem that Talbot had been deficient in any point: he saw

With instantaneous View, the Truth of Things;
Chief what to Human Life and Human Bliss
Pertains, the kindest Science, fit for Man.[1]

It would be hard to find in the eighteenth century a more extravagant attempt to identify a particular man with the ideal of the universal observer who 'superior to the little Fray' of competing interests, understands the relations among them all. And this was not, Thomson insists, a simply latent, a barren ability fostered by and developed in an independence which might also have been a detachment from the society he observed. Talbot did not lie 'in studious Shade', in 'soft Retirement'; he was not 'indolently pleas'd With selfish Peace'; instead, he was active, industrious in the task, not simply of understanding the mixed elements of society, but of reconciling them by teaching the lesson of social love:

> An empty Form,
> Vain is the Virtue, that amid the Shade
> Lamenting lies, with future Schemes amus'd,
> While Wickedness and Folly, kindred Powers,
> Confound the World. A TALBOT'S, different far,
> Sprung into Action.[2]

The point that it is not enough for a man of comprehensive vision to see merely, if he does not also act, may be particularly insisted upon to vindicate Talbot in his willingness to work alongside an administration which Thomson regarded as venal, thus perhaps to correct and regulate, by an impartial occupation of the highest legal office, the consequences of Walpole's government at a time when Thomson's other political associates were more or less affiliated in opposition to Walpole. But it is more than that; for as we shall see Thomson was much concerned, in his three major poems, to argue that it was possible, and still possible, for an individual to have the comprehensive view of society here un-complicatedly ascribed to Talbot, and for him to act on that view, as Talbot had done.

The nature of that first concern will emerge later in this essay; the point of the second can be suggested now if we glance at a poem Thomson published in 1729, addressed to his friend George Bubb Dodington, a Whig politician, sometimes Walpole's opponent but at this time more or less his ally. The poem, a Horatian epistle, is called 'The Happy Man'. It pays an elegant compliment to Dodington by arguing that wealth, by itself, will not make a man 'happy': he must also have a mind which is active and harmoniously balanced.

> He's not the *Happy Man*, to whom is given
> A plenteous Fortune by indulgent *Heaven*;
> Whose gilded Roofs on shining Columns rise,
> And painted Walls enchant the Gazer's Eyes;
> Whose Table flows with hospitable Chear,

And all the various Bounty of the Year;
Whose Vallies smile . . . .

The poem begins apparently by asserting that happiness and riches
are incompatible; but, as the opening sentence continues – there
are five more couplets in the vein of those I have quoted – the
initial 'not' becomes a dimmer and dimmer memory, and the poem
seems to read as a simple celebration of the happiness that money
can buy; which facilitates a position more comforting, we may
imagine, to Dodington; that wealth, if it is not a sufficient, may still
be a necessary condition for happiness, and certainly does not
make it any harder to acquire. Dodington is particularly fortunate:
as well as a fine house, a productive estate, substantial interests in
trade, a full table and cellar, and so on, to him are attributed also
the non-material possessions which elevate the rich man to the
status of a gentleman: for he has a 'Mind'

Where *Judgment* sits clear-sighted, and surveys
The Chain of *Reason* with unerring Gaze;
Where *Fancy* lives, and to the bright'ning Eyes
Bids fairer Scenes, and bolder Figures rise;
Where *social Love* exerts her soft Command
And lays the *Passions* with a tender Hand,
Whence every *Virtue* flows, in rival Strife,
And all the *moral Harmony* of Life.[3]

To survey the 'Chain of *Reason*' is not simply to follow the
connections in a complex argument: it is to survey the world, the
chain of being, and to understand it as the connected production
of the providential Reason of God, so that to survey that chain
'unerringly' is to see the world, as God sees it, as the embodiment
of a perfectly coherent plan, in which everything is as it should be
– an ability which is at once the cause and the effect of happiness,
of that mental balance which plays upon the potentially discordant
passions, and harmonizes them. It is a balance which issues in
'*social* Love', a benevolence which is, in turn, a repetition in the
mind of man of the divine benevolence by which the society of the
world is understood to be bound together in a chain of love.

There may be a problem, then, in the last couplet quoted above
– though it seems to follow unproblematically enough from those
which precede it – which is to guess what opportunity Dodington
finds to exert the other unnamed virtues attributed to him. These

are, presumably, the public virtues proper to the gentleman; but if his judgement, and his benevolence, reveal to him a world already perfect, how can those virtues act on the world to improve it? The poem can only suggest that, somehow, they 'flow' – a verb which directs attention to their source but not to their direction or object; and though the poem seems to be conventional enough in the incense it offers up to a potential patron, it discloses a problem in the ideal identity of the gentleman, as a man of comprehensive vision and also of public virtue. For though it is evidently possible to claim that a particular gentleman is a man of 'wide survey' or of disinterested zeal for the public welfare, it is not easy to see how he can be both, if to see the world clearly is to see it as happy, and to see it as the theatre for public virtue is to see it as urgently in need of reformation.

The Seasons, Thomson's longest and much revised poem, is full, and especially in its final versions of 1744 and 1746,[4] of addresses to lords and gentlemen active in their opposition to Walpole, men to whom is attributed much that Thomson has attributed to Talbot and Dodington; and the more exaggerated each address, the more incompatible may seem to be the tasks which Thomson looks to his ideal gentlemen to perform. It is they who must vindicate the perfection of the social order, and it is they who must rescue society from the corruption which, by the means of political management practised by Walpole, the unmentioned villain of the poem in its later versions, has infected the society of Britain.

Whoever reads *The Seasons* must observe that it appears to be committed to two quite opposite views of history. On the one hand, the history of society has been one of decline, from an age of innocence to a period of luxury and strife; on the other, society has progressed, by the development of political and judicial institutions, of the mechanic and polite arts – and particularly in Britain – to a point of perfection. Thus primitive man can be described, at one point, as the model of the social sense, living in harmonious co-operation with others; and, elsewhere, as the sad barbarian who has never tasted the 'soft Civility of Life',[5] and so has no social sense at all; though in both cases, corruption is the enemy of society, to be found no less in the pre-social world of the savage than – by the alternative account – in the developed states of modern Europe.

The contradiction emerges clearly enough at the start of the poem, in, 'Spring': according to one account of history, the 'first fresh Dawn' of 'uncorrupted Man' was the pattern from which pastoral poets have described the golden age; but now we live in 'iron Times'. The mind has now become 'distemper'd'; it has lost 'that Concord of harmonious Powers', whereas, before, 'Music held the whole in perfect Peace'. The passions are now self-interested only, and 'each social Feeling' is extinct. Love, at best 'a pensive Anguish', is at worst 'sunk to sordid Interest', and men's thoughts are now 'partial', 'cold, and averting from our Neighbour's Good'.[6]

But, 500 lines later, the poet is led

>   to the Mountain-brow
> Where sits the Shepherd on the grassy Turf,
> Inhaling, healthful, the descending Sun.
> Around him feeds his many-bleating Flock,
> Of various Cadence; and his sportive Lambs,
> This way and that convolv'd, in friskful Glee,
> Their Frolicks play. And now the sprightly Race
> Invites them forth; when swift, the Signal given,
> They start away, and sweep the massy Mound
> That runs around the Hill; the Rampart once
> Of iron War, in ancient barbarous Times,
> When disunited BRITAIN ever bled,
> Lost in eternal Broil: ere yet she grew
> To this deep-laid indissoluble State,
> Where *Wealth* and *Commerce* lift the golden Head;
> And, o'er our Labours, *Liberty* and *Law*,
> Impartial, watch, the Wonder of a World!

'The chearful Tendance of the Flock' had been one of the pleasant occupations, earlier, of pre-fallen man; now it seems to be an occupation enjoyed by the modern shepherd precisely because the peace of modern society has left him secure. If in the age of innocence the whole creation was held together in 'Consonance' by the harmony of music, now it seems that harmony is enjoyed by this shepherd too, in the 'various Cadence' of his flock, but can hardly have been earlier, in 'disunited BRITAIN'. Men whose thoughts had earlier been described as partial, are now apparently content to submit themselves to impartial laws. The golden age seems to have been transferred from the past to the present: the gold brought by '*Wealth* and *Commerce*' is brought by peace, and the 'iron Times' of war belong to the very epoch, ancient and barbarous, which had earlier been described as a golden age, and in comparison with which the modern age was of iron.[7]

It is not simply, then, that these two, inconsistent accounts can appear side by side in the same book of *The Seasons;* but that many of the terms which are first used to differentiate a primaeval golden from a modern iron age have been preserved in the second, alternative account of history, and transferred from one age to the other, in a way that calls attention to the inconsistency of the two accounts; and this is by no means the only occasion when this is done. The effect is to make the inconsistency impossible to ignore; it invites itself to be recognized as a problem, and we are obliged to attempt to decide whether either view is the correct one, or whether, if they are both partial views, they are not reconcilable.

The prospect of Britain We may be able to approach an answer to these questions – though I am not among those who believe the poem to be possessed of a fully 'unifying vision'[8] – if we look at a passage which is the most extended vindication in the poem of modern Britain as a state supremely healthy as well as wealthy. It occurs in 'Summer', and was added to the poem in the edition of 1744, the second last to appear in Thomson's lifetime. The passage begins by describing it as a property of summer evenings that they offer the opportunity to man, in solitude, of composing, of harmonizing his heart, if he will 'seek the distant Hills, and there converse With Nature'. He may then, in 'pathetic Song', communicate 'the Harmony to others', or at least to his 'Social Friends',

Attun'd to happy Unison of Soul;
To whose exalting Eye a fairer World,
Of which the Vulgar never had a Glimpse,
Displays its Charms.

Such friends, already predisposed by their benevolent social sense to receive the harmony to be communicated to them, are further defined as possessed of minds 'richly fraught With Philosophic Stores, superior Light'; in their 'Breast, enthusiastic' is an ardent virtue which 'the Sons of Interest' regard as mere 'Romance'. It seems, then, that to see the world as 'fair', and Britain (as the passage will go on to say) as golden, is open to those who are benevolent, enlightened, virtuous and disinterested; though as we shall see it will not therefore follow that to see modern society in terms of corruption, of a decline from a golden to an iron age, is the lot of those whose social sense is extinct, who have no knowledge of philosophy, who regard virtue as an outdated fiction, and who are, in short, the sons of 'sordid Interest'.[9]

But possibly the most crucial qualification of all to those who wish to see the world as 'fair', is that they should be able to withdraw from it in order to be able to contemplate it as harmonious; and the passage continues by representing the poet and the woman he loves – for lovers are 'sacred to sweet Retirement' – together seeking the hills, from which they attain a view of England which is at once 'boundless' and 'goodly', so that the eye, contemplating it, is 'raptur'd', is 'feasted'. It is a view which first, and briefly, takes in London – 'huge AUGUSTA' – and 'majestic *Windsor*', but then wanders upstream to the rural valley of 'the silver THAMES': and what the 'feasted Eye' discovers there, is a selection of the country seats of various men noted for their opposition, at one time or another, to Walpole. Their estates are understood, however, not as centres of political organization, but as being, like the viewpoint of the lovers, locations of retirement: Harrington's 'Retreat', the 'embowering Walks' of Ham, where the 'worthy QUEENSB'RY' and 'polish'd CORNBURY' are to be found 'in spotless Peace retir'd', the bowers of Twickenham, Pope's miniature landscape garden, where the 'Muses haunt', and the groves of Esher, where Pelham, in 'sweetest Solitude', finds 'Repose'. The account of this prospect ends in sublime exclamation: this is an

Inchanting Vale! beyond whate'er the Muse
Has of *Achaia* or *Hesperia* sung!
O Vale of Bliss! O softly-swelling Hills!
On which the *Power of Cultivation* lies,
And joys to see the Wonders of his Toil.[10]

The view, then, has been described as 'boundless' – it is nowhere occluded by hills that might close the prospect, and, confined only by the limits of human perception, it is, like Talbot's portion of divine wisdom, as comprehensive a view as can be vouchsafed to man. It is perhaps surprising that it should also seem so selective a view: a hasty glance at London, and a brief glimpse of agricultural endeavour, are all that, from the viewpoint of the retired lovers, intrude on the view of the Thames valley as a landscape of pastoral retirement – as, indeed, the most complete example of such a landscape the muse could invent. If to the enlarged view of the retired observer, the world is 'fairer' than it can be to the confined view of the sons of interest, that seems to be because he is able to give his attention only to images which replicate his own situation – or, more specifically, to images of other gentlemen who have withdrawn from the world and can be imagined to have a similarly 'comprehensive' yet partial view of it. Even the '*Power of Cultivation*' itself seems retired: having produced the agricultural and moral wealth of the valley, he lies at ease on the hills, and joins the lovers in their enjoyment of the view.

The view, so far described as boundless, is now, as the paragraph added in 1744 joins up with the earlier text, represented as also harmonious:

> HEAVENS! what a goodly Prospect spreads around,
> Of Hills, and Dales, and Woods, and Lawns, and Spires,
> And glittering Towns, and gilded Streams, till all
> The stretching Landskip into Smoke decays!
> Happy BRITANNIA! where the QUEEN OF ARTS,
> Inspiring Vigor, LIBERTY abroad
> Walks, unconfin'd, even to thy farthest Cotts,
> And scatters Plenty with unsparing Hand.[11]

Another glimpse of towns, glittering in this golden landscape, reveals them as unproblematically consonant with the natural landscape that surrounds them – a landscape in which the distinction between different objects disappears, as they are unified by the vapour which finally conceals it. But if the poet cannot see the goodly prospect continuing beyond the limits of his sight, he can still imagine it. 'LIBERTY' can be described as walking 'unconfin'd' to the remotest corners of Britain, there scattering the wealth which litters the visible portion of the land. If the comprehensiveness of this view is limited by the limits of the poet's perception, he still asserts that he can, in another sense, 'see' the whole country, for what is visible is an accurate microcosmic representation of a prosperous Britain, and the apparently unconfined view can tell him all that an actually comprehensive one would do.

This passage in 'Summer' is closely related with another in 'Spring', an account of the 'infusive Force' which the season has on man, or on some men, by which their 'Being' is 'raised', their soul

made 'serene'. It is a force unfelt by the 'sordid Sons of Earth', who
are 'hard, and unfeeling of Another's Woe'; it works only on

> ye generous Minds, in whose wide Thought,
> Of all his Works, CREATIVE BOUNTY burns
> With warmest Beam.

To such minds, of liberally extended if not quite fully comprehensive
vision, more of creation, more of the providential design of the
universe is visible than to anyone else, so that

> sublim'd
> To Rapture, and enthusiastic Heat,
> We feel the present DEITY, and taste
> The Joy of GOD to see a happy World![12]

To those who can discover, or arrive at some intimation of, the
world as the creation of a benevolent God, Spring brings the gift of
a benevolent vision of the world: like God, they see that it is good.
By changing the pronoun, from 'ye' to 'we', the poet includes
himself among those to whom this vision is available. But 'we' is
hardly a more inclusive term than 'ye', and certainly still excludes
the 'sordid Sons of Earth', who are no doubt the same as the 'Sons'
of 'Interest' (itself earlier described as 'sordid'), by whom the view
of Happy Britannia was also unglimpsed.

The passage continues by attributing the comprehensive vision
of the world, on this occasion, to Thomson's friend Lyttelton, the
secretary of the Prince of Wales, at whose court gathered many of
the principal opponents of Walpole. In the years immediately prior
to the appearance of this passage in 1744, Lyttelton was one of the
leaders of the campaign to impeach Walpole; and in this passage
he is described as straying through his park at Hagley, his 'British
Tempe', and thus a landscape not much less ideal than the valley
of the Thames. There he enjoys the harmonious concert of 'the
various Voice of rural Peace', such as was enjoyed by primaeval
men in the Golden Age; abstracted from this, he contemplates 'the
Philosophic World' and 'Historic Truth', composes a few verses,
and plans

> with warm Benevolence of Mind,
> And honest Zeal unwarp'd by Party-Rage,
> BRITANNIA'S Weal, how from the venal Gulph
> To raise her Virtue, and her Arts revive.

Finally, he and his wife arrive at a high viewpoint, from which a 'bursting Prospect spreads immense around', including harmoniously within its natural landscape

> Villages embosom'd soft in Trees,
> And spiry Towns with surging Columns mark'd
> Of household Smoak.[13]

Thus from the retired viewpoint in his park at Hagley, Lyttelton has a large view of Britannia as happy and harmonious; but like the poet's retired view in 'Summer', it may be a very selective comprehensiveness. It is of course particularly easy to see a vast prospect as a harmonious composition, if in its foreground is a landscaped park designed to organize the world beyond it into a pictorial unity from a carefully chosen station. Thus the retired view of the gentleman is particularly favourable to the attempt to see a 'happy World'. But its happiness depends also on the view, as well as the viewpoint, being largely rural: the villages are marked, it seems, not by their buildings, but by the trees that 'embosom' them; the towns are marked by smoke, which announces their presence in the landscape and also conceals it – a convenience of rural viewpoints noted, at the beginning of the nineteenth century, by Crabbe: the man of landed property can look down from his 'upland Paddock', and 'just perceive the Smoke which hides the Town'.[14]

If the town is where the 'Sons of Interest' are to be found – and it often, but not always is, in Thomson's scheme – one convenience of this retired, comprehensive viewpoint is that it does not comprehend them. In an earlier prospect view in 'Spring', the poet describes himself as leaving the 'noisom Damps' of the town 'buried in Smoke' to climb a hill from which he sees the country 'far-diffus'd around' as 'one boundless Blush'; in the 'fair Profusion' of Spring, his 'raptur'd Eye' can perceive 'yellow Autumn' hiding.[15] Thus from his retired and lofty viewpoint he can see through the apparent vicissitudes of the seasons, which had begun only with the fall of man, and see the modern world, or the rural portion of it, as unfallen, still golden.

The paradox of all this, of course, is that if the 'comprehensive view' is attained only by an act of retirement, it is by an act which seems to acknowledge that view to be partial. It is because the town, buried in smoke and divided by interest, inhibits a clear and disinterested vision of the world, that we must retire to the country to see clearly. A probable justification of this is that, in the sight of God (which becomes in these passages hardly distinguishable from that of the retired man, for both see his Creation as 'good'), the town is in unproblematic harmony with the countryside, and the problem is only to discover the correct viewpoint from which this can be seen to be so. In the town we encounter the 'Sons of Interest'; from the country we discover that they too have their place in the providential plan. But this can appear to be so only because, from a retired viewpoint, the town becomes virtually invisible, its inhabitants entirely so. The retired man, looking down from his landscape garden, and enjoying the 'elegant Sufficiency'[16] that elsewhere in the poem Thomson (as he had done in the epistle to Dodington) adds to the qualifications necessary to the achievement of this benevolent vision, can allot the sons of interest a place in the social scheme precisely because he can no longer see them.

The point is worth underlining: he can no longer *see* them, but this does not mean they are absent from his thoughts, simply that they cannot be included within the prospect view which is committed to showing the world as 'happy', as good. The boundless, the 'immense' prospects which attempt to render the comprehensive vision of the retired man of landed property, can in fact represent only one part of what he knows, and that point is clear from the representation of Lyttelton that we have already quoted. As long as his eye is on the landscape, he sees the world as harmonious, but that vision may be more comfortable than complete; for when he becomes abstracted from the contemplation of nature, he plans, as we have seen, how to raise Britannia from the 'venal Gulph' into which she has fallen; how to rescue her from the apparently invisible sons of interest; and these plans he 'makes with honest Zeal unwarp'd by Party-Rage' – no partial interest actuates *him*. Lyttelton thus becomes a complete, a universal man as Talbot had been, and as are the dedicatees of the various books of *The Seasons*: Dodington again, for instance, in 'Summer', whose virtues are shared by Onslow and Wilmington, addressed respectively in 'Autumn' and 'Winter'. These men, and Lyttelton, are the poem's ideal of the disinterested man of comprehensive vision, fired with patriotic concern for the true interests of the realm.

The use of the 'saving virtues' in a world already saved The problem, however, in the representation of Lyttelton, is that his comprehensive vision, and his disinterested public virtues, both of them traditionally the qualities of a patriot of landed property, seem to be predicated on those contradictory notions of modern society, as ascending and declining, that we have already noted as a characteristic of *The Seasons*. If the world, seen from the viewpoint of retirement, is happy, what need has Lyttelton for his public virtues? How can they be exercised? Why does he need to plan schemes to rescue Britain from the venal gulf of interest? We can imagine, perhaps, that as Thomson argued in his long poem *Liberty* (1735), Britain is indeed happy, and that public virtues are necessary only to keep her so, but that is not Lyttelton's sense of things, by which Britain is at once both happy and corrupt. And a similar problem arises shortly after the prospect, in 'Summer', of the vale of Thames: the rhapsodic address to Happy Britannia is followed by a prayer to God that he will 'send forth the saving VIRTUES round the Land', Peace, Love, Industry, and so on, but led by

That first paternal virtue, public Zeal,
Who throws o'er all an equal wide Survey,
And, ever musing on the common Weal,
Still labours glorious with some great Design.[17]

This design is evidently not directed at making a supremely happy country happier still: for these are the '*saving* VIRTUES' [my italics], their task to recall Britain from a corruption nowhere visible in the prospect of her.

The traditional view of the world and of political society that can understand change only as evidence of moral decline, of corruption, is in awkward competition here with an eighteenth-century rationalism that understands the world as the happy design of a providential deity, and, since society is included in the world, sees it too as happy, because divinely ordered, its increasing wealth the gift of divine benevolence. This competition illuminates the contradiction in the abilities and virtues attributed to the gentleman. On the one hand, the gentleman views the world as happy, as harmonious, and he can hardly be permitted to see it differently, for that is how God too sees his creation. For the gentleman to do otherwise would be mistaken at best, but at worst impious, for he would then become a 'Critic-Fly', whose 'feeble Ray scarce spreads An Inch around'; and 'to tax the Structure of the Whole' would be to exhibit the blindness of the ignorant, the self-interested, and the anti-social.[18] If the gentleman's view of the world is to have an absolute authority, it can do so only so long as it is a harmonious view, and one which, as I suggested in my remarks on the epistle to Dodington, requires the exercise of no virtues other than those necessary to its discovery – an unerring judgement and a generous benevolence.

On the other hand, the 'wide Survey' of such a man is of no value unless it issues in the development and use of the public virtues that are no less an essential attribute of the gentleman than is his breadth of vision; and the existence and exercise of these virtues seem to demand that he see society as in urgent need of his impartial and active zeal. The gentleman, it may seem to us again, may be a detached observer, or an active patriot, but not both; and if he is the first only, his comprehensive knowledge will prompt him to no virtuous action; and if he is only the second, it is not clear that his corrective zeal will be easily distinguishable from that of the 'Critic-Fly'.

We might imagine that this contradiction is merely apparent, and argue that God and those 'generous Minds' of whom Lyttelton is the prime example see a happy, but not a perfect world, which, however, through the exercise of God's providence and their virtues, is steadily progressing towards perfection. But these generous minds represent the height of perfection in the chain of being of a world which is also perfect; for they appear at the culmination of an extended passage in which Thomson's 'Theme ascends' from the 'various vegetative Tribes', and on through the birds and beasts, in a celebration of the 'Master-hand' which has 'the great Whole into *Perfection* touch'd' [my italics], and theirs is the 'sublim'd' vision, the 'purer Eye', to which 'th' informing Author in his Works appears', and to which 'this complex stupendous Scheme of Things' appears to be 'with ... Perfection fram'd'. They themselves exemplify that perfection, both as they are able to observe it, and as they are the active instruments of 'CREATIVE BOUNTY': 'Humanity', wrote Thomson in a letter to Aaron Hill,

is the very smile and Consummation of Virtue; 'tis the Image of that fair Perfection of the Supreme Being, which, while he was infinitely happy in himself, mov'd him to create a World of Beings to make them so.

The humane and bountiful explore the wintry corners of the world in search of those whose distresses they can relieve; but the very need for providence and bounty, and the fact that they can be exercised, must call into question the generous mind's observation of the world as perfect, and God's too.[19] The problem, which arises from a rationalist emphasis on the perfection of Creation and not on its fallen state, can be resolved only by a confession of ignorance and a profession of faith, but, as we shall see, when in *The Seasons* Thomson adopts that solution, he cannot do so in such a way as to suggest that the pure vision of the generous mind might be deceived in seeing the world as perfect.

Nor can the contradiction we have arrived at be resolved by arguing that the natural world, correctly seen, is perfect, and that only man's accretions to that world are evil; for the 'purer Eye' subdues the works of man into the perfect harmony of nature of which they are therefore seen to be a part. Besides, to fail to suggest that the society and government of Britain, that 'ISLAND of Bliss', had not also been framed by the hand of providence, was to surrender one of the most potent weapons for the defence of a mixed constitution and a limited monarchy, which could do '*boundless Good without the Power of Ill* ', and in which therefore Heaven is 'imag'd'.[20] That constitution can of course be threatened – and continually is, in Thomson's works – by corruption; but the problem remains, where in the pure and wide prospect of a gentleman can corruption be glimpsed?

A similar sort of problem, in the task and identity of the gentleman, had been familiar in English political debate for many years before the 1740s, particularly to members of the 'country party', gentlemen of landed property who considered themselves to be the guardians of the traditional political virtues of detachment and disinterestedness: if the ability of the gentleman to judge impartially how to exercise his virtues depends on his vision of the whole, and if that vision depends in turn on his retirement, or at least on a detachment from immediate interests represented by the metaphor of a space between his viewpoint and the field of political conflict, then to descend into that field to pacify and regulate the contestants was surely to resign the detachment which enabled him to know how they should be regulated.[21] The problem is dramatized by its attempted solution in *Liberty*, where Independence and Retirement appear as a 'generous Pair' of personifications, who love the 'simple Life, the quiet whispering Grove', and the pleasures of the 'free-born Soul'. If Independence is 'demanded' to the public scene – for he never appears there undemanded – and must therefore 'quit his *sylvan Friend* a while', he remains still 'active for the Common-Weal', unable to be seduced from his independent standpoint by 'Corruption's Tools'.[22] It seems that, if we can regard the retired man and the patriot as an intimate pair, one can do the observing while the other does the acting; the patriot seeks to actualize the vision of the observer, whose wide survey may direct the actions of the patriot; but the need to imagine the qualities of the universal man as thus divided in their unity, may indicate the difficulty of proposing, in any one man, the ability both to observe and to act rightly.

Heroic portraiture But the problem in that passage from *Liberty* is not exactly the problem as it appears in *The Seasons*, for the latter poem is more committed to a rationalist defence of the world and of society of the kind offered by Pope in the *Essay on Man* or criticized by Voltaire in *Candide*: that this is the best of all possible worlds, and our problem is simply to grasp it as such. The authority of the gentleman now resides in his ability, not simply to see widely and correctly, but correctly to see the 'happy World' that God sees; but as I attempted to argue earlier, the prospects of that world by which its happiness is represented to the rational observer are remarkably partial, and seem only able to justify society as properly natural by submerging the town, the place of interest and faction, into the 'natural' landscape. I want now to suggest that the partial nature of this comprehensive view arises from a difference between what can plausibly be represented as the view of a gentleman, and a rather different view available to the narrator of the poem – a difference which, once it is observed, seems implicitly to question whether the gentleman would not have to be – as eventually he is, in *The Seasons* – considerably redefined and re-presented if the authority attributed to his knowledge and his virtue is to be vindicated.

We can understand the exclusive character of the detached and gentlemanly view of society more clearly, perhaps, if we consider the descriptive terms in which that view is shaped. In the introduction to this book, I argued that it was not until it became possible to understand the structure of modern society in economic terms that the various discrete elements imagined as composing it could be understood as productive of its unity, and not destructive, but that the price of that new understanding was that no one could thenceforth claim to have a complete view of society, because no one could be found whose view could be defined, in these terms, as comprehensive. It may be worth attempting to understand *The Seasons* in terms of that development; for we have seen that in Thomson's representations of society as corrupt, the agents of that corruption are described as opposing 'interests', which, in the language of political theory, produced the need to search for an observer who could claim to be disinterested, and to find him in the man of landed property. In these terms, it is clear that Lyttelton, Talbot and the rest qualify as impartial observers who, detached from the 'little Fray', can observe its structure, and can regulate it. If, on the other hand, the prospects of society they offer us, from the viewpoint of temporary retirement, appear exclusive, that is perhaps because they lack any language, other than that of the prospect-view, to describe the variety of society in terms which will still represent that society as unified and harmonious. The missing term, I suggest, is labour, is industry: the retired gentleman cannot easily see that if society is a unified pattern of opposing elements, that unity proceeds from the variety and therefore the interdependence of its specialized labours, as it is understood in terms of an economic model of society.

If we look, indeed, at representations of 'Happy Britannia' which are not offered in the form of the prospect, we will find that it is exactly in terms of labour that its happiness is described: and in those terms luxury, which from the estate seems an agent of corruption, can be understood not as destructive of industriousness but as its product and reward. When, for example, the prospect of the Thames valley is concluded, it is followed by an account of England as 'teeming' with a wealth produced by the toil of the agricultural labourer, and by the previously invisible 'Sons of Art' in towns and in crowded ports, which 'with Labour burn'. In a long account of the development of civil society, it is entirely by 'Industry' – by mining, smelting, carpentry, masonry, weaving – that society has become united, 'numerous', 'polite' and 'happy'; one in which the merchant is no longer a 'sordid Son of Earth' but properly busy, and where 'the various Voice of fervent Toil' is a harmonious concert, not a threatening discord.[23]

In a society defined by the narrator as a concert of labour, not a conflict of interest, it is not clear what the gentleman can contribute to its happiness. He cannot offer his special faculty of vision, for the details of labour are, the poem manages to suggest, beneath the notice of his elevated viewpoint; he cannot offer his own labour, for his authority and status depend on his performing no task. Nor is it easy to see how he can contribute his patriotic zeal, for its exercise demands that society be divided and corrupt, and not as it appears in this economic account, as unified and blessed by industry. His virtues, like Dodington's in the epistle, can still therefore be praised, but the direction and object of their energy cannot be imagined. In this light the 'gentleman' seems to become an identity in search of a role, and he seems to be threatened by a paralysis which finds its embodiment in Thomson's addresses to various patriotic statesmen in the poem, who are possessed of an impressive range of public virtues which seem to remain, however, latent virtues only, awaiting as it were the corruption of a society which their godlike vision represents to them as supremely healthy and not at all in need of rescue.

We may take as examples the opening addresses in 'Summer', 'Autumn', and 'Winter' – 'Spring' is a different case, for, addressed as it is to the Countess of Hartford, it is obliged to attribute to her only the private, 'soft' virtues appropriate to a noble lady. 'Summer' is addressed to Bubb Dodington, but in terms which do not do much to distinguish him from the statesmen to whom 'Autumn' and 'Winter' are addressed. Dodington is distinguished, indeed, only by his private relation with the poet – he was Thomson's 'youthful Muse's early Friend'; otherwise, he is simply an ideal exemplar of all the public and private virtues that could be elegantly and conveniently listed within a brief address: in him

> the Human Graces all unite:
> Pure Light of Mind, and Tenderness of Heart;
> Genius, and Wisdom; the gay social Sense,
> By Decency chastis'd; Goodness and Wit
> In seldom-meeting Harmony combin'd;
> Unblemish'd Honour, and an active Zeal
> For BRITAIN'S Glory, Liberty, and Man.

'Autumn' is addressed to Arthur Onslow, for more than thirty years speaker of the House of Commons, a position for which disinterestedness is the pre-eminent qualification; he is a man of 'noble Cares', whose thoughts are taken up with 'Patriot-Virtues', and whose parliamentary eloquence is sweeter than the song of Thomson's Muse, though both are zealous for 'public Virtue'. 'Winter' is addressed to Spencer Compton, the Earl of Wilmington, who is skilled in 'awful Schemes', like those planned by Lyttelton, 'to make a mighty People thrive'; and he is marked by 'equal [that is, impartial] Goodness', 'sound Integrity',

A firm unshaken uncorrupted Soul
Amid a sliding Age, and burning strong,
Not vainly blazing, for thy Country's Weal,
A steady Spirit regularly free;
These, each exalting each, the Statesman light
Into the Patriot; these, the publick Hope
And Eye to thee converting, bid the Muse
Record what Envy dares not Flattery call.[24]

That even envy could not describe these addresses as pieces of flattery is perhaps the greatest hyperbole they contain, and one calculated, of course, to secure the less extravagant position, that if anyone *does* call them flattery, it will be out of envy that he does so. And if these addresses do flatter, it is not only by attributing such an ideal blend of virtues to so many Whig politicians, men who have hardly perhaps earned the attribution, either by displaying those virtues in life, or by dying, as Talbot did, and so becoming the subject of a genre of poetry in which anything less than extreme hyperbole can be represented as a lapse of taste – *de mortuis nil nisi optimum*. It is also that, in putting such stress on the importance of public virtue, of disinterested zeal for the national interest, they imply that the presence of such virtues in the gentleman patriot makes all the difference between a society which is chronically sick and one which may possibly recover its health.

No doubt when they first appeared these addresses could have been understood merely as the conventional acts of obeisance of an ambitious young poet. But by the appearance of the 1744 edition of *The Seasons*, Dodington had broken with Walpole, and Wilmington had briefly succeeded Walpole as First Lord of the Treasury; and in the 1744 edition the addresses to these men and to the nobly impartial Onslow appeared in company with a considerable number of passages in praise of men hostile to Walpole and to the system of institutionalized corruption he had developed – Pitt, Lyttelton, Cobham, Chesterfield, Cornbury, and others. It seems likely that all these passages would now have been read as attempts to represent their subjects as members of such an élite as Bolingbroke describes in his *Letter on the Spirit of*

Patriotism, men on whom the 'Author of nature' is 'graciously pleased to bestow a larger proportion of the ethereal spirit, than is given in the ordinary course of his providence to the sons of men'. Such men, in the circle influenced by Bolingbroke, to which in the 1730s Thomson, via Lyttelton, had become attached, were urged to oppose Walpole by becoming 'the guardian angels of the country they inhabit, busy to avert even the most distant evil, and to maintain or to procure peace, plenty, and the greatest of human blessings, liberty': the well-being of the commonwealth was entirely dependent on the vigilant ministrations of such patriots.[25]

That point is well suggested in the address to Lord Chesterfield, in 'Winter', who is described as a man, once again, of great and various accomplishments and virtues, and of a commanding eloquence which is used to further the interests not of any one party but of all men, by an appeal to their best selves:

O THOU, whose Wisdom, solid yet refin'd,
Whose Patriot-Virtues, and consummate Skill
To touch the finer Springs that move the World . . .
Thou to assenting Reason giv'st again
Her own enlighten'd Thoughts; call'd from the Heart,
Th' obedient Passions on thy Voice attend;
And even reluctant Party feels a while
Thy gracious Power . . . .[26]

By this eloquence, disinterestedly employed, Chesterfield can 'touch the finer Springs that move the World' – a line which depends for much of its meaning on a play on the meanings of 'move' and 'World'. Thus the line admits to being read as a fairly conventional compliment to an orator, that his eloquence is found moving, an incitement to right action: but that reading smuggles in a more extravagant one, by which it is Chesterfield's Orphean eloquence which, as we say, 'makes the world go round', which stirs it into the activity necessary for its survival.

The world is thus imaginéd, is fictionalized, as if its fate is entirely dependent on men such as Chesterfield, a notion which seems to be challenged, however, by the style of Thomson's addresses, which could be described as the nearest imaginable equivalent, in verse, of the style of heroic, of 'historic' portraiture we associate particularly with Sir Joshua Reynolds. The distinction between one gentleman and another, is, as often in Reynolds's work, less remarkable than what they are represented as having in common – the same blend of the great but few virtues and attributes necessary to the patriot: a piercing intelligence, a patriotic ardour, and a disinterested spirit. That uniformity is imagined as justified in portrait painting by the exemplary functions of the art: the ideal of Reynolds is that portraiture increases in importance as a genre the more nearly it approaches history painting – the more, that is, that it discovers a universal nobility of feature, of character, of virtue in its subjects, and the less therefore that it represents them as particular men.[27] But such idealized portraits, though their distant setting may be – in the case of admirals, for example – a seascape, or – in the case of soldiers – a field of battle, can portray only the character necessary to the performance of great actions, and not the actions their subjects have performed; and to a lesser degree the same is true of history painting itself, which can represent heroic actions only in a motionless epitome of an extended and complex event. But when that point was made in the eighteenth century, it was always by contrast with the ability of writing, to represent men through their actions and not their appearance or their qualities only; so that if Thomson chooses to represent Chesterfield and the others by a means analogous to that of portraiture, the effect is to fix those men, to represent them as ideal blends of latent qualities which cannot be represented as issuing in action, because, as I have suggested, no actions can be envisaged for them which will not be predicated on a view of Britain as corrupt, as other than a Happy Britannia of industry, prosperity, and freedom.

The point can be confirmed if we look at one more account of a great statesman in *The Seasons*, one which is acknowledged to be an extraordinarily special, indeed a unique case, but one which seems to keep alive the possibility that it may still be the patriot, the man of public virtue, to whom even this new version of social unity is apparent. It is, appropriately enough at the very end of the poem, in answer to the question, 'What cannot active Government perform?', that this figure emerges, in the form of Peter the Great, and the answer he offers seems to be 'everything'. For Peter 'left his native throne', spurning 'the slothful pomp of courts',

And roaming every Land, in every Port
His Scepter laid aside, with glorious Hand
Unweary'd plying the mechanic Tool,
Gather'd the Seeds of Trade, of useful Arts,
Of Civil Wisdom, and of Martial Skill.

Instead of observing the world in prospect, Peter descended into the landscape, and roamed it himself, as only Lyttelton's 'eye' roamed it from Hagley; but this was no grand tour, such as Steele's gentleman undertook, for as well as gathering political information and an understanding of military affairs, occupations becoming to a gentleman, Peter himself worked as an artisan, and paid attention also to the arts of commerce. On his return to Russia his empire, 'taught by the ROYAL HAND that rous'd the Whole' became 'One Scene of Arts, of Arms, of rising Trade'[28] – a unified polity, not threatened but confirmed by the range of occupations every one of which Peter himself had practised: and more influential on the development of his Empire than his wisdom was his example – his attempt to be a universal man skilled in all the arts now perceived to be essential to a happy land.

The example of Peter was important to the period we are studying, because it appeared to solve so many problems in the notion of what a 'compleat gentleman' might be. He was 'fir'd', wrote Defoe, who in 1722 had produced *An Impartial History* of his career, 'with resolutions of improving himself that he might improv his whole empire'.

He sought wisdom, thro' the whole world; he applyed for knowledge in every branch of science. He knew he wanted it before, and he knew it was to be obtained, and this made him unwearied in his applicacion to encrease his knowledge, to cultivate his understanding. This made him resolv to travell, that he might furnish his head with knowledge: the want of it made him uneasie and unsatisfy'd with himself and with his whole empire: he abhorr'd to be ignorant of any thing, and from hence he resolv'd to see every thing that was to be seen, hear every thing that was to be heard, know every thing that was to be known and learn every thing that was to be taught... he built himself a yacht or pleasure boat, and had allmost drown'd himself to learn how to work it. [29]

This special case, this aristocrat of comprehensive view and public virtue who is also a migrant jack-of-all-trades, is an improbable fiction enough, but one so eminently useful if the possibility of a comprehensive, authoritative and optimistic understanding of a society, now perceived as infinitely complex, is to be preserved, that we shall meet versions of him twice more in the course of this study.

The passage from Thomson is not a portrait of Peter, a static arrangement of his virtues, but a narrative account of his actions; however if it has the effect, intended or not, of admonishing the

British statesmen represented elsewhere in the poem, it does not leave them with much opportunity to profit by the lesson. For the career of Peter, the tireless exercise of virtue, is dependent on a representation of Russia before his reign as 'a huge neglected Empire', whose people were 'savage from remotest Time', living in 'Gothic Darkness'; it is because in Britain and the other countries he visits a 'Plan of State' has been developed,[30] and the arts of commerce and industry are already advanced, that Peter is able to profit from his travels, and can attempt to attract to his own nation a felicity already enjoyed in other countries.

The example of Peter the Great, however, makes more than one comment on the gentleman statesman as he is represented in *The Seasons*, or in the epistle to Dodington: it suggests not simply how he might, though only in other circumstances, employ his virtues, but also how he might develop a less selective view of the society he observes – as I have suggested, by abandoning his fixed viewpoint, and descending into the prospect itself. This lesson too is a hard one for the gentleman to learn – for it was precisely the fixed nature of his viewpoint which seemed to guarantee its authority – its attachment to fixed property, not the moveable property of the merchant, and therefore to the permanent, not temporary, interests of the realm. It was not for nothing that the 'Spectator' claimed, in the first number of his periodical, that his 'small hereditary Estate' had survived 'whole and entire' for six hundred years, without a single field or meadow acquired or lost. The fixed nature of landed property made it arguably analogous to that viewpoint, beyond space and time, from which God surveyed his creation – an analogy that, as Pocock has shown, had long been a crucial element in the claim for the disinterestedness of the man of landed property.[31] To abandon the viewpoint provided by the estate may therefore be to forfeit not only one's claim to have any general view of the world and of society, but also one's identity as a gentleman, as Peter himself had done, if only temporarily, when he laid aside his sceptre, plied 'the mechanic Tool', and thus passed through a succession of occupations whose characteristic, as we saw in the introduction, was that they occluded a view of the world from any other aspect than that demanded by the interests of the occupation.

There is of course one other figure in the poem who sees the world from a succession of changing viewpoints, but who, engaged in no particular occupation and laying claim to no specific identity, appears to have the ability to perceive them all, and thus perhaps to see them as unified in a coherent vision of society. This figure is the narrator, to whom Ralph Cohen, the most thorough and the most perceptive of recent commentators on *The Seasons*, ascribes a good deal of the responsibility for the unity he discovers in the poem. To Cohen, the retired estate offers a purely ideal look-out point on society, one too comfortable to be more than *a* perspective on the world, and with no especial claim to pre-eminence. If any mortal within the poem is possessed of a truly 'unifying vision', it is, argues Cohen, 'the speaker-commentator, the man of many muses or roles', who 'for all his changes', remains consistent in his values. He recognizes 'the tendencies in man for good and evil' – he sees the world as happy and as corrupt – while urging a 'belief in God's wisdom and benevolence': by 'his class anonymity', he 'provides a possibility of moving unnoticed among all classes',[32] and thus is capable of a more comprehensive vision of society than is available to Lyttelton, or to any other patriotic gentleman except, perhaps, Peter.

There is much in this that I would agree with, but I would question for whom it is that the retired estate appears to offer an *ideal* viewpoint: it may do so for us, and evidently my account of the poem is concerned to show it to be just that. It is less clear that Thomson himself could have acknowledged its purely ideal status, in that, as I have suggested, to do so would be to challenge the authority of the gentleman when it is exactly that, I will suggest later, that he is, through whatever difficulties, concerned to protect – and if the gentleman is one who can 'taste The Joy of GOD to see a happy World', Cohen's argument could be taken to question the pre-eminence of the viewpoint of God himself. Nor am I convinced by the claim Cohen makes for the vision of the narrator. If his values remain consistent, that is perhaps to say no more than that he is consistent in the habit of continually alternating views of society as happy, and as corrupt; and if, in order to develop these opposing views, he must employ, as he so frequently does, the image of his Muse as a bird, capable therefore of wandering everywhere and anywhere in search of the comprehensive knowledge available to the bird's-eye view; and if he must continually change his role, in order to represent, by an effort of imaginative sympathy, the different perspectives on society that he describes, it is still not clear that the 'balanced' view that his sympathy enables him to develop is therefore a unified and not simply a

various one. It is clear that the condition of writing the poem is a
wide survey, but it may not therefore be a comprehensive one; and
if the narrator himself, who is occasionally able to grasp the
structure of society in terms of the unity of co-operative labour,
cannot always convince himself that by those terms the divisions,
the 'Fray' of interest is overcome, it may be that no one can now
develop a convincing view of the order of society, and that the
poem exemplifies the impasse described in the introduction,
whereby, as society is discovered to be increasingly complex and
divided, no one is left able to comprehend it.

The prospect: bounded or boundless?   That answer – that a
knowledge of the order of the universe, and of society, is
unattainable – is offered by the poem too, though out of deference
more to the transcendent knowledge of God than to the complexity
of society. It is offered by the poet on a number of occasions when,
as Cohen puts it, he 'urges belief in God's wisdom and benevolence',
and accepts the limitations of human knowledge in the assertion
that only God can see the whole. In 'Winter', for example, the poet
considers what he, and other men who aspire to public virtues,
might profitably do in a period of retirement. They might try

> to scan the *moral World,*
> Which, tho' to us it seems embroil'd, moves on
> In higher Order; fitted, and impell'd,
> By WISDOM's finest Hand, and issuing all
> In *general Good.*

That even those whose fortune allows them to aspire to the public
virtues of the patriot can only 'try' to grasp the design of moral,
and therefore of social life, which to them, even in retirement,
'seems embroil'd' – would appear to be as clear an announcement
as one could wish of the impossibility of any mortal attempt to
grasp fully that design, and of the poet's resignation to that
impossibility, in the faith that God grasps it, and impels the world
towards '*general Good*'. At the end of 'Winter', the necessity for
faith and patience is urged on us again; our vision is now imperfect,
even deluded, and we must leave the task of seeing the world
correctly to God, whose vision we will share only at the second
coming, when we will understand the apparent imperfections and
inequalities of the social world as part of '*the great eternal Scheme*'

as our limited prospect 'wider spreads' until 'one unbounded SPRING' will 'encircle All',[33] and our view becomes truly unconfined, unbounded, comprehensive.

Such declarations of ignorance seem to be necessary, not only to forestall the charge of impiety that might be incurred by the claim that any human being, however illustrious, can see as God sees, but also to reconcile the contradictions within the poem's account of human society, as progressive or in decline, that we have been examining throughout this essay. For if even the gentleman, the man of public virtue, can see the world both as happy and as corrupt, this is a mystery, the solution of which can only be left to the omniscience of God. It is a solution which, however, seems simply to generate another contradiction. For if Lyttelton, or Talbot, or even the poet himself, can sometimes or often see the world as good, it is not clear that, on such occasions, their view can be either confined or mistaken, and Thomson is often at pains to argue that it is not either of those things. The promise of the new vision we will enjoy at the second coming, when the mist at the horizon that now confines our understanding is removed, is hard to distinguish from the account, in 'Spring', of the comprehensive and benevolent view of the universe enjoyed by Lyttelton and by the poet himself. And when, in 'Summer', the poet asks the rhetorical question:

And lives the Man, whose universal Eye
Has swept at once th'unbounded Scheme of Things?

we may be reminded of the confident assertion in the memorial verses to Talbot, who saw

With instantaneous View, the Truth of Things;
Chief what to Human Life and Human Bliss
Pertains [34]

– not much, if anything in the '*moral World*', seems to have been concealed from the late Lord Chancellor.

We seem to be being asked to believe two incompatible assertions, that the gentleman and patriot, when he sees the world as happy, sees it as God sees it; and that only God can see the world as good, because only he can see it as a whole. The second of these assertions is, within the terms of Thomson's theology, not open to question; but we never seem invited to believe that the benevolent and comprehensive view of the gentleman patriot – however partial it might seem to us, on a critical reading – is mistaken at those moments when it seems to reveal to him just that happy design in the universe that God sees in it. There can be no resolution of this contradiction, but perhaps, when we have made an attempt to account for its presence, and its function in the poem, we will be able to see that it is a contradiction which, as long as it remains unobserved, is more convenient than embarrassing, and convenient particularly to safeguard the position of those to whom the poem is addressed – not simply of Dodington, Onslow, Wilmington, Chesterfield, Pitt, Lyttelton, but of all that splendid constellation of the aristocratic and gentle, of whatever party (and Walpole himself among them) who subscribed to the first complete edition of *The Seasons* in 1730.

We have seen that, however much the view from the estate may appear to us a partial view, it was, when evoked in Hagley Park, accorded a high degree of authority, a high degree of compatibility, that is, with God's vision of the world. And however much the prospects seen from such a retired pastoral viewpoint may depend for their harmony on an ambiguous blurring of the objects in the landscape – a blurring which we may take to indicate that their view is 'boundless', or that it achieves its concord by ignoring the specificities of the images it includes – they do, formally, include village and town among the works of nature and of agriculture, and so may claim to be, formally, a complete, or completely representative, view of the landscape and of the society of Britain. When reflection on that other world, of which the gentleman, in his identity as a man of public virtue, is also aware – the world of opposing interests and of apparent injustice – suggests that human society is less than the concordant pattern seen from Hagley, then, and only then, does Thomson remind us that the world seems to us less than perfect only because we cannot, as he now chooses to argue, grasp the design for creation that can be known only from the viewpoint of its providential creator. Thus if we are puzzled that 'unassuming Worth' should die 'neglected', that the 'lone Widow and her Orphans pin'd In starving Solitude', or that 'Luxury' is permitted to form 'unreal Wants', such mysteries are not capable of being penetrated from our present station, and must wait for solution until the prospect spreads wider, and becomes truly boundless. [35]

There seems to be a certain inconvenience in Thomson's

dependence on the prospect-view as the principal harmonizing strategy of his poem: because that strategy cannot acknowledge imperfection in the universe except by simultaneously requiring us to see that imperfection as, at a higher level, a harmonious part of the providential design, the poem cannot dwell in any detail upon aspects of society which the gentleman has recognized as corruptions and which offer him therefore an opportunity for the exercise of his public virtue. But that inconvenience, which, as we have seen, seems to deprive the gentleman of some part of his moral and political identity, is essential to what is also the convenience of the strategy, and of the contradiction which is the answer to the question, 'Who sees the world fully, and who sees it as good, God only or the gentleman as well?' For the prospect-view encourages us to trust in a view of England seen by the benevolent and retired gentleman, a comprehensive view of a happy world, whose happiness it would be impious for us to question, for it is the nearest approach to God's view available on earth. If we see the world as discord, as a place where it might seem unjust, for example, that extremes of wealth and poverty, idleness and industry should exist, that is either because we are not gentlemen, and cannot see the relations between them, or because, even if we are, we do not yet share the boundless view of God. This argument, which can cheerfully represent the prospect from retirement as 'boundless' at one moment, and at another as limited compared with the boundlessness of God's prospect, is one which in its various versions will be familiar to readers of Augustan verse, of the *Essay on Man* in particular, and has the value of being able to be used as a comprehensive answer to whatever difficulties can be thought up by the ignorant, the presumptuous, or the disaffected.

If we are fortunate enough to be able to see the world as happy, that is because our boundless prospect of it is in line with God's; if we are unfortunate enough to see it as discordant, that is because no one can grasp its true design. The comprehensive viewpoint is suddenly (and, we may feel, arbitrarily) made subject to the limitations of our mortal nature, whenever it threatens to become implausible, and the mist at the horizon can be used to suggest that the prospect is boundless, or subject to the error of imprecision, as it becomes appropriate to do one or the other. It is a naive view of *The Seasons* which imagines that the contradictions in the poem arise from simple negligence on Thomson's part; but it is not much less naive to argue that, by the blurring of values in the prospect view, and by the arbitrary imposition of limits to it, Thomson achieves a humble but profound view of the universe, which comprehends as much of God's mysterious ways as it can, but willingly and obediently gives way before the incomprehensible.

By such means, he can use the prospect-view, now bounded, now boundless, to assert that the order of society is providentially designed, is necessary to the happiness of Britain, and is therefore not open to be changed. The gentleman, by one version of the argument, can see better than anyone else the relations between the various elements that compose society: it is the reward and also the justification of his retirement, that, in Goldsmith's phrase, 'those who think must govern those who toil'.[36] By another version of the poem's argument, no one, not even the gentleman, can see those relations; but in that case we must have recourse to the providential wisdom of God, whom we believe to have created a happy world, even if it does not now appear so to us, and who has therefore created a social order still not open to be changed by human agency: whatever is, is right, whether we can judge it to be so or not. Thus however much, at times, the poem provokes us to question whether the gentleman, who like God sees creation as happy, is right in his view of it, and whether he is not, by his situation, only too favourably disposed to see it as happy, it does not permit us to question his right to the 'elegant Sufficiency' and the retirement he enjoys, which if not justified by his wide thought is justified by God's; and if we, or if the narrator, sometimes seem to see more of the world than he does, this perception is, at best, no more authoritative than the gentleman's, at worst much less so.

The position of the gentleman, the wealth he enjoys and the authority of knowledge he claims, are thus in a manner vindicated; and if his other defining characteristic, his public virtue, seems still insecurely founded, it is asserted by Thomson no less positively for that. It may be that the assertion feeds off the contradiction in the poet's opposed accounts of society, or feeds, rather, off the *visibility* of that contradiction, which directs attention to a deficiency in his view of the world rather than in the gentleman's, and yet manages to insert into the poem the image of a society in alarming decline which the patriot can then be represented as anxious to reverse, and which can only be reversed by him. The contradiction, I am saying, seems to operate in the world as it is seen by the poet – this is where it is always discovered by critics of Thomson – and not in the world inhabited by the gentleman of 'wide Survey' and 'public Virtue'. It is that deflection which therefore allows the gentleman still to appear in that double identity, as the benevolent observer of Britain's happiness, who tells us that the nation is in need of no social or political rearrangement, and as the stern bulwark against corruption, who informs us that his virtues, and his alone, can rescue a nation in decline.

'The Castle of Indolence' The issues we have noticed in *The Seasons*: the comprehensiveness of the view of the gentleman, and how his privileged viewpoint is to be justified; the problem of whether, if he sees the world as 'happy', he does not need to see it also as corrupt if he is to exercise his virtue; and the suggestion, in the account of Peter the Great, that if we are to see society as happy, we must understand its component parts not as competing interests but as co-operating labours, these all are raised in Thomson's last poem, *The Castle of Indolence* (1748), an allegorical narrative in the stanza, and in a version of the language, of Spenser. This poem, even more explicitly than *The Seasons*, calls attention to its mixture of pastoral and georgic elements, the more explicitly perhaps because its official purpose seems to be to question, much more directly, the authority of the happy prospect as it appears to the retired gentleman, and to suggest that the pastoral life he enjoys may sap that sense of duty, that strength of will on which the achievements of a progressive society must be based.

The poem tells a story, which it will be convenient briefly to summarize. There is somewhere, apparently in England, a castle owned by the wizard Indolence, a poet with the power to enchant those who hear his song and are touched by his 'unhallow'd Paw'.[37] The castle offers those who enter it a life of perfect luxury and ease, in the most beautiful pastoral surroundings, at least for so long as the willing inmates remain pleasing and healthy: when they cease to be so, they are locked in a dungeon beneath the castle. In the second of the two cantos, the Knight of Industry, who has civilized the civilized world, and especially Britain, retires from his labours to a country estate, where he is told that, such is the wizard's success, the stability of British society, and the continued progress of the realm are seriously threatened – in particular, the wizard has infected the labouring classes with resentment at the apparent indolence of their masters. With the help of a dwarfish patriotic bard, probably a representation of Pope, the knight goes to the castle and overcomes the wizard. Of the inmates, those who repent in time he leads to lives of useful toil, while those who repent too late are driven through a muddy, boggy land, the opposite of the pastoral landscape they had previously enjoyed, and one which teaches them, indeed, what the natural landscape would be like, if it had not been cultivated by the labour of others.

The first canto, in which the life of Indolence is described, offers two very different accounts of the human condition, which correspond with the two alternative accounts of human history as they were set out in 'Spring'. According to the voice of the poem, in the very first stanza, man lives by toil, is sentenced to labour forever, but this 'hard Estate' is better than its unattainable opposite, a life of ease, which would bring far greater evils than man at present puts up with. This beginning may seem to present so straightforwardly georgic a vision of human life that when the wizard produces his alternative the relation between the two must seem to be as that of truth to falsehood, reality to dream – but the situation is more complex than that. The wizard argues that we do indeed have a choice about how we live – we may work, or if we wish we may live a life of idleness.[38] It may occur to us, of course, that each of these accounts may be true according to who is imagined to be addressed, the practitioner of a particular occupation or the gentleman of none, producer or consumer, but that, it would seem, is not the official point of the contrast. The life of idleness is presented by the wizard as a life of luxury, and as one which may be chosen by all those, whatever their station in life, who are persuaded to enter the castle.

Thus the inmates include representatives of the highest and lowest degrees of men –

> From Kings, and those who at the Helm appear,
> To Gipsies brown, in Summer-Glades who bask . . . .[39]

– though of course the choice of gipsies to represent the lowest class is rather forced on Thomson, because, as they do not visibly engage in any employment, they are the members of that class who can most easily be represented as idle by choice. The advantage of the wizard's introducing the notion of choice is clear; for while the first stanza presents the producer, at least, as merely *obliged* to work out a sentence which he may suspect, as he looks around, to have fallen unequally on him and on those who consume the product of his labour, the wizard, apparently more destructive of the order of society, is in fact simply more artful in its defence. The poorest and most laborious of men, his song manages to suggest, has *chosen* to reject a life of idleness, not for the danger of starvation it brings, but for the enervating luxury it would force upon him. He may feel that he envies the idle and luxurious, but his own choice of an arduous existence shows that that he knows, in spite of his immediate inclinations, what is really worth having and what is not.

The identification of a life of indolence as a life also of luxury is not made at the start of the poem. In the early stanzas, Thomson concentrates on the landscape round the castle, and describes it as one in which is lived the soft and simple life of pastoral eclogue: all men rest in flowery fields, lulled by the conventional concert of rural sounds led by the pipes of 'vacant Shepherds'. The sense of an effortless pastoral existence, as unencumbered by luxury as by labour, is continued by the beguiling song of the wizard, who compares the human lot unfavourably with that of the butterfly, whose pleasures are 'unearn'd';[40] the birds, he goes on, like the lilies of the field, 'neither plough, nor sow',

> Yet theirs each Harvest dancing in the Gale,
> Whatever crowns the Hill, or smiles along the Vale.[41]

Thus gifted by nature, they 'hymn their good GOD', and the wizard is not ashamed to present this life of easy pleasure as a moral life, and a religious one: for 'What', he asks, 'is Virtue but Repose of Mind?' – a question that has been asked so often before, by so many poets of rural life, that it may threaten the eventually industrious moral of the poem more than it discredits the wizard's pastoral alternative.[42] If it does not, this is because, once the wizard's song has ended, the Castle appears in a quite different light – no longer as an old-time poetic fantasy, but, quite recognizably, as an eighteenth-century country house, in which time hangs so heavily on the hands of the inmates that they find no repose of mind or body.

The life of indolence In becoming a more eighteenth-century life, the life in the castle does not become less pastoral: rather, the ideal of pastoral ease and the 'Splendor, the luxurious State' enjoyed by the English aristocracy become impossible to separate. Thus the 'huge Tables' in the castle are 'crown'd' with 'Wines high-flavour'd and rich Viands', all 'silently display'd' by 'some Hand unseen' – food produced and served without visible effort as in the Golden Age, but of a delicacy and range unknown before the eighteenth century. Life is occupied in eating, drinking, loving, and singing, as it was in Arcadia, the hospitality so lavish and free that victuals appear simply as they are desired, and one is spared the effort even of expressing desire. The castle, like an English country house, contains a collection of paintings by the most fashionable artists, '*Lorrain*', 'savage *Rosa*', and 'learned *Poussin*'; and the costly tapestries with which the walls are hung depict Arcadian or Sicilian scenes, according as to whether they are presumed to illustrate the eclogues of Virgil or the idylls of Theocritus; others show the patriarchal age of Abraham, when 'Toil was not', and when, in most theories of aristocratic Pastoral, the best of men were shepherds, and society was divided by rank but not by occupation. The furnishings of the castle are modern, yet encourage a properly pastoral, or, more than that, an 'oriental' indolence:

> Soft Quilts on Quilts, on Carpets Carpets spread,
> And Couches stretch around in seemly Band;
> And endless Pillows rise to prop the Head;
So that each spacious Room was one full-swelling Bed.[43]

The comparison thus made between the castle and the country house allows the poem to represent the idle life as a plausible and a thoroughly attractive one, even to the poet himself, who can only produce the second canto of the poem, in praise of the Knight of Industry, when he has escaped from the Castle. But however attractive the pastoral life enjoyed by the aristocracy, it may not always be admired, and not enjoyed, perhaps, for long: so that although the light exercise of gardening is permitted to those who would not be entirely inactive, even those who perform it, 'Bevies of dainty Dames, of high Degree' whose 'only Labour was to kill the Time', are shown as making at best 'a vain Shew of Work' – 'to knot, to twist, to range the vernal Bloom'; or else they simply 'saunter forth' into the park, 'with tottering Step and slow', but finding even this 'too rude an Exercise', go indoors and lie down.[44]

In the terms of this essay, the life in the castle may be most particularly identified with that enjoyed by the aristocracy in retirement when the wizard himself puts forward an account of the history of society as one of progressive corruption, which necessitates a withdrawal from the world: for it was when 'hard-hearted

Interest' began 'to poison Earth' that '*Astraea* left the Plain'. The castle thus represents not only a pastoral refuge from a society divided by competing interests, and thus an opportunity to step out of history, but also a place of disinterestedness, 'above the Reach' of 'wild Ambition', and above those Passions that this World deform'. The retired man is thus the happy man, enjoying a repose of mind which is a gift of the repose of his body – for this is before we have begun to be shown how that repose enervates rather than recreates him – a gift of his freedom from the necessity to pass 'the joyless Day' in 'various Stounds', the misfortunes of various forms of employment. It is because he does nothing that he is disinterested, and it is because from the castle of 'tender Indolence' are banished 'Interest, Envy, Pride, and Strife' that the inmates can discover there a life 'sooth'd and sweeten'd by the social Sense', that benevolence particularly attributed to the retired gentleman in *The Seasons.* Those in the castle are as much removed from the 'filthy Fray' as Talbot was superior to the 'little Fray' of competing political interests.[45]

It is worth pointing out, for it will be of some importance later, that this life of indolence is offered more to the polite, some of whom enjoy it already, than to the vulgar, who do not – the point is made by the series of promises, of freedom from labour, made by the wizard. Those who enter the castle need not 'rise at early Dawn' to follow employments which, if they are not the exclusive 'employments' of the rich, are exclusively those of the polite, or the literate; who take their rounds in the City, pay visits, 'proul in Courts of Law', or 'in venal Senate thieve'; and when, in contrasting the soft pastoral harmony of the castle with the discords of active life, the wizard seems to promise a freedom from labour to the 'Swain', it soon turns out to be a promise that the castle is soundproofed from the noises of vulgar labour that normally disturb the rest of the genteel:

> No Cocks, with me, to rustic Labour call,
> From Village on to Village sounding clear;
> To tardy Swain no shrill-voic'd Matrons squall . . .
> Ne noisy Tradesman your sweet Slumbers start,
> With Sounds that are a Misery to hear.[46]

One favourite occupation of the inmates was

> In a huge crystal magic Globe to spy,
> Still as you turn'd it, all Things that do pass

Upon this Ant-Hill Earth; where constantly
Of Idly-busy Men the restless Fry
Run bustling to and fro with foolish Haste,
In search of Pleasures vain, that from them fly.

In this glass, '*of Vanity the Mirror*', were visible the various occupations (not all of them laborious) of the men described as ants here, as 'Emmets' in the first stanza of the poem, from which the inmates were free: the 'Muckworm' (or, as we say, 'money-grubber') 'at his dull Desk, amid his Legers', repeating the prudential maxim of Sir Andrew Freeport in the *Spectator*, 'A Penny saved is a Penny got'; the 'spendthrift Heir', and the 'Pimps, Lawyers, Stewards, Harlots' and 'thieving Tradesmen' who help him to ruin himself; 'the Race of learned Men'; the 'prowling Crew' of the 'splendid City', who 'prey', 'each on each'; and the 'puzzling Sons of Party'.[47] It is a world in which all compete in the vain pursuit of private ends, of the 'wild Ambition' which the 'sons of Indolence', unlike those of interest, are so far above.

It is thus not only by identifying the castle with the country house that the poem seeks to identify the 'Sons of INDOLENCE' with the retired gentleman; it is also by emphasizing the lack of occupation of such a man, and that his understanding of the world is framed in terms of a fray of interests which he is 'above'. If those whom the wizard of the castle has enchanted are to be saved from their sloth, it will have to be, it seems, by someone who is more than a retired and therefore happy man; and, as we shall see, the ideal gentleman that this poem proposes, in its second canto, as the saviour of Britain – not now from venal interests, but from indolence – is another Peter the Great, who sees society not as divided by competing interests but as unified by co-operative labours, all of which he can himself perform.

The life of industry The second canto, officially at least, shows the wizard overcome by the Knight of Industry, and the ideal of an indolent life replaced by that of a life dedicated to the improvement of nature and the production of wealth. It opens with a mythological account of the development of the arts, and of the progress of civilization, both of them engineered by the Knight, who contains within him a number of separate aspects, at once the manager of labour and the labourer, the theoretician of the applied arts and the artisan. He is the son of Selvaggio, man natural and unimproved,

and of Dame Poverty, the mother of invention; and, as he grows
up, he becomes expert

> In every Science, and in every Art,
> By which Mankind the thoughtless Brutes excel,
> That can or Use, or Joy, or Grace impart,
> Disclosing all the Powers of Head and Heart.
> Ne were the goodly Exercises spar'd
> That brace the Nerves, or make the Limbs alert,
> And mix elastic Force with Firmness hard:
Was never Knight on Ground mote be with him compar'd.

The Knight of Industry is thus a universal man as unusual in his
abilities and attainments – we might say as unique – as Talbot, or
as Peter the Great: he is a skilled and enthusiastic hunter, a well-
practised soldier, a philosopher natural and moral who has examined
whatever Nature contains 'in th'Etherial Round' and beneath 'her
verdant Floor', as well as 'those moral Seeds whence we heroic
Actions reap'. To those high, and perhaps proper gentlemanly
pursuits, this allegorical figure has added others less polite: wrestling,
building houses and sailing ships, 'plying' the spade, or plough, or
'strong mechanic Tool' – a phrase we met before, appropriately
enough, in the account of Peter the Great. He can paint, so well as
to vie with nature; he can sculpt, and is a complete and various
musician. The epitome, thus, as his allegorical status demands that
he should be, of every imaginable art except those which, like law
or physic, depend for their existence on the corruption, not the
health of society, he sets out 'a barbarous World to civilize'.[48] By
comparison, Lyttelton, in *The Seasons*, seems woefully ill equipped
to 'revive' Britannia's arts from 'the venal Gulph', as well he might
be, not being a custom-built allegorical ideal. But as we shall see,
the Knight of Industry becomes something more than that, and, as
he does, he seems both to vindicate and to challenge the ability of
such a statesman as Lyttelton to perform his public duties.

The Knight of Industry finds the world for the most part
primitive and violent; he leaves it civilized and peaceable; and it is
only when this has been achieved that the story told in this canto
unites with that of the first. The Knight completes his labours with
the civilization of Britain, a comparatively easy and (he might have
reflected) a partly unnecessary task, for in Britain there was, it
seems, none of the savage strife that characterized primitive life in
other countries. That done, he retires, as an honest statesman

should, to his rural estate, where, unlike the statesman however, he continues to be at once chief, patriot, and swain too. But he is soon 'demanded' from his retirement, for on his estate he is informed that Britain is in danger of relapsing into sloth, and that the 'lowest' members of society are questioning the division of privilege which exempts the 'Lord' from practising the industrious virtue he enjoins on his 'Lacquey'[49] – it is the social order, and particularly the privilege of the gentleman, that has been challenged, and which the Knight must therefore vindicate and confirm; and if he is to vindicate it, it must be by insisting that the lord as well as the lacquey must practise industry, or, rather, that he generally *does* practise it.

The necessity of industry to society, and the nature of the responsible and industrious life, are described by the bard in a song which answers that of the wizard in the first canto, and by which the bard attempts to persuade those the wizard has enthralled to recover the freedom of their will, and thus to rediscover their duty. The Bard is modelled on the character and appearance of Pope no doubt because of Pope's reputation as an opponent of the venality practised and encouraged by Walpole, and because he had seemed to inaugurate a new genre of poetry in English, the moral essay, by which the claim of poetry to teach as well as to please had particularly been vindicated. He describes civil society in his song, not as corrupted by the vain pursuit of material gain by the 'idly-busy', but as entirely dependent for its support on their labours:

> It was not by vile Loitering in Ease,
> That GREECE obtain'd the brighter Palm of Art . . .
> It was not thence majestic ROME arose . . . .

– and the inmates of the castle must 'Toil, and be glad', for 'who does not act is dead'.[50]

Just as, in the first canto, members of all classes were described as having chosen a life of indolence, but the indolence of the polite seemed to be particularly at issue, so here it is by blandishments particularly designed to persuade the polite to labour that the life of industry is recommended; for the rewards of labour are described as opulence, and especially, renown, to be won not by ploughing and digging, but by bold enterprise in statesmanship and the polite arts. And yet, as the model of indolence was the luxurious life lived in country houses, the corresponding model of industry, as the bard describes it, is the life enjoyed by the 'toiling Swain'

> Who vigorous plies the Plough, the Team, or Car;
> Who houghs the Field, or ditches in the Glen.

This man is 'perhaps the luckiest of the Sons of Men': he is content to live on no more than the simplest fare, preferring the 'native Cup' of ale or cider, to the 'Wines of *France*', and plain bread to the 'Glutton's Cates'; and this moderation together with the habit of daily industry means that he enjoys a degree of health that the richer and less fortunate cannot hope for.[51] But what is this paragon of industry meant to represent when his example is held up not just to gipsies, or to the 'vulgar Men' who are now demanding a share of pastoral ease, but also to the would-be virtuous rich? In Thomson's effort to show how the swain is to be reconciled to his lot, the rewards and blandishments of his life – a simple, healthy, vigorous existence – are presented as the rewards of physical labour, unavailable and inappropriate to those who do not perform it, whether they live as do the inmates of the castle, or lead a less exaggeratedly comfortable existence in the real world – an existence which from the perspective of the toiling swain is no doubt indistinguishable from that led in the castle. What can the rich do, to be as happy and as virtuous as the poor? And by what comparable labour can they earn the opulence they enjoy, and the renown they are to be persuaded to crave, as the swain earns his health by hedging and ditching?

The answer appears a few stanzas later in the bard's song: the Knight of Industry, he announces, will lead the inmates of the castle, some to 'Courts' and some to 'Camps',

> To Senates Some, and public sage Debates,
> Where, by the solemn Gleam of Midnight-Lamps,
> The World is pois'd, and manag'd mighty States;
> To high Discovery Some, that new-creates
> The Face of Earth; Some to the thriving Mart. . . .

– all will be led to work of some sort or another, in a differentiated, organized, and thriving society; and all apparently to a life as industrious as that of the toiling swain, and perhaps more so; for some, the stanza continues, will be led 'to the Rural Reign, and softer Fates'. This line may apply to those engaged in the activities of agriculture, so often seen through the glass of Pastoral as more indolent than those of the town. If the responsibilities of the great are such that they must toil in courts, in camps and in midnight debates, then the life of the swain, at first the emblem of the most arduous labour, is now seen as an easy option, so that one wonders why the 'Lord' himself, and not his 'Lacquey', had not originally been used as an example of one 'whom Toil has brac'd'.[52] But that he was not makes it equally plausible that it is the rich who are here being offered a life of rural retirement and repose – a promise smuggled into this list of social duties as if it was truly one of them. The line can be read either way: it can reassure the poor that they work no harder than the rich; and it can hint to the rich that they need not work at all.

We may now begin to see that the song of the bard not only counters but complements the song of the wizard. The latter suggests that the indolent pleasures we associate with the life of the rich may be shared by all; the bard replies that the simple virtues of the ploughman are equally available to all. By the first argument, the equality of society in Britain is asserted, for all could live in idle luxury if they chose; by the second, the social structure is defended from the demands of the vulgar for a more equal distribution of privileges; for all men earn their bread in different ways but in one way or another, and none is more idle than another. It is officially denied that repose and industry are the particular characteristics of the life of different classes, the duties and pleasures of life being shared among all members of the united kingdom of Britain – an equality of effort we may feel is undermined, however, by the hint we have just examined, and by the fact that the images that typify industry and idleness are on the one hand the doggedly laborious 'Swain', on the other the luxurious country house.

The Castle of Indolence is by reputation a very ambiguous poem, and a number of critics have felt this ambiguity to be so great as to preclude the poem from making any unified or coherent statement about the issues it seems to be discussing. The problem, if it is one, is in Thomson's social vision before it is in the poem, for his understanding of the unity of Britain can be presented only by ambiguities which, once perceived, are indeed likely to destroy the apparent unity of the narrative. For industry means different things to different people: a life of continuous labour for the toiling swain, a life of public service to the senator, sweetened by the promise of future retirement. If Thomson reproves the life in the country house, it is with the aim of persuading us of the importance of the swain's labours; if he appears to approve it, as he does, for example, in the account of the well-merited retirement of the Knight, it is with the sense of that polite existence as the flower and ornament of Britain's wealth and civilization. Such ambiguities proceed from the nature of the task that Thomson has set himself, of justifying the fruits of social division, while denying at the same time that any serious social divisions exist.

In order to perform that task, however, Thomson has been obliged to create a figure in whom the power of unifying society resides, who is quite as implausible a construction as Peter the Great. For the Knight is an allegorical figure whose status as allegory, in a literature which by the eighteenth century had come to expect such figures to act as more or less motionless personifications, becomes less and less apparent to us as the poem proceeds; by the end of the second canto, he looks more like an ideal patriot who is rescuing Britain, as Lyttelton had only planned to do, from the corruptions of luxury. But it is on the nature of his education, at the start of the canto, when he was most evidently being treated allegorically, that his claim to be equal to his task is founded. It is his own willingness to perform every occupation necessary to a flourishing society which gives him a knowledge of the importance of industry, and of society as dependent for its health on the co-operation of its members all seen, ideally, as workers. It is not then a disinterestedness which bases its claim to a comprehensive understanding on being placed above the merely mechanical occupations of 'idly-busy' men – that is the delusion of the 'Sons of Indolence' – but one which is based on a practical understanding of all those occupations.

By increasingly representing the Knight of Industry as the ideal of a patriotic statesman, who is 'demanded' from his retirement to reanimate the public and private virtues of society, Thomson can preserve the notion that it is still the gentleman who sees the whole, and thus can vindicate, by another means, the elevation of the gentleman above the competition of interests. But the price of doing that is to redefine him as a quite improbably universal and laborious gentleman, a man who does everything, not nothing; for only thus can his claim to understand the relations within a society unified by labour, not divided by interest, be made good. He makes the blurred prospects of the retired observer more precise by his detailed knowledge, but can only escape the partial view of the practitioner of one particular task by performing them all – and the gentleman whose authority he has vindicated is set an example of the comprehensiveness necessary to maintain that authority in a complex modern society, but an example which is, only too evidently, an impossible fiction.

'The Fleece'   In *The Castle of Indolence* Thomson offers an account of society as united by labour, not divided by interest: Britannia becomes happy, not on Lyttelton's terms, by which the oppositions of interests among men could be blurred by blurring together the different landscapes they had created, but by acknowledging that different tasks are allotted to different men, and that it is on this basis that they are able to co-operate. However, that vision is dependent on the creation of an observer, the Knight himself, whose qualifications to understand the whole are imaginable only in such an allegorical construction as he is; that understanding does not seem available to the poet himself, who can understand the *notion* of diverse but co-operative labour, but who, if he is to be able to create that unifying allegory, must write in a genre and language hospitable, at best, only to the naming of the different tasks of society, not to the description of them and of the relations between them. The idea of social unity that we must assume is an immediate reality to the Knight can be communicated to us only as an idea, whose validity we take on trust only because not to do so is perhaps to condemn ourselves as indolent survivors from a world in which those tasks were understood only as the selfish pursuits of 'idly-busy Men'.

The only genre of poetry in which the task of realizing that idea could have been attempted was the formal Georgic, more or less in the manner of Virgil, a genre officially committed to the fairly detailed description of, in particular, rural labours, and a view of modern society as progressive by its labour. But in the early eighteenth century, Georgic is still evidently embarrassed by the freedom permitted to it of describing mean tasks in detail; for poetry, if it was to be worthy of the name, must please as well as instruct, and could instruct only about what was thought worth knowing. Thus much early eighteenth-century Georgic is written, it seems, as an exercise of style, concerned to substitute '*Metaphors, Grecisms* and *Circumlocutions*' for the terms of art, to avoid sinking into a '*Plebian* Stile', to 'toss the dung about with an air of gracefulness', and not to soil its hands by the close description of the mean tasks it proposed as its official subject.[53] It was not until a language had been developed by which society could be described in economic, rather than in philosophical or political theoretical terms, that Georgic could describe, without mock heroic apology, the various tasks of industry in some detail. Until then, the belief that such description would be as mean as the tasks it described was reinforced by an uncertainty as to whether it would be conducive to a representation of Britain as harmonious, as well as wealthy. For a proliferation of local detail was inimical to knowledge of the universal principles by which social organization was to be understood, and by which many of the newly important occupations of modern society were understood more readily as evidence of its corruption, not of its health.

The sense that the lowliness of mechanical occupations would communicate itself to the verse in which they were described was never entirely overcome: of John Dyer, the author of *The Fleece* (1757) Johnson wrote in 1781, 'the meanness naturally adhering, and the irreverence habitually annexed to trade and manufacture, sink him under insuperable oppression'.[54] But *The Fleece* itself was written at a moment when polite literature had achieved a considerable freedom to discuss such 'mean' topics, as *The Rambler* itself bears witness; a freedom lost to it again later in the century when, by the division of literary labours, poetry was left with the task of offering a sentimental critique of modern society whose organization was left to be described and vindicated in the various discourses of social philosophy, and most notably, of course, in the writings of political economists.

Of all the poets writing in mid eighteenth-century England, Dyer is the one most willing to acknowledge divisions in society: *The Fleece* sets out to demonstrate a unity of interest among the practitioners of different occupations whose attitudes to work and whose styles of life seem utterly opposed. The scope of the poem is as wide as that of *The Seasons*. We follow the fleece from the valleys of Herefordshire, through the industrial towns, to the ends of the most exploratory trade routes; it is wide, too, in the number of occupations it can thus reveal as unified by the parts they play, in the production and distribution of wool, in a pattern of economic and therefore also of social interdependence. That the main

concern of the poem is to represent Britain as unified in its
divisions is well suggested by the variety of occupations and social
classes gathered into the poem's opening address:

The care of Sheep, the labors of the Loom,
And arts of Trade, I sing. Ye rural nymphs,
Ye swains, and princely merchants, aid the verse;
And ye, high-trusted guardians of our isle,
Whom publick voice approves; or lot of birth
To the great charge assigns: ye good, of all
Degrees, all sects, be present to my song. [55]

These lines propose a community of concern among shepherds,
industrial workers, merchants, elected and hereditary members of
Parliament – between, finally, men of good will from all social
classes and all religious groups.

The task of the poem is then to discuss how a society fragmented,
in the terms of Ferguson, by the 'separation of arts and professions',
can be understood as still coherent. The society of eighteenth-
century Britain as both Dyer and Ferguson describe it is one in
which individuals all pursue their own interests and perform their
particular functions, without thought for the well-being of the state
as a whole; which is nevertheless guaranteed precisely by the
single-minded diligence with which each man faithfully carries out
his allotted task. The 'dignity, and grace, And weal, of human life'
are owing to the 'strong contrarious bents' which create, on the
one hand, 'vain wants' as well as 'real exigencies', and thus create
also the artisans and merchants to satisfy them; and which, on the
other hand, permit producers to do good to all as well as to
themselves by the labours they pursue, though all may be
'unconscious of the union', which is certainly invisible 'to vulgar
eyes'. The processes of wool production and processing are thus of
particular interest to Dyer as they define the structure of English
society as a whole, in which 'all seek for help, all press for social
aid', and so in which 'various professions ... unite: For each on
each depends'. Thus as Ferguson believes that only the statesman
may have 'a wide comprehension of human affairs', in a society
organized after this fashion, 'while the tools he employs are
ignorant of the system in which they are themselves combined', so
Dyer ends his opening address to the various classes and professions
of England by invoking the aid of the king, the 'people's shepherd',
who 'eminently plac'd Over the numerous swains of ev'ry vale', can

use his benevolent authority and watchful eye to ensure the prosperity of all his subjects.[56]

Dyer's decision to write a poem about sheep-farming, that branch of agriculture which, in pastoral poetry, is normally conducted in an atmosphere of relaxation or indolence, invites us to expect a conflict of values between his pastoral subject and his georgic verse. The first book, the only one in which rural life and shepherding are the main subjects, though it is willing to describe the tasks the shepherd must perform, is at the end most concerned to leave us with an image of the shepherd's lot as still something very much like it was in Arcadia. At least, shepherding in England is like that; for with a proper patriotism Dyer suggests that this easy life is a gift bestowed on England by her healthful climate and enviable political institutions; and even within England itself, Dyer suggests, the Arcadian life is lived especially on the uplands, where the healthy sheep do not disturb the pastoral pipe with 'hoarse cough'; more especially still in Siluria, 'the part of England that lies west of the Severn, viz., Herefordshire, Monmouthshire, &c'. The Wye, the Severn, the upland estates of Herefordshire and Shropshire, these places are the centre of the poem, with which as foreground Dyer looks out over the rest of 'noble Albion' and discovers a prospect as rich, as populous, as happy as Thomson's 'Happy Britannia' or Virgil's Italy: [57] from here he can see the whole world, indeed, as a prospect organized to facilitate the distribution of English wool.

This division between Siluria and the rest of England is underlined, for example, in Dyer's discussion of the various breeds of sheep:

But hills of milder air, that gently rise
O'er dewy dales, a fairer species boast,
Of shorter limb, and frontlet more ornate;
Such the Silurian. If thy farm extends
Near Cotswold downs, or the delicious groves
Of Symmonds, honour'd through the sandy soil
Of elmy Ross, or Devon's myrtle vales,
That drink clear rivers near the glassy sea;
Regard this sort, and hence thy sire of lambs
Select: his tawny fleece in ringlets curls;
Long swings his slender tail; his front is fenc'd
With horns Ammonian, circulating twice
Around each open ear, like those fair scrolls
That grace the columns of th'Iönic dome.

Yet should thy fertile glebe be marly clay,
Like Melton pastures, or Tripontian fields,
Where ever-gliding Avon's limpid wave
Thwarts the long course of dusty Watling-street;
That larger sort, of head defenceless, seek,
Whose fleece is deep and clammy, close and plain:
The ram short-limb'd, whose form compact describes
One level line along his spacious back;
Of full and ruddy eye, large ears, stretch'd head,
Nostrils dilated, breast and shoulders broad,
And spacious haunches, and a lofty dock. [58]

There are quite clearly two tones and two sorts of diction in these two paragraphs. In the first, the Silurian sheep, a 'fairer species' than the mountain breeds of sheep just discussed, is described in a diction as ornate and classicizing as, according to Dyer, its own appearance is. Its fleece is tawny (*fulvus*), curled in ringlets, and its horns curled also, in the shape of the horns of Jupiter Ammon, or the scrolls of an Ionic column. This writing is formal enough, but has nothing mock epic about it, none of that disdain for rural matters that informs the remarks quoted earlier on the language of Georgic. It is a language which, not especially simple in itself, directs attention to the simplicity of the shepherd's lot: if his sheep are Silurian, he need concern himself, it seems, with their beauty only, while less fortunately situated shepherds must worry about profitability.

The larger, nameless breed, on the other hand, recommended in the second paragraph to those with the soil to suit it, is described in a language altogether more appropriate to the pretensions of Georgic to be genuinely concerned with instruction. This language is even less concerned to conceal the details of rural life from the fastidious reader; it calls attention to its ability to say exactly what has to be said to the practical man. It is a language an auctioneer would understand, although in fact it is imitated from Virgil's similarly downright instructions on breeds of horses, as, in earlier English Georgics, are Thomas Tickell's and William Somervile's accounts of the points to look for in various kinds of hounds, and as is also, appropriately, James Grainger's advice on choosing slaves:

Must thou from Africk reinforce thy gang?
Let health and youth their every sinew firm;
Clear roll their ample eye; their tongue be red;

Broad swell their chest; their shoulders wide expand;
Not prominent their belly; clean and strong
Their thighs and legs, in just proportion rise. [59]

The first two editions of *The Fleece* were both issued with
frontispieces of sheep grazing. The first edition showed a breed
unrecognizable at least from the various descriptions of sheep
Dyer gives in his poem; the second shows one which is recognizably
the Silurian – its tail thin, its fleece curled, and the ram with
Ammonian horns. In bothering to get the illustration changed,
Dyer or his publishers, the Dodsleys, underlined the fact that the
poem's centre was Siluria.

These two styles are played off against each other in the first
book, sometimes to distinguish Siluria from the rest of England as
a particularly favoured and Arcadian region, and sometimes to
indicate more broadly the two opposed ideas of the shepherd's life
– as indolent or as industrious – which Dyer attempts to unify as
he later attempts to unify also the pastoral life as a whole with that
of industry and commerce. The language of that second paragraph
thus reappears whenever Dyer is most concerned that the precept
should predominate over the poetry, so that he avoids the epic
circumlocution, the coy mock heroic, in which all earlier writers of
Georgic couch their more practical passages. When Dyer describes
work, it can never be mistaken for play:

To mend thy mounds, to trench, to clear, to soil
Thy grateful fields, to medicate thy sheep,
Hurdles to weave, and chearly shelters raise,
Thy vacant hours require. [60]

In passages such as this, the shepherd's lot is suddenly attended
with hard, but dignified labour: this list is of jobs he must do in his
'vacant hours'. This insistence on arduous labour reads oddly
alongside the assurance, in the lines quoted earlier, that the life of
British swains was one of 'little care'. What is perhaps most
significant, though, is not that these two styles and the values we
associate with them can co-exist – that much is an aspect of the
occasional blurring of Georgic and Pastoral that is, I have argued
elsewhere, a particular characteristic of English Georgic – but that
the transitions between them are achieved, as we shall see, with an
ease, a sang-froid that reveals how assured is Dyer that the
opposition between them can be resolved.

The most extended passage in an explicitly pastoral mode is the description of the sheep-shearing feast, in which 'we think the golden age again return'd', so easily can the young swains, or their nymphs at least, be mistaken for the 'Dryades' themselves:

> While th' old apart, upon a bank reclin'd,
> Attend the tuneful carol, softly mixt
> With ev'ry murmur of the sliding wave,
> With ev'ry warble of the feather'd choir;
> Music of paradise! which still is heard,
> When the heart listens; still the views appear
> Of the first happy garden, when content
> To nature's flow'ry scenes directs the sight.
> Yet we abandon those Elysian walks,
> Then idly for the lost delight repine:
> As greedy mariners, whose desp'rate sails
> Skim o'er the billows of the foamy flood,
> Fancy they see the less'ning shores retire,
> And sigh a farewell to the sinking hills. [61]

This golden age, still to be found in the English valleys, is presented, by the references to Eden, to Paradise, as a stage in our own life, which we grow out of, or away from. It is something we leave behind in time, and in space too; the pastoral world, the Golden Age, is home, and the process of growing up is one of leaving home and innocence for a wider universe – for a delusive goal made attractive to us by our own perversity. The greedy mariners we thus resemble, however, are the same who, later in the poem, will be extolled for taking British wool to the ends of the earth, and pushing back the frontiers of the known world.

We have a clear set of oppositions before us now: between the pastoral and the mercantile life, Siluria and the rest of England, English valleys and the rest of the world, youth and age, all evaluated by the further opposition between innocence and greed; but in the very act of defining these conflicts, Dyer is suggesting a relation between them, by setting the English pastoral landscape and the infinite sea, pastoral innocence and acquisitive guilt, in the context of one process, one movement, one life. This spatial continuity between opposed sets of values, imagined in the familiar form of a world-wide prospect through space and time, becomes the basis of the unifying vision of society which emerges from the poem as a whole; so that what is, from the point of view of Siluria, a greedy quest for a delusive goal becomes, from an urban and mercantile perspective, a patriotic exploration, an expansion of the trade which is the life blood of Siluria and the world.

At this point, Dyer himself intrudes into the poem, as one who, like the greedy mariners, has left Siluria, and so as one for whom the description of the sheep-shearing feast involves a difficult act of memory. He manages it, however, and thus manages to reaffirm a continuity between his own individual experience of the two opposed worlds. What he remembers is a thoroughly conventional dialogue in the form of a pastoral eclogue, between two Silurian shepherds, Damon and Colin, on the Wrekin: a dialogue concerning the disadvantages of urban life, its luxury and squalor, about which neither seems disposed to disagree. The benefits of all but the pastoral life are dismissed, and it seems unlikely that any poem devoted to the arts of trade as well as of agriculture could recover from such a deliberate polarization of values and of activities. Indeed, from the prospect of this first, pastoral book, Dyer himself claims to be unable to comprehend how the 'verdurous' lawns and 'spacious flocks of sheep' can be held together in the same prospect with 'frequent towns superb of busy trade', 'ports magnific' and 'stately ships Innumerous': he represents himself as, in imagination, straying from Siluria to London, roving 'wild' among 'groves immense of masts', 'crouds, bales, cars ... wharfs, and squares, and palaces, & domes', like a naive stranger,

> unable yet to fix
> His raptur'd mind, or scan in order'd course
> Each object singly. [62]

The first book narrows its focus progressively, forgetting, in its introduction of the pastoral eclogue, the pastoral feast, that it had earlier shown the shepherd's life to be arduous, and forgetting, as its pastoral becomes exclusively Silurian, that there is an England elsewhere: it is as hard to anticipate how the valleys of Herefordshire will be shown to be promoting the same social interest as the towns of the north of England, as it is for the stranger to find an order in the immensity of urban life. And yet, by the end of the eclogue, Dyer is already at work reconstituting the society he has so deliberately polarized:

> The jolly chear,
> Spread on a mossy bank, untouch'd abides,
> Till cease the rites: and now the mossy bank

Is gayly circled, and the jolly chear
Dispers'd in copious measure; early fruits,
And those of frugal store, in husk or rind;
Steep'd grain, and curdled milk with dulcet cream
Soft temper'd, in full merriment they quaff,
And cast about their gibes; and some apace
Whistle to roundelays: their little ones
Look on delighted: while the mountain-woods,
And winding vallies, with the various notes
Of pipe, sheep, kine, and birds, and liquid brooks,
Unite their echoes: near at hand the wide
Majestic wave of Severn slowly rolls
Along the deep-divided glebe: the flood,
And trading bark with low contracted sail,
Linger among the reeds and copsy banks
To listen; and to view the joyous scene. [63]

This extraordinary sentence ends the first book, and the section of
the poem specifically related to the pastoral life. It begins with a
description of rural 'cates' such as we are familiar with from
Elizabethan Pastoral, which is recalled, too, by the mention of
'roundelays'. But now the focus of the description becomes wider,
the observer more removed: a prospect begins to form, in which
the mossy bank where the picnic is laid out is seen first in the
context of the mountain woods and winding valleys, a landscape
harmonized by the united orchestra of sheep, cattle, birds, brooks,
and shepherds' pipes; and then in the context also of the Severn
and the trading bark. In this latter movement there is a bold
attempt to harmonize the pastoral landscape with the local river
which is also the start of the trade route from Siluria to the world,
by accommodating the pastoral feast and the trading vessel – itself
modestly contracting its sail, not wishing to cut too assertive a
figure in the scene – within the same spatial continuum. This
seems a much more successful use of the prospect-view to harmonize
opposing images than Thomson's, because, as I mentioned earlier,
it does not attempt to conceal the conflicts it tries to resolve. For
us, the bark and the shepherds are part of a continuous and
harmonious landscape, unified by Dyer's inclusive syntax; but for
the bark itself the hill and its shepherds are something apart, a
scene over there which the bark itself is observing, itself unobserved
except by us. The shepherds, then, and the bark, see themselves as
entirely separate from each other; but our elevated position allows

us an overview, from which we can grasp the relations between them. It is a success which will convince us only for as long as we neglect to ask the question, who are *we*?

Trade and manufactures The elevated viewpoint which Dyer has now adopted, so that he no longer looks out on the world from within Siluria, is the one from which the rest of the poem is written, for the poem is as necessarily divided as is the labour involved in the production and distribution of wool. Thus, as well as the care of sheep, the poem represents, in more or less detail, the tasks of wool-combing, carding, spinning, weaving, fulling, the occupations of hatter, hosier, clothier, burler, dyer, wool buyer, factor and merchant seaman. And, turning for a moment to the weaver in particular, Dyer enumerates the various occupations that must combine to produce a loom – carpenter, smith, turner and graver – so that the poem seems as if written to echo that rhapsodic exclamation – 'What a Bustle is there to be made ... before a Fine Scarlet or Crimson Cloth can be produc'd, what Multiplicity of Trades and Artifices must be employ'd!' – quoted, in the introduction, from Mandeville, whose theory of luxury and desire Dyer is clearly familiar with. [64]

In Book II, the trading bark appears again:

When many-colour'd ev'ning sinks behind
The purple woods and hills, and opposite
Rises, full-orb'd, the silver harvest-moon,
To light th' unwearied farmer, late afield
His scatter'd sheaves collecting; then expect
The artists, bent on speed, from pop'lous Leeds,
Norwich, or Froome; they traverse ev'ry plain,
And ev'ry dale, where farm or cottage smokes:
Reject them not; and let the season's price
Win thy soft treasures: let the bulky wain
Through dusty roads roll nodding; or the bark,
That silently adown the cerule stream
Glides with white sails, dispense the downy freight
To copsy villages on either side,
And spiry towns, where ready diligence,
The grateful burden to receive, awaits,
Like strong BRIAREUS, with his hundred hands. [65]

This all takes place at evening, the time which, in eclogue, usually brings to an end such light labours as the shepherd has to perform, and sends him home to bed. This evening, however, the harvest moon is shining, and sees the farmer, unwearied, still gathering in the sheaves; and the pastoralized reference to work allows a smooth transition whereby the busy wool buyers can enter this subdued landscape. The paragraph continues, modulating unobtrusively between images of a soft pastoral life, and an active industrial one: elements of the language of both worlds are juxtaposed without discord: 'let the *season's price Win* thy *soft treasures*', '*downy freight*'. The progress of the bark, still modest, and gliding silently down the stream, makes a continuum of the landscape as it nevertheless becomes steadily less pastoral. The fleece is delivered, first, to copsy villages, and then to spiry towns, the proper component of the penultimate distance in a landscape by Claude or Thomson, where, however, a mass labour force is, as it were, lying in wait, to seize the fleece and to process it. The sense of a unity between the rural evening landscape and the industrial town is managed without shocks until the last line seems to insist on the conflict of styles, if not of interests. If we compare this with a prospect of Thomson's, we will see that whereas in *The Seasons* towns are firmly relegated to the penultimate distance, in this passage foreground and distance are at the end reversed – the town is suddenly right before us, and the harmony of the landscape almost endangered by Dyer's willingness to emphasize the opposition.

There is a variety of passages in the poem where Dyer makes what seem to be provisional, or incomplete gestures towards the resolution of pastoral and mercantile, or Pastoral and Georgic, that finally emerges only at the very end of the poem: for example, the occasional attempts to endow industrial processes with a seasonal rhythm appropriate to the cycle of agriculture only. Weaving, fulling, and so on proceed, he argues, from day to day, season to season – 'So the husbandman Pursues his cares' and so on.[66] It is a strange argument, that the very division of labour that has freed the industrial arts from the tyranny of cyclical organization, can be seen as precisely what relates them to the rhythm of agriculture – for by watching one fleece through several processes and several hands, Dyer imagines he is watching a process analogous to that by which the farmer divides his work into separate, seasonal activities.

In another attempt, at the resolution this time of trade with agriculture, Dyer retells, in a digression licensed by Virgil and by every other writer of Georgic, the myth of the Golden Fleece. In the first book, by modulating from the georgic manner to the pastoral, from pastoral simplicity back to the industrious values of Georgic, Dyer seemed to be presenting an idea of the pastoral life in which innocence and joy were the rewards of industry. In that way he managed to set up two separate ideas of the characteristic virtues of rural life; simplicity, when that life was seen in opposition to trade, and to London; but when it was seen as itself, a simplicity moderated by care and diligence. In the same way, in the second and third books, we are offered an idea of trade as characterized by busy activity, and thus opposed to the quietness of the shepherd's life; but when we look at trade in itself, we are repeatedly warned that it must be moderated by a pastoral simplicity, if it is not to be seduced, by the wealth it creates, into luxury and idleness. It is as a warning against this development that the myth of Jason is retold. When Jason arrives in Colchis, the land is already half corrupted, and the wealth that trade has brought is encouraging the people to neglect the shepherd's art. This process is completed by the theft of the fleece, by which is symbolized the final departure of the pastoral virtues from Colchis, and which necessarily brings about a decay in its trade also; for Dyer, as for other writers on economics in the century, trade can be lastingly beneficial only when founded on the secure base of a flourishing agriculture.

But the most impressive attempt to find an expression which will harmonize the separate activities that Dyer describes, and yet acknowledge the oppositions between them, occurs at the end of the poem, and employs the same spatial terms we saw used at the end of the first book, where the separation between Siluria and the trade-bearing Severn did not preclude an awareness of continuity between them. This last book is written in a headlong, rapturous manner, no longer pastoral at all, but 'daring, and sublime', as Grainger described it, occasionally troubled by warnings of luxury, but always finding new momentum in imitation of the relentless movement of trade. Dyer notices, for example, that there are few outlets for the fleece on the shores of Africa, in the land

>   of savage Hottentots,
> Whose hands unnatural hasten to the grave
> Their aged parents: what barbarity
> And brutal ignorance, where social trade
> Is held contemptible![67]

– where the abhorrence which at first seems to be a reaction to the

unnatural practices of the Hottentots, is in fact inspired by shock
at their indifference to English wool. This fourth book becomes a
description of the entire globe, as we follow the progress of the
fleece from the ports of England to China, Patagonia, and wherever
else English trading vessels have penetrated. And it is repeatedly
emphasized that it is the 'homely' fleece, the link between Siluria
and the furthest outpost of trade, that makes possible this
exploration, this triumph of progressive civilization.

In the last paragraph of the poem, Dyer returns in imagination
to Siluria, by a movement entirely conventional and entirely
appropriate to the homing instinct of Pastoral and Georgic alike,
when the Muse has flown beyond the limited compass that decorum
allows her:

> That portion too of land, a tract immense,
> Beneath th' Antarctic spread, shall then be known,
> And new plantations on its coast arise.
> Then rigid winter's ice no more shall wound
> The only naked animal; but man
> With the soft fleece shall every-where be cloath'd.
> Th' exulting muse shall then, in vigor fresh,
> Her flight renew. Mean-while, with weary wing,
> O'er ocean's wave returning, she explores
> Siluria's flow'ry vales, her old delight,
> The shepherd's haunts, where the first springs arise
> Of Britain's happy trade, now spreading wide,
> Wide as th' Atlantic and Pacific seas,
> Or as air's vital fluid o'er the globe.

This passage is closely reminiscent of the close of the *Georgics*, as
also are the concluding lines of Pope's *Windsor Forest* (1713). As
Siluria is linked with the furthest outposts of the developing
empire by the fleece, so Pope imagines a similarly concrete
connection between the forest and the mercantile world beyond it
(it is Thames who speaks):

> Thy Trees, fair *Windsor*! now shall leave their Woods,
> And half thy Forests rush into my Floods,

– as they are converted, of course, into sea-going ships. This
couplet is followed by a vision of a future *pax Britannica* in which
seas will 'but join the Regions they divide', and 'Earth's distant

Ends' will behold the glory of Britain. But after this flight into an epic future, Pope's 'humble Muse' gratefully returns to the silent shades of the forest, described in the conventional value-language of Pastoral – 'unambitious', 'sweet', 'careless';[68] and a quite unexpected division appears between the Thames and the Forest, between commerce and retirement, which can be accounted for only by the witty frailty of the union Pope had proposed between them.

The prophetic strain in this concluding passage is reminiscent also of the end of John Philips's *Cyder* (1708), except that Philips does not incline, as Pope does, to a pastoral nostalgia at the end. For him, the recent Act of Union of England with Scotland is an emblem of the unity of the British people as a whole, and guarantees their strength. In some belligerent writing he looks forward to a time when

> uncontroul'd
> The *British* Navy thro' the Ocean vast
> Shall wave her double Cross, t'extreamest Climes
> Terrific, and return with odorous Spoils
> Of *Araby* well fraught, or *Indus*' Wealth,
> Pearl, and Barbaric Gold.

This jingoism can spare a thought for agriculture as well as trade, for meanwhile, continues Philips, the swains at home shall reap 'unmolested', and Silurian cider will be borne to the utmost bounds of the globe, to triumph over the (French) vine.[69] This is an entirely unproblematic vision of the unity of Britain, and of the eventual unity of the world, in which all Britons will struggle for the same patriotic and imperial ideals.

Dyer avoids the opposite extremes of Pope and Philips by a dialectical *coup* which is the final and perfect expression of what I have been describing as his sense of the opposition of values, but unity of effort, in English society. At the end of *The Fleece*, the Muse returns to Siluria; but Siluria is no longer seen simply as a retreat, a place of retirement – the place that the greedy mariners or humble muse left, as they should not, perhaps, but still must do. Siluria is now seen, after this movement across the world and back, as at once a retreat, and as the source of all the energy behind that rapturous movement that Dyer has been describing and enacting. The valleys of Siluria are now both a refuge from the mercantile world, and the origin of all mercantile wealth. Trade, by its activity, is opposed to the state of rest that Dyer now looks for in the agricultural landscape, but is founded upon it; a volatile gas which energizes the entire world, yet a stable element too, because founded on a permanent agricultural base, as the Roman Empire is in Virgil's *Georgics*.

Two kinds of observer: gentleman and poet   *The Fleece* offers us, it may seem, the most whole vision of eighteenth-century English society that is offered anywhere in its poetry, holding together rural and industrial, industrial and mercantile, domestic and imperial concerns – yet, however remarkably it does this, we are likely to come away from a comparison of *The Fleece* and the poems of Thomson with a conviction that Thomson is by far the more complex and more artful poet. Dyer, while appearing much more willing than Thomson to admit the fact of division in society, is in fact so concerned to identify those divisions in terms of differences of occupation, as if to show how these can be reconciled is all that is needed to reveal the society of Britain as unified, to the extent that he is able to overlook other, more divisive aspects of society which were, however, evidently a problem in *The Castle of Indolence*, and would have seemed so also in *The Seasons*, had space permitted a more extended account of that poem. The opposition between Georgic and Pastoral, which is an important issue in all three poems, is at heart an opposition between two ideals of how life might best be lived, indolently or laboriously; but unlike Thomson, Dyer is content to share the terms 'indolence' and 'industry' exclusively among the producers and active distributors of Britain's wealth – the shepherds, weavers, merchants, and greedy mariners. In the later books of the poem, in particular, from the perspective of trade and manufactures, idleness is attributed to the shepherd's life, industry to trade and manufacture, and the content of this opposition is exhausted without any consideration of those who take no part in the productive effort of society.

The consumers of Britain's wealth do however occupy an important place within the poem, if not therefore within the society it describes. As we noticed earlier, the opening address, to all degrees of men, concludes with an appeal to the king himself:

But chiefly THOU,
The people's shepherd, eminently plac'd

Over the num'rous swains of ev'ry vale,
With well-permitted pow'r and watchful eye,
On each gay field to shed beneficence,
Celestial office! THOU protect the song.

Like Ferguson's statesman, the king, it is claimed, can oversee the activity of every vale in England, because he can see over all divisions – over all the upland areas, so to speak, which divide the country into separate and self-regarding valleys unaware of their place within the national economy and the national life. It is not an overview that pastoral Colin has when later in the first book he climbs 'huge Breaden's stony summit':

What various views unnumber'd spread beneath!
Woods, tow'rs, vales, caves, dells, cliffs, and torrent floods;
And here & there, between the spiry rocks,
The broad flat sea.

The 'various views' are exclusively rural except for that glimpse of the empty sea, and are the 'nobler', as Colin insists, for not including 'dusty towns'[70] – this is an expression of the shepherd's contentment with the narrowness, not the breadth, of his vision.

But it is not only the king who occupies the favoured viewpoint 'over the num'rous swains of ev'ry vale'; for, like Thomson, Dyer is happy to offer that station also to a number of aristocrats commended in the first book of the poem for owning upland estates which not only protect their sheep from rot, but also permit them an extensive view of England, a view of 'regions on regions blended in the clouds'[71] – a comprehensive view, like Lyttelton's, apparently at once boundless and harmonious because the opposition of regions, of which the poet is aware, is blurred.

It seems that if the reader also is to grasp the harmony of the 'social bond' – if he is to see with more than the 'vulgar eye' of those who, like 'sedulous ants',[72] stay close to the ground, so preoccupied by their immediate tasks that they are unconscious of the union in which they are involved, parts of this landscape, not observers of it – he must join the king and the men of landed property on the eminence they share. For except at one moment, which I shall discuss in a while, it seems that this is the only position from which a comprehensive understanding of English society is available. It is nowhere suggested by Dyer that the reader might, if he wishes, climb higher still, and see the observers of the landscape of Britain as also part of the view – as, at the end of the first book, the trading bark was at once observer and observed. But if they are to be also a part of the view, it must be, in this economic account of society, not simply as patrons of England's prosperity, 'shedding beneficence on each gay field', but also as the consumers of the wealth of each field, and rather more difficult to absorb into the landscape than the shepherds and mariners were. For Dyer has defined the unity of Britain in terms of a community of producers, some apparently more idle than others, but all finally industrious, and there seems to be no place in the prospect for those who merely observe it – which is perhaps why after all, Dyer has almost entirely left them out. It appears as though his candour, in admitting as boldly as he does the division between idleness (as enjoyed by the shepherds of Herefordshire) and industry (as performed by industrial workers and seamen) has had the effect of concealing from him another and more important division, between those who merely fill the poem, and those who read it.

If, in the attempts he makes to argue that the society of Britain is harmonious and unified, Thomson, and especially in *The Seasons*, appears to fail where Dyer seems to succeed, it is because he is only too aware, that the conflict between industry and idleness is not primarily a conflict of concepts, or of different productive occupations, but of classes. This is not something that can easily be avowed, though it always seems imminent in *The Castle of Indolence*; and Thomson seems obliged to conceal the oppositions his poems explore, not because, as he pretends, he knows too little of the workings of the world, but because he knows too much. What looked to be, in the context of Thomson's work considered in isolation, a willing agnosticism, becomes in a comparison with *The Fleece*, an awareness of problems of social organization in England that Dyer never approaches; and the far greater success of *The Seasons* in the eighteenth century was perhaps due in part to his ability to take up issues far more sensitive to the polite than those which Dyer examined so fully, and to drop them again tactfully beyond the horizon.

There is, however, one position in *The Fleece* from which Dyer's belief in the adequacy of the comprehensive, if blurred view of the aristocrat appears to be questioned. It occurs in the second book, where the poet describes himself in the process of collecting materials for the poem, whose aim is described as to teach the virtues of industry by which it can be argued that 'each man's born For the high purpose of the public good':

> For this, I wake the weary hours of rest;
> With this desire, the merchant I attend;
> By this impell'd, the shepherd's hut I seek,
> And, as he tends his flock, his lectures hear
> Attentive, pleas'd with pure simplicity,
> And rules divulg'd beneficent to sheep:
> Or turn the compass o'er the painted chart,
> To mark the ways of traffic; Volga's stream,
> Cold Hudson's cloudy streights, warm Afric's cape,
> Latium's firm roads, the Ptolemean fosse,
> And China's long canals; those noble works,
> Those high effects of civilizing trade,
> Employ me, sedulous of public weal:
> Yet not unmindful of my sacred charge.[73]

Without neglecting his duties as a clergyman, Dyer reassures us, he has himself worked to produce the poem, and in his spare time: conversing with the merchant, the shepherd, and, no doubt, the manufacturer, studying the trade routes, and so on. The knowledge that has enabled him to write what is certainly the most comprehensive and well-informed Georgic in English has been won by effort, and not simply given to him by virtue of any disinterested and capacious viewpoint he might have been privileged to occupy. The lines may remind us of Johnson: of those passages in his periodical essays where he emphasizes the degrees of effort necessary to an understanding of any extended activity, but of a passage also, in the *Preface* to the *Dictionary*, which we shall examine in the next essay, where defending his refusal to include the 'fugitive cant' of the 'laborious and mercantile part of the people' in the vocabulary, he announces it to have been unavoidable: 'I could not visit caverns to learn the miner's language, ... nor visit the warehouses of merchants, and shops of artificers'.[74] To define the language of the gentleman, who does nothing, such excursions are unnecessary; but to arrive at an understanding of social and economic organization, they are as essential to the Rambler as Dyer claims they are to him.

It is on the strength of his own efforts to understand Britain as a republic of industry that Dyer can claim himself to be 'sedulous of public weal'; and if to be so depends, in the society he has described, on thus occupying oneself, it is hard to see how public virtues can now be regarded as exclusively the preserve of the gentleman patriot. For by a move which was to become increasingly familiar in the late eighteenth century, Dyer redefines the private virtues of industry, fair-dealing, freedom from vain ambition, as public virtues, which now appear to belong to 'each man' but only if he works, as each man does, arguably, at the end of *The Castle of Indolence*: so that, from the perspective of this passage, the eminent seem now to be excluded from a society which they cannot clearly observe, and in which they are offered a role neither as producers nor consumers. These reflections are not offered by the poet, who is happy to reserve the position of knowledge to the king and to the great estate; but if Dyer takes none of the pains taken by Thomson, to justify those positions as still adequate to the task assigned to them, that is perhaps because it is hard to see how, in a society now exclusively defined as a community of productive labour, they could be justified at all.

In the mid eighteenth century Georgic was the dominant mode of the poetry of rural life; possibly, after the death of Pope in 1744, the dominant mode of poetry. But the applause for Happy Britannia was not joined by everyone: poets such as Thomas Gray and William Collins, unwilling or unable to support themselves in Grub Street or to compete for the dwindling patronage of the great, had less inclination to exult in the prosperity, or to believe in the unity, of Britain. Gray was more interested in the virtues of more impoverished, primitive communities, where the poet instead of celebrating what the polite chose to hear as the harmony of a nation which, from that primitivist viewpoint, was evidently discordant, could be the spokesman of a community less differentiated by rank or occupation. But he recognized, as did Collins, that the druidical, celtic or otherwise primitive communities he admired had disappeared from Britain: the last such community was being systematically destroyed and 'modernised' even as Collins was describing it in his 'Ode on the Popular Superstitions of the Highlands' (*c.* 1749). The writing of such poets seems reduced to questioning the possibilities of writing 'true' poetry at all in a 'progressive' age: it does not so much challenge the confident vision of Georgic, as resent it.

There was room, even in so nationalistic a culture as that of mid eighteenth-century England, for such muted utterances of resentment, but they could be made only, and only heard, in a tone and space acknowledged by all to be *private*. Thus the 'Elegy Written in a Country Church-yard' (1751) is composed as a soliloquy, as the interior monologue of a man who, no matter whom the poem appears to address, is speaking only to himself; the ode by Collins is in the form of a private letter to his friend John Home, a Scot who is therefore presumed still able to describe a world which is lost to Collins. The distinction, between such largely or wholly 'public' discourses as *The Seasons* and *The Fleece*, and discourses to which the freedom of disaffection is accorded on the understanding that they are private, is a complicated one beyond the scope of this book. But it needs to be noticed here, for by the mid century it was only in the private space that it was possible to acknowledge, at once openly and, as it were, *sotto voce*, that modern society was not just increasingly corrupt, but increasingly incapable of being understood: the society of primitive men, undifferentiated by occupation and divided, if at all, only by the luminous distinction of leader and faithful follower, is an ideal which announces that a society is healthy only when its simple structure is visible to all its members.

2 The language properly so-called: the authority of common usage

Law and language   In *The Castle of Indolence* Thomson was concerned to persuade us that the society of Britain was unified, at an economic level, by the co-operative industry of its members. Though he does not make much of the point, he also represents Britain as unified, on a political level, by the Law, before which all were equal. The basis of this political unity was the particular nature of the British constitution:

> A matchless Form of glorious Government;
> In which the sovereign Laws alone command,
> Laws stablish'd by the public free Consent,
> Whose Majesty is to the Sceptre lent.[1]

The laws command, not the King; they command the King too, whose majesty (as the rhyme word 'lent' insists) is borrowed from the people, who make the laws by their 'free Consent' and so are sovereign, and themselves free. The question this raises, of course, is 'Who are the people?' – a question that will preoccupy us throughout this essay. In this case, the answer is ambiguous, in Thomson's best manner: the people are, at once, all those with the right to vote, and thus with the power to give their 'free Consent' to the laws which govern them; and they are all the people privileged to live in such a society, voters and non-voters alike; for democratic theory in the eighteenth century had developed some subtle arguments to establish that the unenfranchised, those not directly but 'virtually' represented in Parliament, were free and consenting parties to the laws which governed them. It is, the poem argues, the law which governs all: those with votes, in consenting to surrender their sovereignty to the laws, make themselves (except, as we shall see, in extreme circumstances) as much subject to them as those without; all are equal before the law, and so Britain is an egalitarian society of free men.

This sort of argument – we will soon have occasion to examine it in more detail – was one of the main strategies by which the ideal political unity of Britain was asserted as showing through the actual and evident divisions between voter and non-voter, rich and poor, anglican and dissenter, metropolitan and provincial, in the period we are studying. But in this essay I want to study in particular how, by analogy with the unifying power of the law and the constitution, the language of Britain also was seen and was used as a means of impressing on the inhabitants of the country the idea of their unity, while at the same time it could be used (as it still is, of course) as a means of confirming, also, the divisions it pretended to heal.

The possibility of using the language of Britain as a means of confirming the unity of the nation is a frequent theme of writers on language in the eighteenth century, and is put most clearly perhaps by Thomas Sheridan, a teacher of elocution and rhetoric, and father of the dramatist. Noting that while other countries of Europe had refined, corrected, and ascertained their languages by 'fixed and stated rules', the 'English alone left theirs to the power of chance and caprice', he finds this fact all the more astonishing in that the cultivation of the language seems 'to be of more absolute necessity to us, than to any other nation'. This he explains by various reasons, among them the fact that 'Britain' had been composed of four distinct nations, three of whom 'spoke in tongues different from the English', and who

were far from being firmly united with them in inclinations, and of course were pursuing different interests. To accomplish an entire union with these people, was of the utmost importance to them, to which nothing could have more effectually contributed, than the universality of one common language .... Add to this, that even in England itself for want of such a method, there were such various dialects spoken, that persons born and bred in different and distant shires, could scarce any more understand each others speech, than they could that of a foreigner, which is notorious even now.

As the constitution has the power to unify those who 'pursue different interests' and who belong to different classes, so the language, properly standardized and reduced to rule, should have the power to unify, we might interpret this to say, the different interests of the different regions and classes of society beneath an apparent unity of expression.

Such a programme can be interpreted in a number of ways. We could see it, as Sheridan sometimes and as the radical philosopher Joseph Priestley always did, as a democratic and genuinely egalitarian aspiration, contributing to 'put an end to the odious distinction kept up between the subjects of the same king', and, by fitting all men to communicate with each other on the equal terms of reason, enabling not only those 'bred up at court' but 'the millions who speak the same tongue' to have the same opportunity of political self-realization as at present only the political élite enjoyed.[2] Or we can see it as an attempt to reduce, to subjugate, varieties of provincial English, and the modes of expression of different social classes, to the norms of that élite, and so to conceal beneath a veneer of universally adopted 'correct' English the different local cultures, as well as actual regional and economic inequalities, of Britain and her dependencies. This is certainly how it must have appeared after Culloden, to the Gaelic-speaking schoolchildren of the Highlands obliged to be educated in English; and this is how, in the early nineteenth century, John Clare was to take the attempts of his publisher to make his own dialect conform with what was then sufficiently established as the national standard of correct English:

grammer in learning is like tyranny in government – confound the bitch I'll never be her slave.[3]

Clare's recognition of the political designs of the grammarians is not a flash of revelation, the sudden discovery of a concealed conspiracy, for throughout the eighteenth century writers on language practice – and it is such writers on whom, for reasons of space, I have chosen to concentrate in this essay, to the exclusion of theoretical linguists[4] – had been comparing the language of England with its constitution; they continually exploited the comparisons possible between the laws of England and the rules of good English, with the aim of revealing that the language community could be understood to be structured as a political community, and more specifically as the political community of eighteenth-century England.

The language, like the constitution, had its theoretical origin in contract, its actual origin in custom. It had its bodies of customary and of statute law; the canons of 'common usage' were described in terms of the common law (in one or other of its various definitions), and against whose edicts, as in law, it was possible to appeal to the principles of 'equity' – 'the correction of that wherein the law (by reason of its universality) is deficient'.[5] The language, like the constitution, 'breathed a spirit of liberty', a liberty traceable to the Anglo-Saxon origin of both, sometimes threatened, sometimes confirmed by 'Norman innovation'. Legal maxims were adapted as maxims of grammar. The defence of the authority of common usage over rational analogy was modelled at the start of the century on arguments endorsing the resistance of the English to the absolutist designs of the Stuart monarchy, at the end, on those by which the customary practices and arrangements in the law and the constitution were defended against the suggested improvements of enlightened reformers. Most important, for our purposes, though all men were understood to be governed by the laws of the language – which, like the laws of the land, were claimed to have been established by 'the public free Consent' – some members of the language community were enfranchised, and could use their voice in making the laws which bound them, and some were not. Some, in the words of the educationalist, James Nelson, were 'born rather ... to be obedient to the Laws', others 'to be the Dispensers of them';[6] and between these two groups was a third, to whom most works on language practice were addressed, who might hope, by the acquisition of the linguistic equivalent of a property qualification, to become fully enfranchised members of the language community.

Locke: language and politics We will find the comparison between the language and the constitution in the works of numerous writers on language, of all political persuasions, throughout the century. Here, for example, is Addison, writing in 1711:

I have often wished, that as in our Constitution there are several Persons whose Business it is to watch over our Laws, our Liberties and Commerce, certain Men might be set apart, as Superintendants of our Language, to hinder any Words of a Foreign Coin from passing among us.

This, nearly fifty years later, is Johnson:

tongues, like governments, have a natural tendency to degeneration; we have long preserved our constitution, let us make some struggles for our language.

And this, in the last decade of the century, is Tom Paine:

The American constitutions were to liberty, what a grammar is to language: they define its parts of speech, and practically construct them into syntax.[7]

The analogy between law and language was not an invention of such men: it is at least as old as Plato, and had been used by Bacon and Hobbes, among others, in seventeenth-century England.[8] What is important however is the frequency of its use in the period we are studying, and the fact that – with occasional exceptions, as in the example from Paine – it has a particularly English character in this period, by which I mean that those who use the analogy are not much concerned with any general comparability between laws and political institutions, on the one hand, and languages on the other; they are making a specific comparison between the English political and legal system and the English language.

The analogy seems to be suggested to them by two sources in particular. The first is the writings on civil government of John Locke, particularly as, in defining an ideal political system, they may be taken also as describing the political system of England after the Glorious Revolution; also his discussion, in the third book of his *Essay concerning Human Understanding*, of language. The second is a long tradition, one particularly rich in the seventeenth and eighteenth centuries, of ideas about the nature of Englishness – of the national institutions; ideas which, in the eighteenth century, were contributing to the newly assertive nationalism of post-revolutionary England. As we shall see, both the writings of Locke, and the nationalist tradition to which I have just referred, came together in confirming what is the most fundamental and widely shared belief of writers in our period, that, in the words of Horace, 'use is the law and custom of speech';[9] or that, in the terms of the analogy of law and language, in linguistic matters no less than in legal the characteristically English tradition of common law is an authority preferable to that of the statutes. But as we shall see, this belief was based on a conflation of two notions of common law which, as they could be applied to the language, seem to be in contradiction with each other: common law as a system of customary practices 'used so long, that the memory of man runneth not to the contrary', so that 'if any one can shew the beginning of it, it is no good custom';[10] and common law in the sense of its not being 'local' but 'common' to the whole kingdom. I want to look first at the notion of custom, in matters of language practice, as it was expressed for the eighteenth century by Locke, in whose writings I want to point out also certain relations of political and linguistic theory, and a number of ambiguities, real or imaginary, in his theory, which were variously interpreted by different writers on language, all of whom however accept with various qualifications the authority of customary usage in determining disputes in matters of language.

In opposition to political philosophers of the restoration and earlier – specifically Sir Robert Filmer – who had argued for the absolute sovereignty, by divine right, of the monarch, the basis of Locke's theory of government was the consent of the governed. Men are naturally free, and in the state of nature they have specific freedoms which on their entry into civil society they resign to the appointed magistrate, but only in order to make them more secure. Men enter society primarily for the protection of their property: this is the chief end of civil society. If those to whom, by consent, by the choice of the majority, they have delegated authority, infringe the trust placed in them, or – not occasionally but consistently – use their power in such a way as not to protect but to put at risk the property of the governed, the compact on which society is based is dissolved, the state of nature is come again, and men are free to choose new governors, and even to make a fresh system of government on whatever terms they can agree to. Final authority is in the people, and Locke specifically presented his *Two Treatises of Government* as an attempt to establish

the Throne of our Great Restorer, Our present King *William*; to make good his Title, in the Consent of the People, which being the only one of all lawful Governments, he has more fully and clearly than any Prince in *Christendom*.[11]

It is a theory of government which, by locating sovereignty in the people, and by establishing the basis of government in consent, was presented as justifying the revolution of 1688, and any further revolution also, in the event of a consistent abuse of power on the part of the governors.

'Consent' is equally the basis of Locke's theory of language. For Locke, man is designed by God to be a 'sociable Creature', with a necessity and inclination to have fellowship with others of his own kind; he was furnished with language 'which was to be the great Instrument, and common Tye of Society'. Or not exactly with language, but with the ability to make articulate sounds, and to make these stand as signs for internal conceptions, as marks for the ideas in his own mind, by which he could make them known to others. Crucial to Locke's theory of language (as to his theory of knowledge) is that words are not the signs of things, but of ideas, and this insistence is related to another, that words do not come to stand for ideas by virtue of any natural connection (of the kind that might be suggested, for example, by onomatopoiea, and was the basis of some seventeenth-century theories of universal language) between words and ideas, for then all languages would be the same, but by a 'voluntary Imposition, whereby such a Word is made arbitrarily the mark of such an *Idea*.' Language is then the creation of men within a society, who agree, who voluntarily consent that words should stand for certain ideas; presupposing of course – and this is a large problem in Locke's notion of communication – that they know to what idea they agree to apply each word.[12]

From this it follows that the 'rules' they assent to establish are revealed in their customary linguistic practice, and not by what grammarians of the period referred to as 'analogy' – the form of language that *ought* to apply, on the belief that language is, of its essence, an internally consistent and coherent system, or that, as it is the vehicle of communication among rational men, it should be *made* consistent; a belief which prior to our period had been held by some renaissance writers on language, whether because they also believed that language was an invention and a gift of God, and therefore perfect at least until the 'second fall' at Babel; or because of a more humanistic belief in the necessary progress of science.[13] For Locke, if the users of language consent to irregularities, there is no appeal to the superior authority of what they *ought* to say, except arguably in the case of speakers who do not conform with the practice of the majority. There is no authority in the divine analogy of language, which is, like the divine right of kings, a figment.

The analogy between Locke's theories of government and of language can be taken further, in that the latter like the former contains a relation between a state of nature and a state of civil society, and the notion of a movement from one to the other.

Thus, no one 'hath the Power to make others have the same *Ideas* in their Minds, that he has, when they use the same Words, that he does'; and so 'every Man' has 'an inviolable Liberty' to 'make words stand for what *Ideas* he pleases'. But, Locke goes on – and here, by implication, speaking of uses of language in civil society – 'common use, by a tacit Consent, appropriates certain Sounds to certain *Ideas* in all Languages': for social purposes we tend to use the same words for the same ideas, not because we are compelled, but because we consent to do so:

That same Liberty also, that *Adam* had of affixing any new name to any *Idea*; the same has any one still, (especially the beginners of Languages, if we can imagine any such,) but only with this difference, that in Places, where Men in Society have already established a Language amongst them, the significations of Words are very warily and sparingly to be alter'd. Because Men being furnished already with names for their *Ideas*, and common Use having appropriated known Names to certain *Ideas*, an affected misapplication of them cannot but be very ridiculous. He that hath new Notions, will, perhaps, venture sometimes on the coining new Terms to express them: But Men think it a Boldness, and 'tis uncertain, whether common Use will ever make them pass for current. But in Communication with others, it is necessary, that we conform the *Ideas* we make the vulgar Words of any Language stand for, to their known proper Significations, (which I have explain'd at large already,) or else to make known that new Signification, we apply them to.[14]

There are, however, dangers for certain of the purposes of language in taking common usage as our standard, as Locke goes on to point out. It is true, he says, that '*common Use*

regulates the meaning of Words pretty well for common Conversation; but no body having an Authority to establish the precise signification of Words, nor determine to what *Ideas* any one shall annex them, common Use is not sufficient to adjust them to philosophical Discourses .... Besides, the rule and measure of Propriety it self being no where established, it is often matter of dispute, whether this or that way of using a Word, be propriety of Speech, or no.[15]

The point here is of course primarily to distinguish between the sort of precision required for everyday conversation, and for philosophical discourse – Locke's discovery of the inadequacy of the meanings provided by common usage being what had led him into the discussion of language in Book III of his *Essay*. But his point has another and (for us) more important implication. Common usage – say, a generally, and tacitly agreed definition of a word – is a good standard for everyday conversation as long as we simply accept it, and don't say what it is: as soon as we define a word by common usage, we substitute for common usage our own authority, and no one has the authority to do that. Nor can we therefore even agree what common usage is – not just what the common meaning of this or that word is, but what the concept, common usage, is in itself – whose usage is common usage?

It comes down to the question I touched on earlier: who are the people? In his own writings, Locke's answer to that question is entirely ambiguous. It may seem that when Locke speaks of the sovereignty of the people, the consent of the majority, he is speaking of all the people; on the other hand, as he repeatedly insists that the chief end for which men formed themselves into societies was the protection of property, it was easy for his followers in the eighteenth century to consider that the consent he looks for to validate government is the consent of substantial owners of property – more or less, of those in England who could vote. To that it can be replied that Locke's definition of property is pointedly capacious – it is the 'Lives, Liberties and Estates' of the governed, and does not apply simply to property owners. But again, it is clear that Locke (and by 1750 or so almost everyone) regarded the title of William III after the Glorious Revolution to reside in the 'consent of the people', whereas in fact it had undoubtedly resided if anywhere at all in the consent of the convention parliament, a body which, though described by such an authoritative defender of the Revolution as Sir William Blackstone as 'representing the whole society,' was plainly representative only of the enfranchised owners of property. In any case 'consent' in Locke is itself often a tendentiously capacious term, not much to do with the right to vote, so that for Locke a man may be said to consent to the government of a country if he walks along a highway, or does not emigrate.[16] It seems hard therefore to see how the people as a whole can ever have the right to *dissent* (except by emigration) from a government, a right which would have to be the basis of their consent, and one, of course, which the voter does have, in some measure at least.

None of this is irrelevant to the problems in the notions of consent and common usage, as those standards were accepted in the eighteenth century by grammarians who appear to derive much of their theory of language, if they have one, primarily from Locke. For example, it makes possible the assertion that a man who speaks a language, as a man who travels freely on a highway, in doing so must consent to accept the rules of that language, as he must consent to obey the laws of the country, though he has no say in the formation of either rule or law. As far as language goes, that may seem fair enough, for no one, it must be argued by the proponents of 'usage' and 'custom', has a say in the rules of language – all must conform with the customs of the country. But as Locke himself points out, what custom is in language, is up to whoever says what it is – he sets up the rules, and claims our assent to what he claims we cannot *but* assent to. In any case, as we shall see, it was agreed by Locke as by almost everyone else with an opinion on the matter, that the customs of the vulgar have no authority whatsoever in determining matters of correct usage. It cannot have been with any very democratic notion of 'common usage' in mind that Locke argued, in his *Conduct of the Understanding*, that the children of the poor ought not to be taught reading, but only religion, knitting, spinning, and so on, because

for a man to understand fully the business of his particular calling in the commonwealth, and of religion, which is his calling as he is a man in the world, is usually enough to take up his whole time.[17]

The genius of the English The second source of ideas for writers on language practice anxious to stress the supremacy of 'custom' in matters of correct usage, and the particular appropriateness of regarding custom as supreme in relation to the language of a country regarded as once more, or as newly, democratic, was the tradition by which the English were seen as, *by nature*, the most tenacious of liberty among all the civilized nations. The English have, as it were, a characteristic inherited disposition to be free: in the words of *The Castle of Indolence*, the 'Genius' of Britain is 'to Freedom apt' (Canto II, stanza xvii); in those of Blackstone, the 'spirit of liberty is ... deeply implanted in our constitution, and rooted even in our very soil'; and that freedom, manifested at least from the time of the Anglo-Saxons and the free institutions established then, and ever after tenaciously protected, was seen as a divine gift to a chosen people:

When Britain first, at heaven's command,
  Arose from out the azure main;
This was the charter of the land,
  And guardian Angels sang *this* strain:
    'Rule, *Britannia*, rule the waves;
    Britons never will be slaves'.[18]

In comparison with the French, who are 'servile' and who easily put up with the restraints and humiliations attendant upon life beneath an absolute monarch, the English are 'impatient of restraint'. This is a characteristic attended by certain inconveniences, as we shall see, but one universally praised throughout the century, even by those such as Johnson who are most concerned to stress those inconveniences.

It is a characteristic which shows equally in the nature of the English political system, and in the language. England has no written constitution – when the English, or a few of them, had the opportunity, in 1688, of writing one, they chose not to do so. The English constitution is instead a dispersed body of common and statute law, of precedents judicial and institutional, of institutions and their customary relations with each other. It is indeed based on custom, and its nature, apparently accidental and contingent, but to some 'the absolute perfection of reason',[19] expresses the unwillingness of the English to submit to having their liberties codified, methodized, and in that way given firm definition, with both senses of that word equally applicable – clarified, and limited. That unwillingness is confirmed by the preference of lawyers such as Sir Edward Coke and Blackstone for the common, and as it were unwritten law, *leges non scriptae*, over statute law, *leges scriptae*. According to Sir John Davies (*Report des Cases*, 1615), the English common law

is so framed and fitted to the nature & disposition of this people, as wee may properly say, it is *connaturall* to the Nation, so as it cannot possibly bee ruled by any other lawe;

and forty years later William Prynne also was praising the 'connaturalness', the 'conveniency of the Laws of England to Englishmens tempers'.[20] Experience of the 'usurpations' of the seventeenth century established this natural and 'connatural' aspect of the common law so firmly, that even for the elected representatives of the people in the House of Commons to attempt to alter the 'immemorial' customs of the nation could be seen as dangerous and even illegal, the customary being regarded as the *direct* manifestation of the will of the people, voter and non-voter alike, and so of the political liberty of *all* Englishmen. According to Blackstone

it is one of the characteristic marks of English liberty, that our common law depends upon custom; which carries this internal evidence of freedom along with it, that it probably was introduced by the voluntary consent of the people.

This notion of the customary is an aspect of English culture, as Christopher Hill has demonstrated,[21] remarkable for its adaptability: from the seventeenth through to the nineteenth century it could be used to authorize an astonishingly wide range of ideologies, from a moderate conservatism to an extreme and sometimes republican radicalism.

Continuously related to the idea of the characteristic freedom of the English people is a notion of the 'freedom' of the English language. This relation could be invoked, and often was, to argue against the superimposition of foreign, especially French, words on the purity of the Anglo-Saxon mother tongue, as an aspect of the superimposition of Norman feudalism on the democratic institutions of Anglo-Saxon England – a tradition, this, going at least as far back as the early sixteenth century, and referred to by Blackstone in noting that after the Conquest legal decisions were recorded in 'law French', a 'barbarous dialect', and 'an evident and shameful badge ... of tyranny and foreign servitude'.[22] Or the freedom of the language could be seen, on the contrary, to have been enhanced by the greater variety and copiousness of expression introduced by the Normans, an argument used by Francis Bacon and in our period, for example, by Isaac Watts:

The *English* Tongue being composed out of many Languages, enjoys indeed a Variety of their Beauties; but by this means it becomes also so exceedingly irregular, that no perfect Account of it can be given in ... Rules.[23]

Watts is here repeating a common argument of the preceeding century, that in comparison, for example, with the classical languages, but also with French or Italian, English was characterized by an apparent lack of rule, or method, most evident in its lack of case endings, in its apparently casual formation of tenses by auxiliary verbs, and in its multiplicity of idioms and irregularities; with the result that while other languages appear to be governed by analogy, which in almost all cases is identical with the custom of language users, in English we can rarely use analogy as a standard, and must accept not what ought, logically or analogically, to be correct, but what is the practice of speakers and writers whether in a philosophical view it should be or not. This casual and immethodical aspect of English is often argued as a product of the free spirit of the English, one still evident, for example, in the casual orthography and even grammar of seventeenth- and early eighteenth-century authors, who spelled as they pleased and not as they 'should'.

The question of the 'freedom' of English is taken up by the notable critic and grammarian Bishop Lowth, in his *Short Introduction to English Grammar* (1761). Arguing against Swift's insistence that English, 'in many Instances ... offends against every Part of Grammar', he asks:

Does it mean, that the *English* Language as it is spoken by the politest part of the nation, and as it stands in the writings of our most approved authors, oftentimes offends against every part of Grammar? Thus far, I am afraid, the charge is true. Or does it further imply, that our Language is in its nature irregular and capricious; not subject, or not easily reduceable, to a System of rules? In this respect, I am persuaded, the charge is wholly without foundation .... It is not the Language, but the practice, that is in fault.[24]

As Lowth, and as we shall see as Swift understood the question, the 'freedom' of English, whether it resides, as Watts sees it, in the nature of the language itself, or, as Lowth, in the practice of those who use it, is not a matter for the unambiguous praise which is to be accorded the English for their disposition to *political* freedom. Such writers are not among those who choose to employ the analogy of language and constitution; and yet it may be as implicit in their writings – particularly in Swift's – as it is explicit in those who do find reasons to praise English liberty as it finds expression in the language. For such writers are able to express in their writings attitudes which, if extended by analogy to politics, would have been recognizable as open dissent from the increasingly unchallengeable belief in the perfectly libertarian nature of the English constitution – recognizable, that is, as counter-revolutionary.

The key phrase to decipher, in discussions of language and liberty in our period, is one used by numerous writers on language: 'the "genius" of the tongue', a phrase related to the 'genius' of the land, of the nation, as it occurs in political writings. For writers such as Swift or Lowth, the genius of the tongue was to be understood as its ideal, analogical structure, all too rarely embodied in actual usage; it was what the language ought, ideally, to be, in accordance with the rules of universal grammar, and not what by accident or negligence it had actually become. This is what Lowth is thinking of in his distinction between the 'language' and the (mere) 'practice' of it; and what he intends us to understand by such a remark, in his *Grammar*, as 'Adjectives are sometimes employed as Adverbs; improperly, and not agreeably to the Genius of the English Language.'[25] The 'genius' of the language, on this showing, is the opposite of practice, or usage; it is the ideal, theoretical form of the grammar, as God or reason would have it.

But the majority of the writers we have to consider use the term with a quite opposite meaning, and by the middle of the century, Lowth notwithstanding, the 'genius' of the language is to be looked for not in its supposed analogical and rational structure – which, if rational, must be supposed the same for all languages – but in its characteristic idioms and expressions as these have been developed by customary usage. The distinction between the two notions is explained by James Buchanan, a schoolmaster, lexicographer, elocutionist and grammarian, in this way:

As far as Human Nature and the primary Genera both of Substance and Accident are the same in all Places, and have been so through all Ages; so far all Languages share one common Identity. As far as peculiar Species of Substance occur in different Countries, and much more, as far as the positive Institutions of religious and civil Policies are every where different; so far each Language has its peculiar Diversity. To the Causes of Diversity, may be added the distinguishing Character and Genius of every Nation.

Buchanan does not actually use the phrase 'the genius of the language'; but his relating the peculiar diversity of every tongue to the genius of its speakers, as well as to national peculiarities of religion and government, makes it clear that for him, just as each language must share certain general characteristics with every other – must employ, for example, many of the same parts of speech and tenses of the verb – and thus must correspond to what is universal in human nature, so it must also display entirely national characteristics – idioms – which correspond with the peculiarity of the culture of each nation. His jingoistic concern throughout all his writings for the improvement and diffusion of 'the manly diction of BRITONS' makes it equally clear what qualities, for him, are peculiar to the language and character of Britain.[26]

The insistence that English has a genius of its own, distinct from that of other languages, has two related functions. First, it is used to argue the primacy of the study of English grammar over that of Latin, as Blackstone was to argue for the study of English common law over the written 'Roman' law. English should be learned first, grammarians argue with increasing confidence through the century, and many children need learn English only. The case was argued most influentially by Locke, and originally on the grounds that an understanding of grammar is most easily acquired in one's own language, and that such an understanding would then render the acquisition of Latin a good deal easier. 'Can any Thing be more absurd,' absurd asked *The Tatler* in 1710,

than our Way of Proceeding in this Part of Literature? To push tender Wits into the intricate Mazes of Grammar, and of *Latin* Grammar? To learn an unknown Art by an unknown Tongue? To carry them a dark Round-about Way to let them in at a Back-Door? Whereas by teaching them first the Grammar of their Mother-Tongue, so easy to be learned, their Advance to the Grammars of *Latin* and *Greek* would be gradual and easy.

The point is repeated in numerous works on grammar. 'How unaccountable it is', argues the anonymous author of what is known as the Brightland Grammar,

that the Teaching a Good *English* Stile should be no Part of *English* Disciplin; and to put our Youth upon the study of Foreign Languages with the same Discretion that sends them to travel Foreign Countries, before they know the Constitution and Customs of their Own![27]

The second reason for the insistence, increasingly frequent

through the century, on the characteristic genius of the English language, is this: that if correctness of usage is to be judged in terms of a faithfulness to the idioms of English speech rather than by the notionally rational analogies of universal grammar, the way is clear for arguing also that the authority in such matters lies with the 'people' and their own customary means of expressing themselves, and not in the 'arbitrary' edicts of the universal grammarian. Thus grammarians who are concerned to stress the necessary priority of the study of English over Latin are usually careful to insist also that they have not constructed their systems of grammar on the model of Latin, for the 'geniuses' of the two languages are quite different, and English is a preparation for Latin only insofar as it may be established that the languages have common areas of grammatical structure, without 'forcing' our tongue to 'the Method and Form of the *Latin*'.[28] But insofar as the grammar of the languages is different, this must mean – as Buchanan argued – that the two have developed differently, so that the particular genius of English is the product of the particular genius of the English people, and, by the very nature of that free genius, of the particularly powerful influence the English have had on the formation and development of their own language.

The tone of all these opinions is thoroughly nationalistic, and in the limited terms of the start of the century, democratic. It is to be understood in relation to the arguments in the period over the relative merits of ancient and modern culture, and over whether an English national literature should be modelled on the classical writers or should be free to develop its own genres and practice; and it relates, most importantly, to a sense that, since the Revolution, political power had increasingly devolved to the urban bourgeoisie, to the mercantile class, to the City. Those who argue, then, for the priority of classical over modern literature, for a classical over an 'English' education, for 'civil' over 'municipal' law, are seeking to mystify learning, and the law in particular, and so to keep political power with the old court aristocracy and their scholar clients – with, in short, the very class whose power had been partially curtailed at the Revolution, when the 'people' of England had insisted on the 'restoration' of the 'customary usage' of government.

The Brightland Grammar, first published in 1711, is politically conscious in just this nationalistic and democratic spirit. The author satirizes, for example, the contemporary grammarian Maittaire, whom he seems to regard as a commercial competitor, for believing that those of 'every station' should learn Latin and Greek, and in doing so he claims to speak for those with less leisure than the sons of the nobility:

Much the greater Part of Mankind can by no means spare 10 or 11 Years of their Lives in learning those dead Languages, to arrive at a perfect Knowledge of their Own.

His militant Englishness does not allow him to be seduced from his modernism, however, in the case of Anglo-Saxon – one might argue that if the learning of Latin is not essential to an understanding of modern English, Anglo-Saxon is more so; but 'the *Saxon* can be no Rule to us,' for the 'very Nature and Genius of our Language is almost entirely alter'd since that Speech was disus'd … it is the present Tongue that is the only Object of our Consideration', which is to write a grammar comprehensible to those 'desirous to know the *Grammar* of their own *Mother-Tongue* only'.[29]

The appeal from other ancient languages to English is made in terms calculated to excite a more wordly audience than Latin grammars are designed for:

But after all (because Arguements from Interest are most persuasive) I would ask those Parents, who have their Children bred Scholars chiefly for a Livelihood, In what Language is the Thriving Business of our Nation transacted? And, Whether a voluble *English Tongue* in their Head will not carry them farther in the ways of Profit and Preferment, than all the *Learned Languages*?

Generous Spirits will always have a Concern for the Benefit and Credit of their Country! And how far the Honour and Interest of *Great Britain* are concern'd in the Cultivating of Our Language, I presume not to say; only, That a neighbouring Nation has taken Care of Theirs, and found their Accounts in't.[30]

Here, even the familiar contractions of the past tense 'concern'd', and of the final phrase, are calculated to appeal to the pragmatic and hard-headed merchant, to make him see that he is being offered a bargain. And it may be with a similarly helpful eye on the interests of the less sophisticated that in the first edition of the Brightland Grammar there are published the 'secret hands' – pipe, exchequer, and so on – in which court records and other official documents were still to be written until the middle of the century.

The proposal for an Academy The conflict between such modern, aggressive, pragmatic grammarians as this, and those who looked elsewhere for the 'genius of the language' than to current usage, was fought most notably on the issue of whether or not an Academy should be established in England, to improve and to regulate the English language, on the model of the French Academy which had been founded by Royal Charter in 1635. The suggestion for an Academy had been made on several occasions in the decades around 1700,[31] notably by Dryden and Defoe, and by Addison, who had proposed that it might, 'by rules drawn from the Analogy of Languages ... settle all Controversies between Grammar and Idiom'.[32] But it was with the publication in 1712 of Swift's *Proposal for Correcting, Improving and Ascertaining the English Tongue* that the issue clearly emerged as a political one. Swift argued that English was an 'extremely imperfect' tongue, becoming daily more so. He regarded it as a great misfortune that the occupation of Britain by the Romans had begun after the Golden Age of Latin, and also that their language had never come to be spoken by the 'vulgar' in occupied Britain as it had done in Gaul and Spain. On the departure of the legions, the Britons were forced to call in the Saxons to protect them from the Picts, and the Saxons imposed their customs, religion and language on the country.

Swift's hostility to the Saxons is considerable – it contrasts notably with, say, Coke's, Thomson's or Blackstone's attitude to them – and is no doubt to do with the mythological position attributed to them in English history, as the founders of the 'democratic part' of the English constitution. The Saxon language, for Swift, was *naturally* imperfect on account of the preponderance in it of harsh, multi-consonantal monosyllables, which he interprets as a mark of northern 'Barbarity'; and the implication is that the nations and the polysyllabic languages of Southern Europe are more civilized than those of the North. The monosyllabic nature of Saxon is reinforced by a national habit of reducing all words as far as possible to monosyllables, or at least to a clenched aggregate of harsh consonants: Swift affects to be appalled by the abbreviation of words in fashionable conversation, and by the habit of omitting the vowel in the final syllable of verb forms in '-ed', first introduced he imagines by poets for the sake of the metre, but now 'every where to be met with in Prose as well as Verse'. These and other faults of the language, seemingly trivial enough, had according to

Swift been increasing since the period of the 'Great Rebellion', before which, in the reigns of Elizabeth and James I, the 'English Tongue received most Improvement'.[33]

The 'improvements' and 'corrections' Swift himself had in mind were matters of grammar and of vocabulary: in the former, 'wherein we are allowed to be very defective', there are many 'gross Improprieties', which 'however authorised by Practice, and grown familiar, ought to be discarded'. As far as vocabulary was concerned, there were 'many Words

that deserve to be utterly thrown out of our Language, many more to be corrected; and perhaps not a few, long since antiquated, which ought to be restored, on account of their Energy and Sound.[34]

The remedy he proposes is the establishment, on the French model, of an Academy which, having once corrected the language, would preserve it as far as possible from future degeneration.

Swift's *Proposal* elicited replies from militant Whig pamphleteers, the scornful tone of which to some extent he provoked himself, for though he envisaged an Academy composed of 'such Persons, as are generally allowed to be best qualified for such a Work, without any regard to Quality, Party, or Profession', he was particularly anxious that the institution and patronage of the Academy should be managed by the then Tory ministry, and in particular by the Earl of Oxford whom in the course of his proposal he fulsomely congratulated for having 'saved his Country, which . . . was almost ruined by a *Foreign War*, and a *Domestick Faction*'. To some extent, also, the Whig ripostes were provoked by the publication, in a foreign newspaper, of a list of the Academy's prospective members, all of them members also of a Tory dining club but few of them probably regarded by Swift himself as 'qualified for such a Work'. [35]

But the Whig objections to Swift's proposal were more funda-mental than these matters of the leadership and membership of the Academy, and reveal the degree to which the matter of language also involved important issues of political principle or ideology, centred on Swift's notion of the 'improvement' and 'correction' of the language. To say that English 'offends against every Part of Grammar', that it is 'very defective', however 'familiar' its defects have become in 'practice', is to appeal to the notion of universal grammar, governed strictly by analogy, that we have already glanced at. It is based on the notion that there is some other authority than custom, and that authority must be, ultimately, divine – language is (though Swift does not say so outright) of divine origin, and not, as it was for Locke, the invention of man. Swift's remarks on the barbarity of the Saxons, on the barbarisms introduced into English by the 'Great Rebellion', make it quite clear that he could envisage a language being perfected and preserved from decay most easily in a version of the hierarchical system of government that obtained in France; though he is wary of attributing too much success to the enemies of England in achieving the reform and preservation of their own language.

If his proposal, then, was unacceptable to his Whig opponents, it was mostly because the theory left implicit in his writing, of the divine origin of language, was too uncomfortably related to the notion of the divine right of kings, God's ministers on earth. The latter notion had been resisted at the 'Great Rebellion' and again in 1688, as the notion that had justified the attack, by Charles I and then by James II, on the customary freedom of the English people; and by extension the appeal to the divine authority of analogy was an attack on the customary freedom of English speakers.

This is evidently the position taken by John Oldmixon, in his *Reflections on Dr. Swift's Letter* (1712). Oldmixon sees the proposal for an Academy, for 'pinning down our Language', as a conspiracy of Tories

who would lord it over us in every Thing, and not only force their Principles upon us, but their Language, wherein they endeavour to ape their good Friends the *French*, who for these three or fourscore Years have been attempting to make their Tongue as Imperious as their Power.

Swift wishes the English to 'submit to the Arbitrary Government of an Ignorant and Tyrannical Faction' who have no 'Tast of any books but *Eikon Basilike*, and the *Thirtieth* of *January* Sermons'. Such men, who have 'for above Fourscore Years' (that is, since the reign of Charles I) 'been doing their utmost to Enslave us',

shou'd always have a Contempt for Wit and Eloquence, which ever have been the Friends of Reason and Liberty.

Oldmixon ridicules Swift's objection to the familiar contraction of verb forms, which is a reformation, not achieved by the

Arbitrary Fancy of a Few, who would impose their own Private Opinions and Practices upon the rest of their Countrymen, but grounded on the Authority of *Horace,* who tells us in his Epistle *de arte Poetica,* that Present Use is the final Judge of Language ... and on the common Reason of Mankind, which forbids us those antiquated and obsolete Idioms of Speech, whose worth Time has worn out.

The dicta of such an Academy as Swift proposes, he argues, would indeed be arbitrary: their 'Rules' would 'grow obsolete as well as their Words'; and his final judgement anticipates that to be passed later by Johnson on Swift's proposal:

What Law of ours Impowers any body to order our Language to be *Inspected,* and who is there that wou'd think himself oblig'd to obey him in it? Is there no difference between the Ministers of a Despotick Monarchy, and the Servants of a limited one, who have no Rule but the Law, and are as accountable to it as the vilest of their Flatterers? We see how our Tongue would be improv'd and enlarg'd, had the Doctor and his Brethren the ordering of it. He has already impos'd on us the Court Style of France, and their Politicks wou'd soon come after it. [36]

The proposal for an Academy continued to be revived from time to time during the eighteenth century, but by no one with the influence of Swift, and when it was advanced, it was generally on reduced terms. The Academy might seek to ascertain the language, not to correct or improve it; and to 'ascertain' was simply to establish what usages, grammatical or semantic, were now 'customary', and to establish that in the hope of retarding what was generally seen as a more or less inevitable change – no longer necessarily a *decline* – of language in use. From the early years of the century, however, custom and use become almost universally accepted by writers of whatever political persuasion, as 'sovereign' in matters of language; and it is accepted almost as generally that, just as the responsibility for deciding how the language is to be used now lies with the users of it, so the credit for its invention should be attributed to man and not to God; and the language of Locke, of 'consent' and 'compact' is used to proclaim the fact:

Words are distinct articulate Sounds, implying by common Consent, some Thoughts or Operations of the Mind, express'd by certain Marks, Figures, or Characters agreed on by Men, as the visible Signs of those Sounds and Thoughts.

Grammar . . . [is] an *Art*, founded on *Compact*, or *Agreement* of Men of such or such a Place or Country, to express such *Ideas*, by such words.

Words are articulate sounds, used by common consent as signs of ideas, or notions.[37]

The notion of 'consent' here is to be understood as very close to the 'consent' of the people in whom Locke had proclaimed William III's title to have been founded, and of the 'public free Consent' in which, according to Thomson and Blackstone, the laws of England, and especially the common law, were established. 'The meaning of language is derived, not from nature, but from compact' asserts Buchanan; 'it is generally imagined', writes John Rice in 1765 (though it no longer was)

that, in our ordinary Discourse, and the common Narrative Stile in Writing, the Words follow each other in a *natural* Order. It will appear, however, on closer Examination, that instead of *natural*, we should say *habitual:* for this Order is different in different Languages.[38]

This is not to say that some grammarians convinced of the divine origin of language or of its ideally analogical character did not survive; nor that among those who accepted the compact theory there are not to be found grammarians who in their *practice* behave as if language could still be corrected by analogy, as a few pages back we saw Lowth attempting to do – as if it could be fitted out where it is defective with new forms analogically derived. There was, for example, a habit of inventing fictitious verb forms: Buchanan is one of a number of grammarians who offer as the pluperfect subjunctive, active and passive, the forms 'I might (would, should) had burned', and 'I might (would, should) had been burned';[39] and John Ash, a conscious disciple of Locke, quotes an earlier analogical grammarian approvingly on the need to 'improve' the tongue, to bring it to 'a regular and compleat system in all its parts'. Ash, too, regrets the insertion of the apostrophe in the genitive singular as a 'corrupt custom'; and that 'corrupt customs' could be discontinued was provided for by a legal maxim which some writers on language were pleased to assert as a grammatical maxim also: *malus usus abolendus est*, a bad custom is to be abolished. Such lapses, and such aspirations, are to be registered as, at most, marks of an unwilling acknowledgement, but an acknowledgement nevertheless, of the newly restricted authority of the grammarian, whose task is now 'to find out, and not to make, the laws of a language'. He must not 'assume the character of a legislator' but must become 'a faithful compiler of the scattered laws' just as, for Blackstone, a judge 'is only to *declare* and *pronounce*, not to *make* or *new-model*, the law.[40]

The model for the grammarian or lexicogapher is now no longer the academician who enjoys the patronage of an absolute monarch; it is quite evidently, in such phrases as I have quoted, such a figure as Sir Edward Coke, the compiler and commentator upon English law, and the anti-absolutist defender of common law and of 'custom' as 'the best interpreter of law'. Coke, like the grammarians and lawyers of the middle decades of the eighteenth century, was unwilling to see the customary law subject to the schemes of improvers: 'it cannot', he wrote, 'without great hazard be altered or changed', though it might perhaps be organized more methodically; his own opinions were, he insisted, of importance only when there arose 'variety of opinions' about the law, when he might try 'to reconcile doubts'.[41]

The most approved writers and speakers But we should beware of rejoicing too wholeheartedly at this apparent triumph of democracy. We should first ask, for example, precisely what is meant by 'custom'; perhaps also why the concept of 'law' remains one still so dear to the mid century grammarians – why do they still cling so tenaciously to the analogy of language and constitution? The first of these questions is a complex one, but we can begin to answer it by making the simple observation that, however 'general' the consent by which language was supposed first to have been instituted, the custom now to be observed in its use was that only of the 'best' speakers and writers. There was a passage from Quintilian, quoted for example by James Greenwood in his *Practical English Grammar* (1711), which was a reassuring pendant to the more widely known dictum of Horace about use being the arbiter of speech: 'custom', in Greenwood's version of the passage, is 'a very dangerous and bad Influence' if

it should take its Name from the Practice of the Majority .... In Discourse, if there be any thing that has corruptly prevail'd among the Multitude, we must not receive or embrace that for the Rule or Standard of Speech .... I shall therefore call the Custom of Speech, the Agreement of the Learned.[42]

This account of custom in language is almost universally accepted throughout the century: the majority have no 'legislative voice in language' and are, as it were, not yet arrived at voting age. Thus the rhetorician George Campbell, who offers the most extended account of what custom is and of whose usage should be taken as customary, writes:

The tattle of children hath a currency, but, however universal their manner of corrupting words may be among themselves, it can never establish what is accounted use in language. Now, what children are to men, that precisely the ignorant are to the knowing.

This type of argument has its equivalent also in the study of law: Coke and Blackstone assert that the rationality of a custom is not to be judged by 'every unlearned man's reason', but by 'artificial and legal reason', the property only of the initiated.[43]

The learned, however, may include not only those whose knowledge of the best part of language has been derived from study; for among their number may also be men whose claim to represent the standard of proper usage is based on their rank and on their acquaintance with the polite world. Thus the 'best' users of the language are variously defined as the 'most polish'd speakers . . . residing in the Metropolis', 'Men of Letters and Education at Court', the 'learned and polite', 'the most approved writers and speakers', those 'in London, the Universities, or at Court', the 'best speakers, and not . . . the Mob'.[44] The enfranchised members of the language community must have been, on this showing, far fewer in number than those of the political community: Campbell estimated that only one in a hundred could speak the 'reputable', 'national', and 'current' language, 'the language, properly so-called', but his estimate is certainly a generous one. For though, as we shall see, there was some disagreement about who spoke or wrote it, most writers would seem to imply that it could only be attributed to those with the opportunity to reside in the metropolis, and thus to preserve their language from provincial vulgarity. For though what 'is properly styled the language' is to be found particularly in London and also perhaps at Oxford and Cambridge, it is not the dialect of any specific locality – its claim to be the 'national' language is based on the belief that 'it commands a circulation incomparably wider' than the words and phrases spoken in any narrow locality: it is 'found current, especially in the upper and middle ranks, over the whole British Empire',[45] and though its users may not understand the speakers of local dialects, those speakers universally understand the language of the polite.

Another qualification necessary to the authoritative users of the language was a private income substantial enough to free them from the need to work for a living, so that their vocabulary could be protected from contamination by the terms of particular arts and occupations, as well as from the poverty of knowledge characteristic of those who 'toil for bread, almost incessantly, in some narrow occupation', and who thus can come to know only a 'very scanty' portion of the language.[46] Johnson is characteristically ambiguous about whether the terms of art may be included in 'the' language, for as we have seen he has no great belief in the value of a 'comprehensive' knowledge empty of particulars. 'They that content themselves with general ideas', he writes, 'may rest in general terms; but those whose studies or employments force them upon closer inspection, must have names for particular parts, and words by which they may express various modes of combination'. Such words belong only in the context of the arts they describe, and it seems that Johnson, like Campbell, regards the national language as derived from a world apart from and above the languages of those who follow particular callings, who will 'make their knowledge ridiculous' by the 'injudicious obtrusion' of terms, into conversations with those who do not follow the same calling; so that it seems the only safe guide to what is the universal language must be the language of one who follows, or is supposed to follow, no calling at all. Who this might be is, however, a problem for Johnson: among the 'fraternities' whom he describes as having 'a cast of talk peculiar' to them, he lists, along with the sailor, lawyer, and mechanic, the academic and the courtier [47] – a pleasant dig at the usual definitions of the best users of language, and one which may suggest either that the writer, at least one who lives in the world and not in the cloister, is now the only authority, or – and this would be in line with the opinions we examined in the introduction – that perhaps no one can now claim that his own language is the national language.

This doubt came to be entertained by a few other writers on language practice after Johnson, but we can defer its discussion for a while, for the great majority of those who considered the question were not troubled by it. They were generally in agreement, however, that money, and an extended knowledge at least of the

polite world, were not enough to qualify a man to be regarded as a
model of correct usage: the enfranchised members of the language
community must also have access to books, to acquaint themselves
with the language of the most reputable authors – they must,
indeed, have had a 'liberal education', by which only can they be
'presumed to be best acquainted with men and things'. But if,
remarks Campbell,

in this particular there be any deference to the practice of the great and
rich, it is not ultimately because they are greater and richer than others,
but because, from their greatness and riches, they are imagined to be
wiser and more knowing.

In practice, writers on language sometimes differ as to whether
these qualifications are more likely to be found among gentlemen
or among established authors, according to whether they have the
spoken or the written language most in mind, or whether it is the
gentlemanly freedom from occupation, or the benefits of education
and the stability of the written word that seem more likely to
guarantee the purity of the language. For the elocutionist Thomas
Sheridan, for example, the model of correct English was that
spoken at the court of Queen Anne, where great care was taken
over pronunciation; for Campbell, on the other hand, as we have
'more of the republican than of the monarchical' in our 'spirit' as
well as in our constitution, 'there is no remarkable partiality' in
favour of the language of courtiers, and it is 'authors of reputation'
who supply the standard of the written language, though the
conversation of 'men of rank and eminence' is still for him the
'only rule' of pronunciation. Those, however, who favoured the
gentleman were, in this as in political questions, anxious to
separate him from the merely fashionable gentleman, who, according
to Johnson,

instead of endeavouring at purity or propriety, has no other care than to
catch the reigning phrase and current exclamation, till by copying
whatever is peculiar in the talk of all those whose birth or fortune entitle
them to imitation, he has collected every fashionable barbarism of the
present winter.[48]

Such fashionable dialects, repeatedly satirized by Swift and Johnson,
are no part of the language of the 'true gentleman', who must
therefore be defined as a man of education as well as of no

occupation if he is to be taken as a model of 'purity or propriety'.

We might expect the author to replace the gentleman as the prime authority as the century proceeds, and as the gentleman becomes more evidently unable to claim, merely by virtue of his rank, a comprehensive knowledge of 'men and things'; and though this is by and large what happens, the change is complicated by the concern that the language be free not only from provincialisms but from the terms of art. This concern attracted the definition of the reputable writer into that of the gentleman who could afford not to know those terms, in the same way as the definition of the gentleman was attracted into that of the man of liberal education: and, as we have seen, Campbell was capable at once of insisting that authors and not courtiers supplied the standard of written language, and that in determining the standard there was a necessary deference to be paid to the rich and great as having the leisure to acquire a comprehensive knowledge of 'men and things'. Thus, if works on language practice do not uniformly through the century set up the gentleman as the standard of propriety, they cannot easily do without the notion of a gentlemanly elevation above occupation in defining who it was who spoke the national language; and the distinction between gentleman and author, thus redescribed to serve as the models for imitation, is far less remarkable than the similarities between them.

Such polite and independent speakers and writers, in obeying the laws of language, made them; in making them, they obeyed them. The linguistic constitution was a body of law derived from their own customary practice, in no sense a restraint upon them but an expression of their own liberty to continue to speak as they did, if not as they chose. The problem of creating a unified, national language was thus a complex problem of persuasion and obligation: those who were not the best speakers were to be persuaded that the customs of the language had, in the immemorial past, been freely assented to by 'all', by the theoretical totality of the 'people'. Those customs, however, when defined, often turned out to be the recent creation of a minority of speakers only. It was necessary, then, first to persuade the vulgar that these were, in legal terms, 'general', not 'particular' customs, which were binding on everyone, everywhere; and second, to oblige the vulgar to do, in obedience to what is thus represented to them as customary *law*, what the polite did by 'custom' defined for *them* not so much as law but as habit, or as 'second nature', as habit was proverbially defined, and as, among writers on language, the phonetician Abraham Tucker described it. [49]

It is in the demand that the vulgar defer to the customs of the polite, as to law, that the conflation I spoke of earlier, of different notions of the common law, can be seen to operate. The authority of the common law, by one meaning of the term, depended on the 'immemorial' existence of the customs of which it was composed, so that to obey it was to defer to the wisdom of ages; but by no stretching of the term 'customary usage' could it appear that the language customs of the polite had been in use 'time out of mind'. For though some writers, Johnson among them, were sometimes willing to look at least as far back as to the Elizabethan age to find '*the wells of English undefiled* ', many, and often Johnson himself, were concerned to defend a notion of correct English as at once somehow customary and *current* – as a modern language washed as clean as possible of spots of local or provincial barbarity, and of those usages described by Campbell, cunningly reversing the legal definition of custom, as 'laid aside time immemorial'. [50] The claim for the authority of custom, by the legal sense which had in England been attached to Horace's dictum, thus encouraged a deference at once to 'common usage' as to an immemorial authority, and to it also as to a *common* as opposed to a merely *local* usage, and so in effect as to a more recent authority than the local customs of speech developed in this or that part of the kingdom, which were now (as we shall see) to be regarded as obsolete – as no longer current in the polite language, and thus as no part of the national language.

It may be helpful to amplify the suggestion that the vulgar were encouraged to regard the customs of the polite as law, and as common law in the sense of non-local, if I refer briefly to an essay by Robert Malcolmson in which he examines the case of the colliers of Kingswood, near Bristol, in the eighteenth century, and sees it as an example of how, as he says, though 'in some parts of the country authority was unchallenged and securely enforced, in other areas the exercise of authority was tenuous, uncertain and often ineffectual'. On a number of occasions in the century the Kingswood colliers combined to resist the authorities and the authority of the law, mostly in the matter of the turnpiking of the roads round Bristol; eventually, as Malcolmson puts it, they were 'tamed'; 'the limits of authority had expanded to incorporate Kingswood within its territory of social discipline'. Malcolmson quotes an observer of 1794 much impressed by the new quiescence of the colliers, who

were, 40 or 50 years ago, so barbarous and savage, that they were a terror to the City of Bristol, which they several times invaded; it was dangerous to go among them, and their dialect was the roughest and rudest in the Nation; but by the labours of Mess. Whitefield and Wesley, by the erection of a parish Church and some meeting-houses, and the establishment of several sunday and daily schools, they are much civilized and improved in principles, morals and pronunciation. [51]

It may seem surprising that one of the main charges this observer can allege against the Kingswood colliers is that 'their dialect was the roughest and rudest in the Nation'; or that he can record an improvement in their pronunciation apparently with as much satisfaction as he records the improvement in their principles and morals. But throughout the century, and increasingly towards its end, the way people spoke was regarded as a matter of social, and of moral discipline; and just as magistrates were concerned to see the laws made in the metropolis enforced throughout the provinces, so writers on language practice were anxious to confirm the political unity of Britain by recommending the enforcement, throughout the country, of the laws of good usage and pronunciation, as derived from the custom of 'the most polish'd speakers . . . residing in the Metropolis'.

However, to submit to the custom of the polite could be presented, as I suggested earlier, as a confirmation and not as a loss of freedom. It could put an end to 'odious distinction', in Thomas Sheridan's phrase, and it could seem to promise even an end to political and economic distinctions; for by the extinction of local pronunciation, argued Sheridan, 'all natives of these realms would be restored to their birthright in commonage of language, which has been too long fenced in, and made the property of the few'. The image Sheridan uses is masterly in its means of persuasion: it seems to offer the restoration of ancient rights and customs, the emancipation of the disenfranchised and the dispossessed: but at the price of accepting that 'the language, properly so-called', is that spoken by and in the possession of the metropolitan polite; and that what the vulgar speak is no language at all. In the light of such arguments as this it is not surprising that Joseph Priestley, who is self-consciously if rather warily democratic in his attitudes to language practice, has nothing to say in his *Rudiments of Grammar* about pronunciation, a topic usually found in eighteenth-century grammars: a silence perhaps attributable to the fact that he feels unable either to recommend the dialect of the most powerful as more correct than any other, or to recommend the preservation of local language customs which, in asserting the freedom of their users, would also assert their servitude.[52]

Custom and grammar In the matter of spoken English, the disenfranchised members of the language community were taken to include all those who did not use the pronunciation of the polite, and should be encouraged to do so. In the matter of the written language, those who were to regard the custom of their betters as the law, to which they were obliged to submit, were not taken by many writers to include *all* who were not polite and learned or bred up at court or the universities: here the majority were not thought of as members of the language community at all, as they were not members of the political community. As we have seen, Locke did not think the children of the poor should so much as learn to read; but though those involved in educating the poor, notably in the Charity Schools movement, were aware of the dangers to industry and good order in teaching them to read, many advocated doing so, largely that the children might benefit from the practice of regular reading in the scriptures. Writing, however, was another matter, more controversial and less frequently taught: 'I will by no means contend for Writing as a Matter of equal Necessity or Advantage with that of Reading,' wrote Isaac Watts in his *Essay towards the Encouragement of Charity Schools* (1728); and as late as 1801 Hannah More, defending her method of education to the Bishop of Bath and Wells, assured him: 'I allow of no writing for the poor. My object is not to make fanatics, but to train up the lower classes in habits of industry and piety'. [53] Those who can read only, and cannot write, have no need at all of grammar.

The classes, other than the polite, at whom most works on language practice were directed, were the rising middle classes of the period: shopkeepers, substantial tradesmen and their children – for whom, according to Locke and the author of the Brightland Grammar, it was not worthwhile to learn Latin, but who would benefit financially from the ability to speak and write correct English. William Loughton's aim was to 'fit' the young for 'Trade and Business'; John Collyer writes for schools that 'equip' boys for 'Trades'; John Ash, the simplifier of Lowth's *Grammar*, for 'young Gentlemen designed merely for Trade'. This class, many of them dissenters, most of them voteless unless remarkably successful, were visibly growing in numbers and in economic if not in political power. It is this class – the equivalent in England of the 'taylors' and 'clowns' whom Burke identified with alarm as having 'usurped' power in France in 1790[54] – from whom the radical agitators of the end of the century were many of them recruited; men – and especially the dissenters among them, virtually disbarred from public office and from many public institutions – who had good reason to doubt the perfection of the British Constitution.

There was no desire to avoid educating such people, as there was to avoid initiating the poor into the mysteries of writing; the necessity of trade to Britain's prosperity was an article of faith by the mid century, and as we saw in the previous essay the writers of the middle decades of the century were at great pains to stress the respectability of the calling. It is stressed too by the *number* of grammars produced for the less-than-polite in the period we have to consider – and this only a small part of the educational material produced during the century for the middle class. But though the power of this class is acknowledged by the number of the grammars addressed to them, it is also kept in subjection, by the form and structure of those grammars, which, as we shall see, were concerned to limit the kind and the degree of knowledge about language that they communicated.

The pattern is set by the Brightland grammar, and is explained in its introduction. Each page is divided into a large-print text and small-print notes. The large print consists of rules, and this is all that needs to be read by, in the author's words, 'children and women, and the ignorant of both sexes'. But since

the Rational Grounds of *Grammar* may be thought Useful, we have added them in the *Notes*, as well as the Formation of *Sounds*, which may Instruct the reasonable Teacher in means of informing the Learner in many things necessary in Pronunciation, especially Foreigners, and such as may have any Natural Defect. This being in the *Notes*, does not interrupt the more Ignorant Learner of the Common *Rules* of the *English Grammar*, since those are plain and distinct by themselves.

In short, we hope we have come up to my Friend's Design, and to that we have added a *General Grammar* as we have said, which may improve some, who think themselves better *Grammarians*, than they really are, by letting them into the Reasons of Things, which is as Pleasant as Useful.[55]

Thus, for reasonable beings, the rational grounds of grammar are exhibited; these readers are 'let into the reasons of things' as if into a secret, and are enabled to assent to the rules in the text – to weigh their reasonableness, and to discover a conformity of duty and inclination, pleasure and use, by which they may freely consent to what is in the text. For others, who are, precisely, the unenfranchised – children, women, and the ignorant – the grammar is not, as it is for the readers of the notes, a system that expresses their own freedom to assent to or dissent from the rules of the language community, but a body of law, presented simply as that, to which it is simply assumed they will submit themselves. It is precisely to the point that the statement quoted from this grammar on page 130, about consent and agreement, appears in the *notes* – the unenfranchised are kept ignorant of the freedom theoretically attributed to them in the notes, and which is therefore (it must be assumed) a freedom practically enjoyed by the 'rational' and enfranchised only. As the constitution, so the grammar; and this division, into text and notes, as Murray Cohen has shown,[56] is a characteristic of grammars at the start of the century, which conceive of their aims as two-fold – as a matter of fitting out the sons of the bourgeoisie with a passable grasp of correct English for the purposes of trade, and of debating the rational grounds of grammar. James Buchanan, whose *British Grammar* (1762) has a staggering preponderance of notes to text – sometimes in the proportion of twenty to one – begins his first section, on the vowels, in the catechistic style frequently adopted by the grammars:

How many Sounds has the Vowel a?
It has three.

His note to this 'rule' begins ' "A" has really five different sounds'. [57]

Through the middle and end of the century, though grammarians keep to the established form of text and notes, the function of the notes changes. The text is still generally kept for rules, often presented in dialogue form between an imaginary learner and his knowing teacher – but the notes tend to be used for 'lesser rules', for examples of bad grammar, or to note occasional exceptions. The rational grounds of grammar almost disappear and they come to be regarded as the subject of a different sort of book: Bishop Lowth directs those interested in such matters to James Harris's *Hermes* (1751);[58] and with the disappearance of theory from the grammars, they become simply manuals of rules, teaching how to conform with common usage.

There are of course many ways of explaining the disappearance of theory from the grammars, even from its reduced position in the fine print of the notes. Many of them were written for children, whom it was thought appropriate to instruct by rhyme rather than reason; it may have been, and not simply imagined to have been, a demand from the class of shopkeepers and tradesmen themselves that grammars should become resolutely 'practical': William Loughton and Charles Wiseman both refused to fill their books with 'large critical Notes', which would 'only . . . increase the Bulk and Price of the Book'.[59] But among these explanations there is certainly room for another, which will help us to understand why, for example, writers on language practice were able to arrive, after the bitterness of the Swift–Oldmixon squabble, at such a remarkable consensus on the question of correctness in language – why, that is, almost all grammarians become the champions of custom and common usage from that time onwards, and why – for the question is still pending – it became of such importance for them to present 'customs' in the form of 'laws'. For the removal of controversy from works of practical grammar, while it still has a flourishing life in more expensive works of theoretical linguistics read only by the polite, had the fortunate effect of representing custom, the practice of the polite, as nature, as not open to question. This of course reinforced, and was reinforced by, the representation of the constitution as a natural growth of age-old custom and precedent, 'now arrived to it's full vigour',[60] perfect, and so beyond questioning, and beyond improvement.

It is for this reason that the enfranchised of all political persuasions are so willing to embrace the authority of 'custom'; what had been a libertarian watch-word in the seventeenth century came to serve as effectively as a repressive and reactionary one in the eighteenth. The free genius of the English people, expressing itself in the custom of the language, was defined and codified by the grammar and the dictionary, and used as a standard by which future freedoms claimed, future liberties taken by language users, could be shown to offend against the rules by which freedom was protected and confirmed, and so could be shown to be, if you like, unconstitutional. Liberty could be represented by rules, and departure from those rules could be branded as licence, and not as the continuing expression of the English disposition to freedom. Just as it is opposed to authoritarian prescription from above – from God, or from the edicts of the king his minister on earth expressed in the decisions of such an academy as the French; so it is now also opposed to any dilution by an extension of freedom to those below, who are henceforth to be taught only their duties to the language community, and not, if they had any, their rights. The point, in political terms, is to safeguard the liberty, the 'free consent', of those whose interests were most consulted in the revolution of 1688, but to cancel the possibility of any future revolution, or any extension of the franchise. In the terms of language, it is to justify the usage of those in power, and to inculcate their usage as a rule for those below them, a rule as little as possible subject to future reformation or repeal.

Once we understand the changing political value of 'custom' in language as well as in politics, we are in a position to grasp the significance of another change that occurs in writings on language practice in the mid century. In Oldmixon's answer to Swift, or in the Brightland grammar, custom is invested in the robes of liberty; by later grammarians custom begins to be spoken of in quite different terms. We begin to read of her as an 'Empress'; of the 'despotic sway' of our 'sovereign Lady Custom'; of the 'arbitrary disposition of custom'; of the 'impetuous and prevailing Tide of Custom'; of 'use, the sole arbitress of language'.[61] Some of these phrases may be the expressions of reluctant democrats; usually however their intention, and certainly their effect, must have been to hypostatize the 'freedom' of use against the freedom of the users, at least of those users who do not 'dispense' the laws, but only 'obey them'; or who have, in Blackstone's phrase, 'no will of their own', and so no vote; or who are, in Burke's, 'formed to be instruments, not controls'.[62]

As the value of the notions of 'custom' and 'use' changed, so also did that of terms such as 'reform', 'improvement', and 'correction'. From now on correction is no longer to be resisted as the programme of Jacobites and their sympathizers; Tory and Whig may have disagreed about what had happened in 1688, but whatever it was, both now agreed that, at the least, it could have been much worse. 'Correction', 'improvement' are now seen as the programme of those who are tempted to question the rationality, the architectural or organic perfection, of the constitution – literate dissenters, for example, and (when they finally appear in the last third of the century) the radical disciples of Enlightenment. The most pregnant term in the set becomes 'innovation' – a word which had not lost much of the connection it had certainly had in the seventeenth century with *res novae* (revolution), and which seems to have been used increasingly to refer to a sudden change in the established form of things, imagined as being initiated from – if the term may yet be used – the left; and the terms in which Johnson attacks 'innovation' in language practice are strikingly similar to those in which Burke was later to attack the rationalist pretensions of the Constituent Assembly in revolutionary France.

Johnson: language and politics   The analogy, often submerged, but often visible, between proper language and proper government, is to be found everywhere in Johnson's writings on language; and it will be worth discussing Johnson's attitude to correct English and to linguistic change in some detail, because it seems to have been he who first clearly identified the threat to the custom of language as now to be anticipated as coming from a new quarter. I want to begin the discussion of Johnson with two quotations in which the analogy is not made directly, but which indicate the similarity of Johnson's ways of thinking about government and about language. In the *Plan* of the Dictionary, as it were an advertisement for the work he was beginning to undertake, dedicated to the Earl of Chesterfield and published in 1747, he writes:

To our language may be with great justness applied the observation of *Quintilian*, that speech was not formed by an analogy sent from heaven. It did not descend to us in a state of uniformity and perfection, but was produced by necessity and enlarged by accident, and is therefore composed of dissimilar parts, thrown together by negligence, by affectation, by learning, or by ignorance.

In a much later work, *The False Alarm* of 1770, written to oppose the stand taken by the electors of the County of Middlesex after the exclusion of John Wilkes from the House of Commons, Johnson wrote:

Governments formed by chance, and gradually improved by such expedients, as the successive discovery of their defects happened to suggest, are never to be tried by a regular theory. They are fabricks of dissimilar materials, raised by different architects, upon different plans. We must be content with them as they are; should we attempt to mend their disproportions, we might easily demolish, and difficultly rebuild them.

Laws are now made, and customs are established; these are our rules, and by them we must be guided.[63]

These passages are not of course a perfect match: the accidental nature of language and of government is not the product of causes precisely similar, and Johnson can admit of language, as he could less easily of government, that it has been formed by ignorance as well as by wisdom – it may be, of course, because all men have contributed to the formation of language, but only some to that of the constitution. Besides, as governments are more easily reformed than are languages, the possiblility (or necessity) of reforming them can hardly be insisted upon. But both passages agree in this, that our language and our government cannot be discussed as if they are the products of settled plans. Johnson may sometimes regret this in relation to language, while he seems to approve it in relation to government; but in either case he is clear that we cannot understand and certainly cannot improve language or government by consulting what, on a rational view, *ought* to be the case. The language, however haphazard, is the only one we have; it must be understood in terms of what we do say, not what we should. Our constitution also, however accidentally composed, is perhaps more tendentiously represented as the only one available: 'we must be content . . .', for

laws are now made, and customs established; these are our rules, and by them we must be guided.

Precisely how Johnson defines what custom is, I will discuss later. I first want to point out that this insistence, on the necessity of being content with the language and government we have, enables Johnson to avoid the theoretical questions concerning the origin of language and government that preoccupied so many political thinkers and linguists from Hobbes and Locke and throughout the eighteenth century. In particular, in his writings on the alleged political rights of the American colonists, Johnson departs from the contractual language of Locke and Blackstone and looks forward to Burke in displaying little interest in the notion of the origin of government in the consent of the governed, and therefore in the notion that governments continue to derive their authority from that continued consent. Similarly his adherence to custom, in his discussions of language and politics alike, is not – as it had been to writers earlier in the century – a defence of custom as the expression of what a language community or a political community has *chosen* to do. Custom no doubt may in part owe its origin to choice, to consent; but once established, customs become, in effect, the laws of the state or the rules of the language, which command obedience from the mere fact of their existence, and which should not be regarded as being open to any but the most modest alteration.

Johnson's impatience with the notion of government as founded in consent is clear in his writings on the Middlesex electors who persisted in returning Wilkes as their Member of Parliament in defiance of the will of the Commons, and in his writing against the American colonists, whose defence of the notion was partly derived from a democratic reading of Locke's second *Treatise*. 'The rabble', he says in *The False Alarm*, 'will be always patriots, and always Supporters of the Bill of Rights'; and in *The Patriot* (1774), another anti-Wilkesite pamphlet, he wrote:

he that has been refused a reasonable or unreasonable request, who thinks his merit under-rated, and sees his influence declining, begins soon to talk of natural equality, the absurdity of *many made for one*, the original compact, the foundation of authority, and the majesty of the people.[64]

Some of what this malcontent talks of, of course, is an evidently radical theory of government, but some of it is the general currency of political theory of whatever persuasion: the discussion of a government in the light of general concepts is for Johnson a sufficient mark of a disaffected demagogue, never mind the fact that his particular opinions on those concepts are not to be trusted.

But most clearly, perhaps, he attacks the theory of consent in *Taxation no Tyranny* (1775):

That a free man is governed by himself, or by laws to which he has consented, is a position of mighty sound: but every man that utters it, with whatever confidence, and every man that hears it, with whatever acquiescence, if consent be supposed to imply the power of refusal, feels it to be false. We virtually and implicitly allow the institutions of any Government of which we enjoy the benefit, and solicit the protection. In wide extended dominions, though power has been diffused with the most even hand, yet a very small part of the people are either primarily or secondarily consulted in Legislation. The business of the Publick must be done by delegation. The choice of delegates is made by a select number, and those who are not electors stand idle and helpless spectators of the commonweal, *wholly unconcerned in the government of themselves.*

Of Electors the hap is but little better. They are often far from unanimity in their choice, and where the numbers approach to equality, almost half must be governed not only without, but against their choice.

How any man can have consented to institutions established in distant ages, it will be difficult to explain. In the most favourite residence of liberty, the consent of individuals is merely passive, a tacit admission in every community of the terms which that community grants and requires. As all are born the subjects of some state or other, we may be said to have been all born consenting to some system of Government. Other consent than this, the condition of civil life does not allow. It is the unmeaning clamour of the pedants of policy, the delirious dream of republican fanaticism. [65]

What is remarkable about this, of course, is the way that an account of the *status quo* is assumed to be, at the same time and without further justification, a defence of it. To the argument that every man *ought* to consent to his own government, Johnson simply replies that, in point of fact, every man does not – and the question of whether there ought to be a more active consent than a merely passive and tacit admission is dismissed without argument as unmeaning, the dream of republican fanaticism for a condition that civil life does not allow – so why bother to consider whether it should allow it or not? It is a fact that in populous countries, the voteless and a significant majority of the voters can have no say whatsoever in the government of themselves – and this, Johnson asserts, in countries (and by implication especially in Britain, 'the most favourite residence of liberty') where 'power has been diffused with the most even hand'. Any other means of organizing government is presented, and as a matter of fact, as impossible; and consent can have no meaning unless we take it at its lowest level – non-resistance. He does not consider, for example, whether an extension of the franchise would ensure a greater measure of consent among the governed, because as I have said he has very little interest in the notion of consent, whether it could be made effective or not. This is clearest perhaps in the remark, 'How any man can have consented to institutions established in distant ages, it will be difficult to explain'. When those institutions were established, the argument is, men may possibly have given their consent to them; but though we who inherit them cannot be said to consent to them, we are not therefore free to change them, and there is no point, for Johnson, in even pausing to consider whether that ought to be the case or not.

The same or a similar attitude is evident in the remark from the *Plan* to the Dictionary quoted a few pages back. Language, says Johnson, did not descend from heaven, a perfect system; but it is not, therefore, as Locke had argued, formed by a voluntary agreement among men to make this sound or combination of letters the mark of an idea. Language was produced by necessity and enlarged by accident; there is no view here of the agents – those who *choose* that the language should take this form or that; and though by its very agnosticism this becomes a more credible view of the origin of language than Locke's, it is also a refusal to consider the rights of the language community as an issue of any importance in the questions of how language is to be used, and on whose terms it is to be 'settled'. Johnson clearly regards this position as an important one to establish if he is to avoid suggesting that men are free to decide, or that one man is as free as another to decide what the rules of the language ought to be. However, if the Tory Johnson differs from many more 'Whiggish' supporters of custom in law or language who see its origin in consent, he does so only to make more sure the process by which, in Blackstone's phrase, customs 'receive their binding power, and the force of law'; [66] and what he does is simply to avoid the complications (and, to his credit, the bad faith) involved in the libertarian rhetoric whereby free men are bound by customs they are supposed to have assented to freely, but which they may not dissent from or change. Johnson's notion of language, as of government, is quite openly and frankly one in which the majority should be idle and helpless spectators while the customs of the polite are converted into law.

Improvement and correction In all that I have said so far, however, I have been comparing what Johnson takes to be the immutable actuality of the political situation, with what he hopes might become – but is not yet – the actual state of the language. The present actuality, as Johnson understands it, is of a language in a state of nature still requiring to be 'reduced' to a state of civil society; and it is in terms of the connection between language and government that he makes the nature of his task as a lexicographer fully (but still problematically) explicit:

When I survey the Plan which I have laid before you, I cannot, my Lord, but confess, that I am frighted at its extent, and, like the soldiers of

Caesar, look on Britain as new world, which it is almost madness to invade. But I hope, that though I should not complete the conquest, I shall at least discover the coast, civilise part of the inhabitants, and make it easy for some other adventurer to proceed farther, to reduce them wholly to subjection, and settle them under laws.

There may be, as I believe there often is in Johnson's writings about language, an irony in this – evident perhaps in the words 'frighted', and 'madness' – in which Johnson may be half-mocking the loss of the sense of proportion that he has incurred by devoting himself so entirely to lexicography – he seems to do the same when, in the later *Preface*, he notes wryly that as far as spelling is concerned 'particular combinations of letters' do not have 'much influence on human happiness'.[67] The irony may here be reminding us, and Johnson himself, that this is only a dictionary, and not a constitution. But there is more to it than that: the irony challenges the scale, but not wholly the nature of the comparison, a comparison reinforced by Johnson's ambiguity about what or who it is that he seeks to 'civilize', 'reduce', and 'settle': the 'inhabitants' are, in the first place, presumably the words of the language, to be 'settled' and 'reduced to subjection' by having their spelling, etymology and meanings fixed, and then by being organized alphabetically in the word list. But the anthropomorphism of the passage points also to the political nature of the task – in settling and subduing the language, Johnson will also be settling and subduing the inhabitants of England, the speakers of English. To neither point is it irrelevant that Johnson sees himself as a *Roman* conqueror; though he is insistent that English is not to be regulated by the laws of any other language, the aspiration is that the language, the inhabitants, and their customs, might come under a discipline like that of Latin grammar, the *pax romana,* and the Roman law.

That the English language, if not the English people, is in need of such discipline, is a point continually reiterated by Johnson, in metaphors often openly political; and it is a point which becomes more important to Johnson in the course of his work on the dictionary, and so is much more insisted upon in the *Preface* than in the original *Plan*. In the earlier essay, English is described as 'our licentious language', and Johnson remarks of the syntax, for example, of English, that it 'is too inconstant to be reduced to rules', as also are the inflections of many English verbs. In the *Preface*, the tone of such remarks becomes much more emphatic, in proportion (as we shall see) to Johnson's increasing doubts that there is any possiblility of civilizing the 'inhabitants' of England. English began as a 'wild and barbarous jargon', and has since been

suffered to spread, under the direction of chance, into wild exuberance, resigned to the tyranny of time and fashion, and exposed to the corruptions of ignorance, and caprices of innovation,

with the result that it is now

copious without order, and energetick without rules: wherever I turned my view, there was perplexity to be disentangled, and confusion to be regulated; choice was to be made out of boundless variety, without any established principle of selection.[68]

That Johnson to some extent still regrets what he sees as the unanalogical character of English is everywhere clear from his tone; but what he can do about it, or whether he should do anything, is less clear to him, and at no time less clear than on the completion of the dictionary. The possiblilities are of course for him as they were for Swift: to correct and improve, or simply to ascertain and fix. That Johnson is tempted by the first possibility is clear, but it is one he claims to have rejected. He can expel, as he says he has done in the preface to the popular shortened version of his dictionary, some 'barbarous terms and phrases' – *malus usus abolendus est*; he can attempt to fix spelling by referring more to the etymology of words than to their current pronunciation; but there is much more that he cannot do. Thus, some unanalogical spellings 'are not errours in orthography, but spots of barbarity impressed so deep in the *English* language, that criticism can never wash them away; these, therefore, must be permitted to remain untouched'; and in the grammar prefixed to the dictionary he seems to regret the passing of words such as 'wherewith' and a number of others which were in fact more tenacious of life than Johnson realized – 'thereby', 'whereby', 'hereafter', and so on – words which are 'proper, useful and analogous', but which could not alas be revivified.[69]

In fact, Johnson is usually far from convinced of the value – let alone the possibility – of improvements and corrections in the language, and it is worth paying close attention to the language he uses at such times. He sometimes sees such improvements as the suggestions of pedants, doomed to be ignored by those whose concern with language is practical, not limply theoretical. This is from the 'Grammar':

There have been many schemes offered for the emendation and settlement of our orthography, which, like that of other nations, being formed by chance, or according to the fancy of the earliest writers in rude ages, was at first very various and uncertain, and is yet sufficiently irregular. Of these reformers some have endeavoured to accommodate orthography better to the pronunciation, without considering that this is to measure by a shadow, to take that for a model or standard which is changing while they apply it. Others, less absurdly indeed, but with equal unlikelihood of success, have endeavoured to proportion the number of letters to that of sounds, that every sound may have its own character, and every character a single sound. Such would be the orthography of a new language to be formed by a synod of grammarians upon principles of science. But who can hope to prevail on nations to change their practice, and make all their old books useless? or what advantage would a new orthography procure equivalent to the confusion and perplexity of such an alteration?

The second question here is what gives Johnson's most usual position on what he calls such 'innovations' – in the grammar he goes on to give examples of such schemes, 'as a guide to reformers, or terrour to innovators'. In the *Plan* he had already announced that, in matters of orthography, he proposed to follow the rule

to make no innovation, without a reason sufficient to balance the inconvenience of change; and such reasons I do not expect often to find. All change is of itself an evil, which ought not to be hazarded but for evident advantage; and as inconstancy is in every case a mark of weakness, it will add nothing to the reputation of our tongue.

And the position is most firmly stated in the *Preface* itself, where he advises would-be reformers of language 'not to disturb, upon narrow views or for minute propriety,

the orthography of their fathers. It has been asserted, that for the law to be *known*, is of more importance than to be *right* ....[70]

The similarity between the position here taken by Johnson, and the defence of the common law by Blackstone and of the unreformed House of Commons as it was to be made by Johnson himself, and later by Burke, is sufficiently clear: 'it hath been', wrote Blackstone, an ancient observation of the laws of England, that whenever a standing rule of law, of which the reason perhaps could not be remembered or discerned, hath been wantonly broken in upon by statutes or new resolutions, the wisdom of the rule hath in the end appeared from the inconveniences that have followed the innovation.

Johnson's appeal to the 'orthography of our fathers' is closely related to that deference to the wisdom of our political forefathers in framing the constitution and the law, and it is in this context that Johnson's hostility to 'innovation' is to be understood: he uses the word, as it is sometimes used by Blackstone, often by Burke, and by Johnson himself in his political writings, in contexts where one can hardly doubt that such competent latinists have *res novae* in the back of their minds. [71] It may certainly be so used in the laconic phrase just quoted from the 'Grammar', 'a terrour to innovators' – 'terrour' here has the sense of the threat of severe punishment, even of death, appropriate for revolutionaries but less so for academic linguists.

The correction and improvement of the language is no longer for Johnson, then, primarily to be resisted on the grounds that it was at the start of the century, as an attempt to impose uniformity on language by a divine right of grammarians; it is resisted now on the grounds that 'all change is of itself an evil', which involves an exchange of 'stability' for 'confusion'; and that such remarks have political implications is clear in Johnson's remark that 'for the law to be *known*, is more important than to be *right*'.[72] The fear is of a reorganization of society or of language that may possibly produce better laws, but will more probably produce anarchy. The innovators of language still sometimes retain, for Johnson, the characteristics of pedantic antiquarians with an absurd fondness for the obsolete. More often however, they are revealed as more dangerous modernists with no respect for established forms, in his reaction to whom Johnson himself can take on something of the tone of the antiquarians he ridicules, for example in his willingness to defend the 'corruptions' of language, as he understands them, when they are sanctioned by time, in terms which anticipate to a remarkable degree Burkes's willingness to defend the system of Old Corruption in the unreformed House of Commons – rotten and pocket boroughs, sinecures and pensions – against the reforming zeal of philosophical radicalism. In Johnson's late and very Burke-like political writings, the dangers of pedantry have been entirely forgotten, and 'innovators' in politics are unambiguously identified as inhumane rationalists who cannot grasp the value of the security guaranteed by the persistence of custom, and who do not understand that the constitution, like all the works of merely human tongues and hands, and whatever Coke or Blackstone may say of its 'perfection', *must* be in some measure imperfect.

To Johnson, therefore, the process of fixing and ascertaining the language was not, as it had been to Swift, a part of the same enterprise as that of improving and correcting it; rather its opposite. It is an attempt to ascertain what is customary usage, however vicious it may often seem, and to fix it beyond the reach of reformers and innovators, as well as beyond that of those who, speaking and writing incorrectly, are likely to introduce further corruptions into the language. It is in this context that we should understand Johnson's impatience with theory – his lack of interest in the question of the origin and purpose of language, and his pragmatic insistence on usage – which relates to the sense we discovered in his political writings, that simply to discuss political ideas, regardless of the object, was the mark of a political malcontent. Thus, in the *Preface,* he seems to refer to Locke's notion that words are the signs of *ideas,* but he is insufficiently interested in the notion to avoid expressing the wish, two lines later, that these signs might be made permanent, 'like the *things* (my italics) which they denote' – an expression which entirely misses the point of Locke's definition. 'Grammar', he announces at the start of his own Grammar, *'is the art of using words properly'.*[73] What he means by 'properly' we shall shortly discover, but it is the emphasis on 'use' that I want to point to here. Like other 'practical' grammarians of the mid century, Johnson has no interest in 'rational grammar' or with the theoretical status of grammatical rules, but simply in the necessity of speaking and writing in accordance with those rules, understood as derived from the practice, not the theory, of language.

Johnson announces his intentions as a lexicographer at the start of the *Plan*: his concern is with the 'perpetuity' of the language, and his aim is 'to preserve the purity and ascertain the meaning of our English idiom'. As far as pronunciation goes, he is concerned to 'fix' it, while accepting that such variations as have already come into use cannot perhaps be eradicated; in the matter of the selection of words, careful divisions are to be made, so that they may be kept, between 'words of general use; words employed chiefly in poetry; words obsolete; words which are admitted only by particular writers, yet not in themselves improper; words used only in burlesque writing; and words impure and barbarous'. The latter are 'carefully to be eradicated wherever they are found, and thus

will our language be laid down, distinct in its minutest subdivisions, and resolved into its elemental principles. And who upon this survey can forbear to wish, that these fundamental atoms of our speech might obtain the firmness and immutability of the primogenial and constituent particles of matter, that they might retain their substance while they alter their appearance, and be varied and compounded, yet not destroyed.[74]

This, like the wish in the *Preface* that words might become as permanent as things, is an aspect of that attempt to reify, precisely to 'thingify', the usage of English speakers, so that, as I said earlier, usage is hypostatized and opposed to what people do actually say. Usage becomes, as it were, a general will, how people ought and how ideally they want to speak, whether they do speak or want to speak like that at all. This is related to an important idea of the constitution common to all who, in the eighteenth century, found themselves in the position of having to defend the revolution of 1688, but were anxious to minimize if not to deny the possibility of any future revolution: that the constitution is, so to speak, the established and permanent articulation of our liberty, which guarantees that liberty against our licence, rather than the immediate expression of our freedom, as a changing language or a changing constitution might announce a change in the will of the people. It is an idea of linguistic and political liberty in which most of the rhetoric is entirely concerned with regulation and restraint, such as Cowper uses in his lines on the Gordon Riots:

Let active laws apply the needful curb
To guard the peace that riot would disturb,
And liberty preserv'd from wild excess,
Shall raise no feuds for armies to suppress . . .
She loses in such storms her very name,
And fierce licentiousness should bear the blame.[75]

The attempt is to define a language which will as far as possible (in the words of the Declaration of Right of 1689) bind 'themselves, their heirs and posterities for ever' – the expression made much of by Johnson and Burke in their political writings, and attacked as meaningless by Paine in *The Rights of Man.*

The language of the vulgar Before we examine Johnson's estimate of his likely success in this undertaking, we should look further at his notion of usage, and ask, in particular, whose usage it was that he sought to fix, to make permanent. The immediate and most obvious answer can be found by leafing through the dictionary itself: like the OED, it is to be regarded as a dictionary of the written, not the spoken language, and of the written language as it is to be found in the pages of polite authors, though as far as possible purged of the barbarisms that from time to time even the politest have admitted. The earliest author generally cited is Sidney; and indeed Johnson remarks of writers before the Restoration that their works are '*the wells of English undefiled*', the pure sources of genuine diction;

From the authors which rose in the time of *Elizabeth*, a speech might be formed adequate to all the purposes of use and elegance. If the language of theology were extracted from *Hooker* and the translation of the Bible; the terms of natural knowledge from *Bacon;* the phrases of policy, war and navigation from *Raleigh*; the dialect of poetry and fiction from *Spenser* and *Sidney*; and the diction of common life from *Shakespeare*, few ideas would be lost to mankind, for want of *English* words, in which they might be expressed.

The claim for the authority of such writers, it must be noted, lies for Johnson less perhaps in their politeness than in their evident excellence as writers, and their linguistic purity is seen mostly as a matter of their being (unlike later writers) comparatively free of '*Gallick* structure and phraseology'. From this it would seem that good usage is to be defined nationalistically, and is more likely to be found in a plain than in a sophisticated style – an attitude foreshadowed in such remarks in the *Plan*, as that 'our language [is to] be considered so far as it is our own'.[76] In spite of his including some extraordinary latinisms in his word list – 'dignotion', for example, or 'exolete', or 'incompossible', or 'clancular' – this notion of Englishness seems to suggest that for Johnson good usage is a matter of speaking and writing plainly, without unnecessary sophistication or affectation.[77]

This does not turn out to mean, however, that good usage is the characteristic of a wider social group than that of the 'best speakers' in whom most eighteenth century grammarians locate it; as we will see by observing Johnson's remarks on such topics as dialect words, terms of art, and pronunciation.

> The English language has properly no dialects; the style of writers has no professed diversity in the use of words, or of their flexions, and terminations, nor differs but by different degrees of skill or care. The oral diction is uniform in no spacious country, but has less variation in England than in most other nations of equal extent. The language of the northern counties retains many words now out of use, but which are commonly of the genuine Teutonick race, and is uttered with a pronunciation which now seems harsh and rough, but was probably used by our ancestors. The northern speech is therefore not barbarous but obsolete.[78]

This passage is a remarkable justification for choosing the words to be represented in the dictionary from the diction of the polite, while appearing only to be guided by a consideration of general usage and genuine Englishness. Thus the assertion that English has 'no dialects' is probably aimed at the Scots, and is supported by the belief that regional varieties of English differ only 'by different degrees of skill or care', which must certainly imply that polite writers are the models of good usage, because they are, not the most polite – that is, apparently, not the issue – but the most skilled writers. The value to Johnson of this position is that it represents English, not as a collection of different Englishes, one of them 'official' but each of them with its own integrity and tradition, but as one language only, which some write better than others. The unity of the language community is represented not as something to be struggled for, but as something already there, and at the same time as the unity of all British writers is thereby asserted, the existence of a hierarchy of writers, and of social divisions within that community, is asserted also. The strategy is familiar to us by now: to represent the community as at once naturally unified, and naturally stratified.

Of equal interest is the assertion that the 'oral' language of 'the northern counties' (which may here include lowlands of Scotland) 'retains' many words 'now out of use'. It is not barbarous, and indeed if we were to take here what Johnson proposes as the test of purity in the *Preface* – an adherence to the teutonic original of English, wariness of gallicisms – we might expect it to be commended as purer, certainly more permanent, than metropolitan English. This would be a conclusion clean counter to most contemporary opinions of dialect, which James Buchanan, for example, who sees the imposition of the metropolitan standard of English on Scotland as a means of bringing the two nations into harmony, characterizes not only as 'vicious' but as 'notoriously vague and unstable', 'continually fluctuating'. Johnson knows too much about language to fall into the same error, and can only avoid attributing to the 'language of the northern counties' the virtues of permanence and stability by saying that northern words, apparently barbarous, are in fact 'obsolete': there could be no clearer example, both of usage being defined as only the usage of the polite, and, in the process, of 'usage' being hypostatized in order to be opposed to the words people do actually use. The standard of what is obsolete here can only be current metropolitan language, even though northern dialect words are precisely current, 'retained', in the north. By this strategy Johnson can omit from his word list all sorts of words, of properly teutonic origin, on grounds which thus establish the primacy of polite usage whether it has the sanction of long-established custom or not; and the notions of the customary and the current can now be manipulated in such a way as to ensure that whatever is in London, is right for everywhere else.[79]

Johnson is on easier ground, with Rice and Buchanan, on the matter of pronunciation, the durability of which he believes is of great moment to the durability of the language. Johnson offers as a rule that we should regard those as 'the most elegant speakers' who are found 'to deviate least from the written words': their pronunciation he describes as the 'solemn' one, and he warns against using instead the 'cursory' and 'colloquial' pronunciation as a standard; for though the solemn is by no means 'immutable and permanent', the colloquial is vague and uncertain, and liable to 'capricious innovation'. Grammarians who have based the standard of pronunciation on the cursory have often established 'the jargon of the lowest of the people as the model of speech'.[80]

The polite clearly emerge as the guardians of the customary, and not of the merely current, in Johnson's discussion, in the *Preface*, of whether the specialized vocabularies of various trades, especially mechanical trades, should be included in his word list; and the less than polite now emerge as too fickle, mutable, inconstant, for their vocabularies to form any part of the permanent language. In his discussion of terms of art in general, Johnson applies different standards according to whether he is dealing with the language of the learned professions or of the mechanical trades. The former are generally included if they have acquired metaphorical meanings which have extended their use outside the professional circles in which they were originally used, or if they may be of use to readers or in the business of daily life. Johnson originally intended to include the vocabulary of the trades on the same basis, but found it impossible to do, as he frankly acknowledges – the defect, he insists, was unavoidable:

I could not visit caverns to learn the miner's language, nor take a voyage to perfect my skill in the dialect of navigation, nor visit the warehouses of merchants, and shops of artificers, to gain the names of wares, tools and operations, of which no mention is found in books; what favourable accident, or easy enquiry brought within my reach, has not been neglected; but it had been a hopeless labour to glean up words, by courting living information, and contesting with the sullenness of one, and the roughness of another.[81]

The note of apology, however, with which Johnson introduces his remarks on this topic, soon fades, and he makes it clear that he does not at all 'lament' his 'omissions';

Of the laborious and mercantile part of the people, the diction is in a great measure casual and mutable; many of their terms are formed for some temporary or local convenience, and though current at certain times and places, are in others utterly unknown. This fugitive cant, which is always in a state of increase or decay, cannot be regarded as any part of the durable materials of a language, and therefore must be suffered to perish with other things unworthy of preservation.

Here the 'laborious and mercantile part of the people' appear as a mob, as the *mobile vulgus* – as the rabble whose 'inconstancy' is lengthily described by Johnson in *The False Alarm* and *The Patriot*. The stability of the language of the *polite*, and the stability of their constitution, are alike threatened by the mutability of the people, who properly considered, have no interest in either matter. They are no part of the true language community, which is now a closed circle of the polite whose language is now presented as durable and permanent; and they form no part of the political community – only 'submission' is 'the duty of the ignorant . . . they have no skill in the art of government, nor any interest in the dissensions of the great'.[82]

But however committed he was to the ideal of a permanent and durable language, Johnson was convinced that his labours were doomed to failure, largely because they involved an attempt to establish the written language as a standard for the spoken; and 'sounds are too volatile and subtile for legal restraints'. It is evident that between the written and spoken language there was for Johnson the same opposition as between the polite and durable, and the vulgar and inconstant languages – not least because the most elegant speakers pronounce words in a way closer to how they are spelled. Throughout Johnson's writings on language the greater permanence of the written is opposed to 'the boundless chaos of living speech': the written language is law, the spoken is anarchy; and the dictionary is as it were the written, methodized account of customary usages, *leges non scriptae*, which attempts to preserve our liberties against the anarchic licence of our actual speech. But the attempt, as I have said, is felt to be vain; for there are at work

causes of change, which, though slow in their operation, and invisible in their progress, are perhaps as much superiour to human resistance, as the revolutions of the sky, or intumescence of the tide.

They include the growth and spread of commerce, and so an increasing contact with other languages; the division of society into laborious and leisured classes, whereby the latter have opportunity to expand the stock of knowledge and therefore of words; the increase in politeness, now again represented as a force for mutability, and always liable to introduce capricious figures of speech; and the spread of translations, which adopt too many terms and idioms from their originals. 'If the changes we fear be thus irresistible,' Johnson concludes,

what remains but to acquiesce with silence, as in the other insurmountable distresses of humanity? It remains that we retard what we cannot repel, that we palliate what we cannot cure. Life may be lengthened by care, though death cannot be ultimately defeated: tongues, like governments, have a natural tendency to degeneration; we have long preserved our constitution, let us make some struggles for our language.[83]

But when we remember Johnson's earlier remark, that 'particular combinations of letters' do not have 'much influence on human happiness' we may suspect an irony in Johnson's regret that we must 'acquiesce' in the inevitable transformation of language, 'as in the other insurmountable distresses of humanity'; and the ironic note is confirmed when we recall that at one point Johnson has described the lexicographer's task as to 'embalm' language – the task of securing it from 'corruption and decay' presupposes in these terms that it is already dead, as indeed by one of Johnson's metaphors it is. For the phrase 'the boundless chaos of living speech' suggests precisely that the life of a language is in its speakers, and even, perhaps, in its less polite speakers, who depart most in their pronunciation from the written word, and from whom Johnson was unwilling to court 'living information'. 'No dictionary of a living language ever can be perfect', he writes at the end of the *Preface*, 'since while it is hastening to publication, some words are budding, and some falling away'; and that image of an organic process in language – 'budding' here a metaphor taken from Horace,[84] the best classical authority for the sovereignty of common usage – seems to suggest a pleasure taken in the mutability of language, and not a merely reluctant acquiescence.

It is an attitude reminiscent of one, at least, of Johnson's political essays – an early one, before the Middlesex election and the American War – *The Bravery of the English Common Soldiers* – where he sees that bravery as something achieved not merely in spite of the lack of regularity and discipline in the English army, but because of qualities intimately related to that lack – the independence, even insolence, of the 'English vulgar', who are raised to acts of courage by being 'impatient of reproach'. It is a jingoistic and comforting vision of Englishness, whose trick is to pretend that in a democracy all are *free*, whether enfranchised or not; it confirms the free genius of the English against the servility of the French, and reassures a polite readership that the other ranks are as keen on giving the French a bloody nose as are the officers. It is in terms of the same reverence for English Liberty that Johnson expresses his fervent hope that no academy on the French model would be established in England:

In absolute governments, there is sometimes a general reverence paid to all that has the sanction of power, and the countenance of greatness. How little this is the state of our country needs not to be told. We live in an age in which it is a kind of publick sport to refuse all respect that cannot be enforced. The edicts of an English Academy would probably be read by many, only that they might be sure to disobey them.

If an academy should be established for the cultivation of our stile, which I, who can never wish to see dependence multiplied, hope the spirit of English liberty will hinder or destroy.... [85]

This jingoism, and Johnson's irony alike, may both be defensive, but they serve to complicate the more closed conservatism of most of his writing on politics and language; and they keep in play a libertarian ideology, which could be used, certainly, as a means of curtailing the liberty it pretended to endorse, but whose implications for both politics and language could be taken a good deal further than Johnson himself would have approved.

The grammar of dissent After the publication of the Dictionary, it is clear that to argue against custom as the law of language was to risk being thought an innovator, in politics – such was the strength of the political analogy – perhaps no less than in language. Among the advocates of custom among linguists of the following decades a number may certainly have been reluctant advocates, unwilling to lend their authority, as Johnson so often was, to the unanalogical and irregular practices that had become common usage even among the polite, but much more unwilling to argue for their regulation. 'It is true', writes John Rice,

that Custom hath authorized a Number of Anomalies, or Exceptions, to the natural Rules of Pronunciation: And, as that is the *Jus et norma loquendi*, we must not rebel against such Authority. [86]

According to most histories of eighteenth-century linguistics, the most convinced advocate of the authority of custom in the decades after Johnson was Joseph Priestley, whose *Rudiments of Grammar* appeared in 1761, a little before Lowth's *Short Introduction*. A careful reading of this work, however, and of Priestley's *Course of Lectures on the Theory of Language and Universal Grammar* (1762) reveals his defence of custom to have been much qualified. To begin with, he grasps more clearly than any of Johnson's immediate successors the ideological function of 'custom' as it had been represented by the political analogy in Johnson; for him what is accepted as 'good usage' is simply the most successful, not necessarily the best, version of the language: 'those forms of speech ... grow established', which have 'the most, and the most powerful advocates'. Priestley's *Rudiments* was designed to exhibit only 'the present state of our language', evidently the statement of a man whose concern is exclusively with actual and not with hypostatized custom. The generally permissive tone of the grammar may be gauged from Priestley's attitude to 'rules' – he avoids the term as far as he considers possible: his aim instead is to give 'the youth of our nation an insight into the fundamental principles of their own language'. The concentration on 'fundamental principles' is precisely designed to enable his readers to grasp the reasons behind, not the rules but the 'material observations' that Priestley offers on grammar; so that those left unenfranchised by the Brightland grammar and many of its successors may find their way back into the language community. The word 'rule' indeed, appears on the first page of his preface, and then not again until almost the end of the book, when it is introduced with the greatest reticence: 'it may not be improper, to lay down, in this place, for the use of learners, *Easy rules to distinguish the several parts of speech*'.[87]

Priestley's concern with usage on the one hand, and his insistence on 'principles' on the other, may at first sight seem to lead him into a conflict between his democratism and his rationalism. On the question of an Academy, he presents himself as entirely a respecter of the influence of 'time' – that is, of unregulated usage – as likely to settle all questions of divided use:

I think it not only unsuitable to the genius of a *free nation*, but in itself ill calculated to reform and fix a language. We need make no doubt but that the best forms of speech will, in time, establish themselves by their own superior excellence: and, in all controversies, it is better to wait the decisions of *Time*, which are slow and sure, than to take those of *Synods*, which are often hasty and injudicious. A *manufacture* for which there is a great demand, and a *language* that many persons have leisure to read and write, are both sure to be brought, in time, to all the perfection of which they are capable.

This is not, however, a defence of usage, and a repudiation of academies, in quite the manner of Johnson, or in the manner in which it has generally been taken by writers on Priestley's theory of language. Essential to it is a belief that there are, indeed, best forms of speech, and Priestley is as critical of those who have followed 'the vulgar mode through all its temporary modes and inconstancies' as he is of those whose rules 'do not correspond with the present state of the language, as it is actually spoken and written'. This may suggest that Priestley is offering us the standard of the best authors or the best speakers, but in fact he has nothing to say of good *speakers*, and, as we have already remarked, he has no interest in pronunciation except as it is concerned with emphasis – he notes of dialects that, as a matter of historical fact, they have flourished most in conditions of political freedom. Of good authors Priestley notes that they have 'adopted different forms of speech, and in a case that admits no standard but that of *custom*, one authority may be of as much weight as another'.[88]

In fact, Priestley, whose works on language and rhetoric appeared while he was teaching at the dissenting academy at Warrington,[89] is that portent which Johnson was so uneagerly awaiting, a spokesmen for those educated dissenters who saw little enough reason to revere the language as sharing the virtues of a constitution that had 'degraded' them to 'second-class citizens',[90] wholly or partly excluded from the political community. He is a rationalist, whose standard is usage only insofar as it is the usage of the free and rational man, and whose faith in the triumph of the best forms of speech is based on a faith in the progressive realization of a free and rational society, which he no doubt believes – one can imagine Johnson or Burke shuddering at the comparison – will be achieved as society is 'perfected' as a manufacture is, and as the language will be, in response to a 'great demand'.

Priestley is, indeed, though in small enough ways, prepared to hasten the arrival of the reformed language, by advocating rational analogy as the only arbiter in questions of disputed usage; for

language, to answer the intent of it, which is to express our thoughts with certainty in an intercourse with one another, must be fixed and consistent with itself.

The appeal to analogy itself may not, however, always be decisive, for

if this should decide for neither of two contrary practices, the thing must remain undecided, till all-governing custom shall declare in favour of the one or the other . . .

and in fact, Priestley's appeals to analogy are often also appeals to usage: 'Mr Johnson', he notes, 'assigns no conjunctive form to the *preter tense*' – if I loved, if thou loved, etc. – but the analogy of the language 'seems to require it, and it is found in usage'; he remarks elsewhere that 'many writers of no small reputation say *you was*, when speaking of a single person; but as the word *you* is confessedly *plural*, ought not the *verb*, agreeable to the analogy of all languages, be plural too? Moreover, we always say *you are*.'[91]

Thus the appeal from analogy to usage, of the kind endorsed however reluctantly by Johnson, is based on a mistaken estimate of the degree of rationality in men, and therefore of the likely uniformity and analogical character of their usage: 'the correspondence between every person's thought and language is perhaps more strict, and universal, than is generally imagined.' In as much as we use language incorrectly, that is (as Johnson would no doubt have agreed) because we are using it less than rationally – 'every thing ... that is maimed, distorted, or redundant in a person's Style, must proceed from the same kind and degree of imperfection in his ideas'; but for Priestley, and emphatically not for Johnson, man is by nature rational, and such imperfections of usage are corrigible and will indeed (as we have seen) be corrected in time; perhaps, indeed, by the eventual adoption of a universal language. The diversity of language has in the past been, on balance, an advantage, as it has been a barrier to the contagion of error; in the rationalist future, a universal language may facilitate the communication of truth; but though this attitude enables Priestley to escape, precisely, the 'contagion' of condemning English as it is adopting more foreign words which 'have added considerably to the bulk and gracefulness of our language', his scientific approach to language (he compares it with the study of natural philosophy) tells him that the state of our knowledge of language as an abstract science is not yet sufficiently advanced for us to succeed in formulating a universal language.[92]

As we might expect, Priestley's use of the analogy of language and politics is in conformity with the spirit of democratic rationalism we have so far discovered in him:

In modern and living languages, it is absurd to pretend to set up the compositions of any person or persons whatsoever as the standard of writing, or their conversation as the invariable rule of speaking. With respect to customs, laws, and every thing that is changeable, the body of a people, who, in this respect, cannot but be free, will certainly assert their liberty, in making what innovations they judge to be expedient and useful. The general prevailing custom, wherever it happen to be, can be the only standard for the time that it prevails. And in a case that admits of no authority to controul a man's actions, it is in vain to pretend that any person may not attempt to introduce whatever he thinks to be an improvement. Indeed the fear of becoming ridiculous is sufficient to prevent many very extravagant and absurd proposals.

The chief thing to be attended to in the improvement of a language is the *analogy* of it. The more consistent are its principles, the more it is of a piece with itself, the more commodious it will be for use: and it cannot be looked upon as any great or alarming innovation, meerly to disuse constructions that clash with others, and to confine ones self to one sense of any single word or phrase. [93]

This is precisely the position that Johnson wrote against, and uses precisely that word 'innovation' in its assertion of the inalienable freedom of men to introduce rational changes in the established forms of the language and the law, on the 'mean' considerations, as they are to Burke, of practical utility, of contingent advantage, and with no respect for the practice of generations. Priestley's willingness to innovate according to rational analogy certainly jostles, in his work, with a less confident, more Johnsonian attitude – sometimes language is to be treated as a science, governed by the uniform laws that govern natural phenomena; sometimes it is to be respected as 'the invention

of men, and particularly of rude uncultivated men. We must consider their circumstances, make the best we can of a lame and imperfect subject, and not deny real defects and redundancies, or fruitlessly labour to reconcile manifest inconsistencies, but must ourselves conform to established vicious practices, if we would not make ourselves justly ridiculous by our singularity.

This is perhaps rather to say that in language practice we cannot expect the immediate acceptance of rational innovations; we may propose them, and hope for their acceptance, but cannot, as a matter of *fact*, impose them – as we can, perhaps, in matters of law and the constitution, which Priestley almost polemically (by 1762) is defining as temporary and as changeable, and so, as a proper field (the implication is) for innovation as an assertion of 'liberty'. [94]

A similarly guarded attitude to custom is evident in the *Essay towards an English Grammar*, by the Congregationalist minister and school teacher John Fell, published in 1784 with a preface by his former pupil Richard Sharp. In fact, Sharp borrowed some of the most striking phrases in his preface from George Campbell's *Philosophy of Rhetoric* (1776), the grammatical section of which had purported to present the notion of custom in a thoroughly democratic manner, but had then proceeded to define the term as applying only to usage which was 'reputable' and 'national', as well as 'current'; and in the process, as we have seen, it had excluded from what it refers to as 'the language, properly so-called' the English of 'ninety-nine of a hundred' of English speakers; and the use of even the remaining 1 per cent was still to be regulated by nine qualifying 'canons', probably modelled on Blackstone's seven 'requisites' necessary to make a custom 'good'. [95] In the same year as he published his work on rhetoric, Campbell preached a sermon in Aberdeen on 'the nature, extent, and importance of the duty of allegiance'. By an appeal to the sovereignty of 'immemorial *custom*', by an insistence that the property qualification for members of the House of Commons guaranteed a concern in them for the interests of all those on whose behalf they legislated, and by a demonstration of the incompatibility of republicanism and Christianity, this sermon was calculated to recall the American colonists from revolt; though, as Leslie Stephen laconically remarked, it failed to arouse them to a sense of their duty.

Richard Sharp, who in later life considered writing an approving history of the American struggle for Independence, was, at the time of the publication of Fell's grammar, a dissenter, probably, like Fell, a Congregationalist; during the 1780s he attended meetings of the radical Major Cartwright's Society for the obtaining of Constitutional Information, a body which campaigned for universal manhood suffrage and the repeal of the Test and Corporation Acts; and he may have been the author of an anonymous tract in support of their repeal.[96] The collision between Sharp's ideas and Campbell's illuminates the degree to which in the seventies and eighties the rhetoric of 'liberty' as employed by conservatives and radicals alike could appear almost identical, and can be separated often only by a careful attention to tone and nuance. Both men represent the grammarian, in phrases quoted earlier in this chapter, not as a 'lawgiver' or as one who 'presumes' to 'regulate the customs and fashions of our speech', but as one whose 'only business is to note, collect and methodize' them; thus far both cast themselves as defenders of the customary law, in the manner of Coke and Blackstone, and both agree of customs that the moment they 'become general .. they are the laws of the language'. From the opinions of the grammarian, both agree, an appeal may be made to the 'tribunal of use, as to the supreme authority and last resort'.[97]

They appear to agree, too, about the role of the *critic* of language; though in the matter of what he is to criticize, Sharp seems concerned more with the irrational caprices of polite usage, Campbell with the intrusion of vulgarisms into the language of the polite. In both cases, however, they agree that the critic has no 'censorian power of instant degradation'; he is privileged only to 'petition', and to 'remonstrate'. The passage in which Sharp discusses this issue, however, is expressed in terms which Campbell would hardly endorse, and which take the jolly rhetoric of 'English Liberty' a good deal further than Johnson would now have done, at the same time as Sharp is evidently more guarded about the perfection of that liberty than more orthodox writers on politics or language would have chosen to appear. He is discussing the possiblility of establishing an Academy, a dead letter by now but still a convenient one in which to inscribe one's democratic principles:

To prevent a similar decline of the French language the French Academy has endeavoured to render it at once more pure and more durable: but the republic of letters is a true republic, in its disregard to the arbitrary decrees of usurped authority.   Perhaps such an institution would do still less well with us . . . . The laws of our speech, like the laws of our country, should breathe a spirit of liberty: they should check licentiousness, without restraining freedom. The most effectual method of preserving our language from decay, and preventing a total disregard to the Saxon part of it, is to bring about a revolution in our present mode of education.[98]

What is remarkable here, as so often in the passages we have been considering, will emerge only if we continue to bear in mind the potency and importance of the analogy of language and politics in the century. Thus it is becoming something of a declaration of one's political attitudes to recommend 'revolution' in any sphere, by 1784; and thus also the phrase 'the republic of letters' ('is a true republic') takes on a more threatening aspect 'in its disregard to the arbitrary decrees of usurped authority' than it had ever done in earlier uses of the phrase – for Campbell, custom was an 'Empress'. In the context of a century of approbation of the British constitution as 'the perfection of government', the phrase seems to challenge rather than confirm the limits of English liberty; and in the mouth of such a dissenter as Sharp, the ambiguity of the following phrase is hardly less remarkable: 'the laws of our speech, like those of our country, should breathe a spirit of liberty: they should check licentiousness, without restraining freedom'. The second half of the sentence is unsurprising enough, and we should note of it only that Sharp was a member of a group which demanded full membership of the political community for men who were regarded by many among the conservative, anglican establishment – by Blackstone, for example – as 'peevish or opinionated men', advocates of a licentious dissolution of the bonds of Church and State. [99] But what are we to make of the first half of the sentence: *do* 'the laws of our country … breathe a spirit of liberty?' – or *should* they do so (although in fact they do not)? The sentence is a fine example of the wary ambiguity of much dissenting prose in the period; for dissenters, condemned by the Corporation and Test Acts to being second-class members of the political community, could be at once anxious to demonstrate their political trustworthiness, and thus their right to enter the institutions and public offices from which they were excluded, at the same time as they felt obliged also to express their reprobation of a law by which they were thus excluded. There must be some question about what construction Sharp himself would have put on the remark.

The body of Fell's grammar is remarkable partly for the authors from whom he draws his examples: along with the usual list – the scriptures, Shakespeare, Addison, Pope, Dryden and so on, are Milton, Locke, Algernon Sidney and Junius, the last two certainly not usual choices, and all four of them writers whose approbation of aspects of the English political system could be interpreted in various ways as less than whole-hearted, as Fell's certainly was – in 1797 he was to lose his tutorship at a dissenting academy on account of his republican opinions. [100] It is remarkable also for Fell's unwillingness to submit to custom, as to the law that Sharp himself, following Campbell, had represented it as being: he is more concerned – as in fact Sharp also had claimed to be in his preface – with the assertion of individual liberty against the absolute authority of hypostatized 'custom'. The plea for the authority of custom, as against a narrowly analogical view of propriety, is made urgently enough by both men; and yet it is always inviting us to take it as a plea for individual liberty against prescription – in the spirit of a bourgeois-democratic reading of Locke – whether analogical or customary.

This emerges particularly as a plea for stylistic freedom: of those who have attempted to put a polish on the language by concealing its rough Saxon oak beneath a veneer of Latinisms, Sharp asks:

Perhaps they *may* have cleared it of some cant terms, low phrases, and awkward constructions: but what they may have gained in accuracy, have they not lost in variety? Have they not reduced all kinds of composition to an insipid uniformity? Is not the spirit of our language lowered, its freedom cramped, and its range of expression narrowed?

On a number of occasions Fell makes a similar point:

every writer ought to be the master of his own phrases; and every reader must be left to approve and reject, according to his own judgment and taste.

Of various instances of doubtful usage, he remarks:

It does not appear that any sufficient reason can be assigned, why we should reject some, and receive others, of these instances. But every writer has an undoubted right to be the master of his own style.

There may be an echo, here, of Johnson's statement, at the end of his life of Roscommon, in rejecting the possiblility of an English Academy:

That our language is in perpetual danger of corruption cannot be denied; but what prevention can be found? The present manners of the nation would deride authority, and therefore nothing is left but that every writer should criticise himself.[101]

Johnson, writing now in the late 1770s, is well aware that the hoped-for consensus of custom – the wish that the custom of the polite could indeed be represented as an unalterable nature, from which no appeal was possible – had been challenged, and that the ideological basis of the attempt to fix language was beginning to be grasped by those whom his version of custom would have excluded from the language community. What he represents here, therefore, as a regrettable necessity, Fell claims as an inalienable right. For Johnson, the responsibility of the writer is to check a licentiousness, as he sees it, in the public culture, by a self-restraint, by self-criticism; for Fell, it is to oppose what he sees as the uniformity, imposed by a hypostatized 'custom', with an individualistic assertion of personal liberty.

Politics, pronunciation, and spelling The degree to which Johnson's version of custom had been recognized as a conservative one is nowhere clearer than in various writings on pronunciation that appeared in the 1770s and 1780s. The orthodox, Johnsonian position is well represented by the 'moderate Whig' Abraham Tucker, whose *Vocal Sounds* appeared in 1773, and who was interested in producing a phonetic alphabet, not for general use but as a means of establishing a uniform pronunciation; but he was more anxious not to be accused of trying to promote a 'revolution' in 'literature' any more than in 'church and state'. His is not a method, he explains, of 'innovation' – he no doubt recalls Johnson's playful threat of death to innovators in orthography – but of 'reformation'; he wants to proceed 'gradually'. [102]

A few years later Thomas Spence, the radical pamphleteer and bookseller who was later to be imprisoned for selling *The Rights of Man*, published his *Grand Repository of the English Language* (1775), the first English dictionary to use a 'genuine, scientific, phonetic' alphabet to represent pronunciation; like Thomas Sheridan, but with a wider class of the underprivileged in mind, including 'Negro slaves' and the inhabitants of India, Spence believed that

the darkest hieroglyphics, or most difficult cyphers, which the art of man has hitherto found out, were not better calculated to conceal the sentiments of those who used them, from all who had not the key, than the state of our spelling is, to conceal the true pronunciation from all, except a few well-educated natives.

The diffusion of his various phonetic spelling systems Spence understood as a political act: 'Hwĕn I begăn to stŭde', he wrote in his account of his second trial at the start of the following century,

I fŏwnd ĕvre Thĭng ĕrĕktĕd ŏn sĕrtn ŭnŏltrăbl Prĭnsĭplz. I fŏwnd ĕvre 'Art ănd Siĕns a pĕrfĕkt Hol. Nŏthĭng wŏz ĭn 'Anărke bŭt Lăngwĭj ănd Pŏlĭtĭks: Bŭt both ŏv dhez I hăv rĕdust tw 'Ordr: Dhĕ Wŏn bi a Nu 'Alfĭbet, ănd dhĕ ŭdhr bi a Nu Kŏnstĭtushŭn. [103]

In the reformed spelling edition of his *Supplement to the History of Robinson Crusoe* (1782) – the republic of 'Crusonia' was Spence's version of Utopia – he wrote:

I hăv prĭntĭd thĭs lĭtĭl Pes ĭn thĭ Kruzoneĭn Mănĭr [by this phrase Spence usually referred to his reformed spelling] fŏr thĭ Ez ŏv Fŏrĭnĭrz ănd ŏrdĭnăre Redĭrz. I tharfor ădjur aul Krĭtĭks ănd Skŏlĭrz nŏt too ăprĭhĕnd thar Librarez ĭn Danjĭr, or thĭngk I ĭntĕnd too kŏmpĕl ithĭr thĕm or thar Chĭldrĭn ĭntoo Kŏnsĭstĕnsez. No, I onle ĭntĕnd too fre thĭ Poor ănd thĭ Stranjĭr, thĭ 'Indŭstreŭs ănd thĭ 'Inĭsĭnt frŏm vĕksashŭs, tedeŭs, ănd rĭdĭkĭlĭs 'Absŭrdĭtez .... I doo nŏt men ithĭr too hĭndĭr thĭ Prĭntĭng, Redĭng, ŏr ăgreĭbĭl Kŏntĕmplashĭn ŏv ăne Old Pĕdĭntrez.[104]

The spirit of this reassurance to the polite, that their libraries are not in danger – an echo of Johnson's concern that a reformed orthography would 'make all ... old books useless' – is hardly that of Tucker: there is no reverence for the inconsistencies of language as the mysterious growth of centuries, and Spence describes the absurdities of the spelling he has set out to reform in much the same terms as Paine would ridicule the inconsistencies of the constitution, as they were to be defended by Burke.

Two years later Robert Nares produced his *Elements of Orthoepy* (1784), written as exclusively for the polite as Spence's works were for the vulgar. Nares appears in some histories of the subject as the champion of current usage *par excellence*. His claim to be so is based on his evident awareness of the transient nature of language; in attempting to record, not to regulate usage, he states that his book

will offer a clear and intelligible view of the externals of the English language, as they stand at present: and, should it exist for any length of time, will be a monument of the pronunciation which prevailed in England towards the end of the eighteenth century.

Of this, Murray Cohen remarks, 'This is a remarkable statement ...for its acceptance of change'; and yet this awareness of the inevitability of change does not make Nares any the less anxious to fix pronunciation, not simply as historical evidence, but for prescriptive purposes. The passage I have quoted is followed by an unacknowledged echo of Johnson, regretting rather than merely registering the fact of linguistic change, and hoping that 'we may perhaps retard what we cannot prevent; and we may even prevent some changes, though we cannot lay a prohibition upon all.'[105] In the context of Johnson, the conservatism of this is striking; even Johnson had not long taken seriously the possibility of fixing the spoken, the 'living' language; and yet Nares here is attempting just that, just what, indeed, Johnson doubted his ability to do even for the written.

And yet the tone of Nares's work is remarkably defensive: he writes of the language as if it is under siege:

Language, being perpetually in use, is not easily preserved from corruption. Violent and gross injuries, indeed, such as proceed from the attacks of vulgar or provincial barbarism, are readily perceived and repelled; but there are enemies which act against it more secretly, and therefore more irresistibly.

The 'language' – a term as exclusive and ideal for Nares as it was for Lowth or Campbell – is here represented, almost, as an Abyssinian prince, guarded in some metropolitan citadel by the more responsible members of the language community. This citadel is attacked from without by barbarians – 'vulgar' and 'provincial' – who are however easily 'repelled'; but there are enemies within, too, a treasonous fifth column among the polite speakers themselves. These traitors are of two kinds: the unthinkingly capricious, who may again be recognized and dealt with easily enough, for 'it will generally be perceived that needless irregularity is the worst of all deformities'; but also a much more dangerous group, who are 'excited' by the 'desire of improvement' and 'prompted by zeal'. These men are evidently misguided rationalists, who in their intention to 'perfect the instrument of reason, will deprave and disorder it'. It is to save the language from the 'attempts of innovators'[106] – the word 'attempt' here used as Burke was later to use it, as a 'rash recourse to force' – that Nares has written his book: to show how much the language contains which

being already right, should be defended from change and violation; how much it has that demands amendment; and how much that, for fear of greater inconveniences, must perhaps be left unaltered, though irregular.

The customary orthography, however originally 'arbitrary', must be defended no less than the grammar of the language: here too change is 'attended with considerable inconvenience'. It is therefore necessary to fix the rules of pronunciation as firmly as previous writers have fixed those of the grammar, 'to resist capricious innovation, to direct the efforts of those who would reform, and to remove the difficulties of those who doubt' [107] – the last phrase has clear religious overtones, and implies as it were an apology for the established religion designed to win proselytes from among the more tractable, less 'zealous' of the dissenters.

It is therefore in this context that Nares's defence of custom must be understood: its desparate optimism that the pronunciation can be fixed – at least until some 'political convulsion' silences the language for ever – is expressed in the military imagery of a community under siege, not at all in that of Johnson's *Plan*, of a prospective invader and conqueror. The political nature of this task is quite evident to Nares, the more so because, as his tone suggests, he fears the attempt may have come too late. What is striking about this political awareness is the marked similarity of its expression to that in which Burke, six years later, was to defend the British Constitution in his *Reflections on the Revolution in France* (1790). There is Nares's insistence that the language should be 'for ever settled' as for Burke the constitution had been; the same distrust in Nares of 'system-makers' as Burke evinces of 'theorists', of 'a geometrical and arithmetical' constitution, of the 'systematic', of those who believe that a commonwealth can be reformed on principles 'taught *a priori*'. Nares's fear of 'injudicious innovation' is matched by Burke's description of the 'spirit of innovation' which 'is generally the result of a selfish temper and confined views'; and which seeks to change, 'on slight grounds', and in order to gratify some 'present sense' or 'temporary ideas' of 'convenience', the customs we have inherited from our forefathers – I choose the phrases at random from Nares and Burke.[108] The list of such anticipations and echoes could continue for pages, but the point is perhaps sufficiently established: by the 1780s, as the work of Sharp, Fell, Spence and Nares makes clear, the consensus of custom, invoked by Johnson against the likely attempts of those outside the community of the language, has been threatened from exactly the quarter that Johnson had indicated. The effort to establish custom as 'our second nature', in terms similar to those in which Burke would argue that to change the established constitutions of Europe it would be necessary 'to make a revolution in nature, and provide a new constitution for the human mind', [109] has failed, for the time being at least; and if Johnson was the first to recognize the threat, he was perhaps also, in his life of Roscommon, the first to recognize the failure.

But the failure was only temporary. It is beyond the scope of this book to demonstrate how, in the 1790s, the 'correct' version of the language as prescribed by 'custom' was further challenged; or why, in the following century, the consensus of custom was able to re-emerge as robustly as it did. On the first issue, however, it is perhaps worth pointing to the writings of men such as Paine, Charles Pigott, Horne Tooke and William Godwin, and to the continuing work of Spence. Thomas Paine nowhere writes directly on language, but in *The Rights of Man* in particular he is continually concerned to argue that what was to him, the meaningless use of language by the Ancien Régime in England is an insult to the intelligence of rational men, and an instrument of political control; he attacks the notion, for example, of the 'customary', as one whereby 'precedent, like a dictionary, determines every case.' In much the same spirit, Pigott produced, in 1795, his satirical *Political Dictionary* of the language of the Ancien Régime, on the model of Voltaire's *Philosophical Dictionary*. The influential, strikingly simple, and apparently largely mistaken system of etymology devised by Horne Tooke made the constant implication that uneducated speakers had a better understanding of the meaning of English words than had the lexicographer or grammarian; and William Godwin argued for the absolute superiority of the style and language of his own day, over that of the reigns of Elizabeth or Anne, the models for many proponents of 'custom', on the positivistic grounds of its superiority as a medium for rational communication.[110] In various ways these men represent the language defined by 'common usage' as a language produced at once to secure and to conceal the political objectives of the ruling class – as in a way more familiar to students of English Literature did Blake and arguably (at least until the turn of the century) Wordsworth.

'ESTO PERPETUA', 'may it last forever', wrote Blackstone of the constitution of Britain, with more confidence than Johnson could muster, at the end of his *Preface*, for the perpetuity of the language as defined by his dictionary.[111] As politicians and constitutional lawyers believed that the revolution of 1688, which had brought the political arrangements of Britain to the perfection of mixed government, was also a dangerous precedent which might be appealed to at any time by fickle men, with temporary grievances, who might seek to change the constitution and shake its stability by replacing the corruptions they attacked with the seeds of greater corruption; so most writers on language practice came to fear that if the customs of speech, however irrational, were not given as much stability as would serve to retard change, if not altogether to prevent it, the language would degenerate into an anarchy in which no man could understand or control another. The corruption of the language was awaited, indeed, with the same fear as was that of the state: for the need to establish as a stable, if not permanent, standard of custom, the usage of the polite – of those who, by virtue of their rank and education, could be regarded as independent of the fugitive interests of the mob, and as capable of taking long views uninfluenced by the attractions of short-term 'convenience' – meant of course that if the standard were challenged, the political as well as the linguistic authority of the polite would be at risk, for that authority was founded on similar qualifications in politics and language alike. The representation of the language in terms of the law was thus more than the analogy that, for my own immediate convenience, I have described it as in this essay: it was a part of the attempt to preserve the authority of a political system framed by the polite to protect their interests.

At least as far as the language was concerned, Johnson could have been more sanguine in his expectations: for despite the criticisms of Paine, of Tooke, of Wordsworth, it is clear that by the early decades of the nineteenth century the proper form of the King's English had been 'settled' to a remarkable degree, if not by 'immemorial custom', then by the codifications of the language of the polite by the grammarians, the lexicographers, and elocutionists of the century before.[112] It was then that the standards of 'correctness', which in spite of Johnson's fears still operate officially today, were established, at the expense of whatever differences of provincial and idiosyncratic usage, so that the standard became indisputably recognized, if not universally adopted, as a *national* standard, confirming (as it was imagined) the unity of the nation. I hope to have made it clear that the 'analogy' of law and language was a crucial weapon in the imposition of that standard, for it represented those who offended against the rules of good English, like those who broke the laws of the land, as thereby in some measure excluding themselves from the national community. The benefits of this imposition are obvious, but it is obvious too that it benefited most those who (as Priestley pointed out) were in a position to announce their own language as 'the language, properly so-called'; for at the same time as it offered a notional cultural equality to men of all classes, if they could speak the language, it confirmed the power of those who could speak it over those who could not, and it continues to do so.

3 A diffused picture, an uniform plan: Roderick Random in the labyrinth of Britain

The novel and social unity No form in the eighteenth century represents the diversity of English society – of its identities, occupations, languages – more fully than the novel or raises more sharply the problem of how society can be understood as anything other than diverse. It is usual, indeed, to regard many 'episodic' eighteenth century novels as concerned far more to represent that diversity than to discover any connection or coherence in the society they describe. In a tradition of criticism whose notions of novelistic form have been more influenced by the Victorian than by the eighteenth-century novel, the sense we arrive at in reading a novel, and particularly in approaching its end, of its formal coherence, is closely related to a sense that the society it represents is also in some way coherent. If a novel represents a host of incidents, and thereby introduces a host of characters, who contribute little or nothing to our final sense of the connectedness of the narrative, and who could therefore be omitted without our having any sense that the novel is somehow deficient – then we will not feel that the experiences of its characters, and the positions they occupy at the novel's end, are dependent on, or are to a plausible degree determined by, the social relations the book represents. In such a tradition of criticism, to call a novel 'episodic' is immediately to question whether it can pretend to any marked coherence of structure, and therefore to any account of social experience as other than casual or random. Episodic novels become more or less highly valued, indeed, in part according to the degree to which characters who appear to be introduced casually into the narrative, and to be dismissed from it equally casually, in fact turn out to exercise a determining influence on the progress of the central character: this is perhaps the main reason why *Tom Jones* is generally more valued than, say, *Roderick Random* – a higher proportion of the people encountered by Tom than by Roderick (though not many in either novel) get back into the story: and Fielding no doubt had this in mind when he called his novel *The History of Tom Jones* – a title that suggests that one event will connect with another, rather than that one will simply *follow* another, as is suggested by such titles as *The Adventures of* . . .Peregrine Pickle or Roderick Random.

We have seen, however, in the earlier essays of this book, how for social philosophers, for poets celebrating the social and economic order of eighteenth-century England, and even for writers on language practice, the unity of society is not simply given, or the ability to perceive it is not something given to everyone – it has to be *observed*. They certainly believed that the society of eighteenth-century Britain was 'really', fundamentally, coherent; but their preoccupation was with the problem of the viewpoint, the intellectual or social position, from which that coherence could be observed, and of the language in which it could be described; for from any but the 'right' position, social experience, social events, will appear random, and society will seem a loose and unorganized collection of individuals each pursuing selfish and separate ends. If we compare, say, *The Fleece* and *Middlemarch*, it's clear that for Dyer and Eliot alike the society they create is 'really' coherent, but that, even though for Eliot no less than for Dyer that coherence cannot be observed by everyone, if by anyone at all, within the society of the book, Eliot is far less concerned than is Dyer to examine the viewpoint from which its coherence can be grasped. It seems to me that writers of episodic novels in the eighteenth century share the concerns of Dyer far more than those of George Eliot: they certainly create far less of the sense that she does of society as an intricate network of determining social relations and events; but they are more concerned than she is with the problem of how to define, and how to arrive at, the position from which apparently random and casual experience can be perceived as confirming, and not denying, the fundamental coherence, comprehensibility, describability of the societies they represent. In this essay I want to try to give an idea of how that position could be defined, and of the sense of diversity, confusion even, which can be grasped as coherence from that position and no other; and to that end I shall mainly concentrate on a single novel, Smollett's *Roderick Random,* first published in 1748.

In the first essay of this book, we saw how in order to define that viewpoint from which diversity and confusion appear as coherence and connected order, it usually seemed necessary to Thomson and to Dyer to adopt a position *outside* the society they described. Thomson could most easily imagine that order being perceived from the point of view of a retired country gentleman: the distance such a man can put between himself and the society he observes is what enables him to grasp its harmony, if not its detail. The sense of distance, of perspective, was crucial to Dyer as well, and *The Fleece*, except in the passage when it describes the poet at work collecting the materials of the poem, suggested that it was necessary to be uninvolved in the economic and social relations one was concerned to describe, in order to grasp them as, precisely, relations; so that the aristocracy of England had to be imagined as disengaged from their identity as landlords, as substantial farmers, and as consumers, for them to be represented as observing the unity of the society below them. The function, indeed, of the English aristocracy seemed in *The Fleece* to lie not in their engagement in economic affairs, but solely in their ability to comprehend them; and the function of the poet was to represent for the aristocracy the order they were imagined to observe.

Similarly, in the second essay we saw how the *common* language, that which was at once 'normal', and hypostatized as being 'common' to all, was spoken by the aristocratic and the polite; and that it was common to all by virtue of the fact that it manifested the peculiarities of none. It was not, therefore, contaminated by regional usages or pronunciations, or by the transient habits of vulgar speech, or by the various and specific terms of the various arts and professions. It was defined primarily by negation; and the language that was left over, when the idiosyncrasies of regional, faculty or vulgar usage had been refined away, was appropriately understood to be the language of the gentleman. It was metropolitan, not provincial – and therefore not thought to be attributable to any particular region; it was 'permanent'; and most of all it was not charged with the terms of any specific occupation, and was therefore evidently the language of those who, following no determinate occupation or calling, were themselves therefore not determined, in their notions or in the language they used to express them, by what they did, for they did nothing.

If we put the arguments of those two essays together, we will arrive back at one argument outlined in the introduction, that only the gentleman will be able to *describe* those social connections that only he is privileged to *observe:* the viewpoint, and the language, are both functions of that impartiality which arises from his having no occupation; and to attempt to describe the order of society in a language contaminated by regional or occupational particularities is immediately to announce that one does not speak or write from that impartial position from which alone the order can be comprehended. But throughout the book so far, this position seems to have been questioned as often as it has been asserted: for as society came to be understood more as a mesh of interlocking and co-operative labours than as a conflict of opposing interests, the likely ignorance of the gentleman, when it came to an understanding of that fine mesh of occupations, became an embarrassment to his claim to be able to see the whole: and Thomson was obliged to offer some very special cases of 'gentlemen' – Peter the Great, the Knight of Industry – to validate that claim. Roderick Random is yet another such special case.

A diffused picture: the variety of languages and occupations
The language of *Roderick Random* is remarkable for a diversity which is, however (though to a lesser degree), a feature of Smollett's other novels and of Fielding's as well. Roderick himself is born and brought up in Scotland, and in the early part of the book we are told on a number of occasions that his accent betrays his place of origin. When he and his valet Strap set out from Newcastle on the road to London, they are picked up by a waggon driver in whose speech is phonetically represented the accent of the north-eastern counties. The first word they hear in London, 'Anan', is at once a representation of the vulgar pronunciation of London, and an indication that as Scots they are 'unintelligible' to Londoners – the word translates as 'Eh? What did you say?'[1] When Roderick is applying for a position as surgeon's mate, he is told how to make his application by a fellow applicant who speaks in 'broad Scotch'. The surgeon's mate aboard his ship speaks with the thick Welsh accent of Fluellen, and sings in the Welsh language. An irascible Irishman speaks in the 'true Tipperary cadence', and expresses himself with what Roderick regards as equally typical Irish illogicality; other Irishmen on board Roderick's ship address each other in Erse.[2] When Roderick returns to England after a voyage to the West Indies, the first people he meets are a pair of agricultural labourers, whose Sussex accent is phonetically represented; and their squire speaks an only slightly less broad version of the same accent.[3] A short section of the novel takes place in France, where Roderick hears Dutch spoken as well as French and

English; but even in England itself we hear Latin, Italian, and various versions of French – a sort of *franglais* and the dialect of Gascony.[4] The occupational dialect of various members of the professions is fully represented: the naval language of Roderick's uncle, Tom Bowling, and of the ratings on board the *Thunder*; the terms of law and physic in the mouths of their practitioners; the sermon-like cadences of a parson; the irascible language of junior army officers, and the terms of fortification in the mouth of a general;[5] and the unintelligible accent of a Scottish schoolmaster who offers to teach the 'pronunciation of the English tongue, after a method more speedy and uncommon than any practised heretofore', of whom Roderick remarks, 'three parts in four of his dialect were as unintelligible to me, as if he had spoke in Arabick or Irish.'[6]

In addition to the foreign languages, the regional dialects, and the occupational habits of expression represented or referred to in the narrative, there is a multiplicity of versions of English in one or another way 'uncommon': a vulgar attempt at a genteel love letter, reminiscent of a similar effort in *Jonathan Wild*, and phonetically spelt; the pedantic fustian of the Scottish schoolmaster; the over-refined English of a homosexual naval captain; 'Billingsgate', a generic name for utterances richly profane and obscene; the vulgarly practical language of an over-thrifty apothecary and his wife; and various others.[7] These languages might be imagined to represent Britain as that anarchy of tongues, that Babel, which was the nightmare of the grammarians and the horror, also, of one of the characters in the novel, who fears that 'our language' may become 'a dissonant jargon without standard or propriety'.[8] It would require, it seems, the gift of tongues to understand, let alone to speak all the languages in the novel; for one of the arguments advanced in the century in favour of the need for a 'national' language was that northcountrymen, for example (as Roderick was) could not understand westcountrymen, and that 'even in Kent, and Berkshire, we hear words and sounds, that are not known in Middlesex';[9] whereas the language of the polite was universally understood.

I make no apology for following that list of languages with another, the longest and not the last, by which something of this book's extraordinary determination to represent the diversity of British society can be exemplified; for still more remarkable than the number of languages imitated or referred to in *Roderick*

Random is the number of occupations followed by the characters in the book, or mentioned in the course of the narrative. There can be few works in any period of English literature since the fourteenth century which offer an account of English society as marked as is that of the eighteenth-century episodic novel by what Ferguson was to term 'the separation of arts and professions'.

Of characters, then, with some pretensions to politeness, learning, or skill in the arts, Smollett represents or mentions schoolmasters, a school usher and a teacher of languages, various members of the clergy – rector, vicar, curate, catholic priest; actors, a theatre proprietor and a theatre manager, a musician, a painter, an ambassador and his secretary, a member of parliament, various surgeons and physicians, clerks, a barrister, and various authors – a poet, a historian, and a journalist. Among tradesmen of various ranks we meet, or hear of, barbers, apothecaries, a pedlar, innkeepers, pawnbrokers, a money-lender, a snuff-seller, tailors, a periwig-maker, a wine merchant, a blacksmith, a chandler and a ship's chandler, a jeweller, merchants and merchant adventurers, a used-clothes salesman, a shoemaker, milliner, weaver, butcher, baker, cheese monger, waggon-master, printer, chemist, carpenter, glass-blower, watchmaker, bookseller and ballad-hawker. In addition to merchant seamen, the navy is represented by the ranks and occupations of admiral, captain, lieutenant, chaplain, surgeon, surgeon's mates, midshipman, clerk, boatswain and boatswain's mate, purser, steward, quartermaster, steersman, gunner, foremast man, and cabin boy; together with an officer, sergeant, corporal and drummer of the marines, and at the Admiralty, first-secretary and under-secretary, upper-clerk, under-clerk and beadle. The army is represented by the ranks of general, colonel, lieutenant, ensign, cornet, recruiting sergeant, private soldier and drummer.

Among the occupations of women can be listed bawd, kept woman, prostitute, sweeper, barmaid, chambermaid, dairymaid, cookmaid and cook, housekeeper, governess, midwife, cinder-wench, waiting-woman, milk-woman, oyster-woman, fish-woman, bum-boat woman, and bunter (these last two, respectively, a woman who from a small boat supplies provisions to ships in port, and a woman who lives by picking up rags in the street). In agriculture we meet farmers, labourers, overseers of estates and 'peasants' of unspecified condition. Apart from the farm labourers, others with menial employments include footmen and *valets de chambre*, a drawer, waiters, a tavern porter, street porter and janitor; a coachman to a private family, a stage-coachman, hackney-coachman, carman, draymen, chairmen and a waggon driver; a gardener, ostler, cook, bargees, chimney-sweepers and dustmen; and among those whose profession is to enforce the law or to break it, we can list an exciseman, constables, watchmen, bailiffs, turnkeys, a judge, justices of the peace, highwaymen, a confidence-trickster, card-sharpers, smugglers and foot-pads. This inventory is probably not exhaustive.

At the time that Smollett was writing *Roderick Random*, he was also engaged in the translation from the French of *Gil Blas*, Le Sage's episodic novel of seventeenth-century Spain.[10] Among the various aspects of the influence of *Gil Blas* on *Roderick Random*, the preoccupation with naming and representing the vast variety of occupations in society is one of the most striking. But in Le Sage's novel, though it is over half as long again as Smollett's, this occupational variety is less than in *Roderick Random*; and the practitioners of occupations are far more often merely *named* or referred to, less often represented in the action of the novel, by Le Sage than by Smollett. Nor are they usually so precisely specified – apart from an 'under-candle-snuffer' in a theatre (Smollett's translation), few if any have the richness of definition we find, for example, among Smollett's occupations of women or tradesmen.

What is more, in *Roderick Random* people *are* what they do: the minute differentiation of occupations is reinforced by repre-senting each practitioner to whom Smollett assigns a name as the stereotype of, and so as entirely defined by, their occupations. Tom Bowling is repeatedly referred to, and refers to himself, as a 'tar'; a soldier is a 'son of Mars', 'a gentleman of the Sword'; schoolmasters are 'pedants'; a physician is a 'quack';[11] a squire who 'minded nothing but fox-hunting, and indeed was qualified for nothing else', becomes simply a 'fox-hunter', a 'spark', 'this young Acteon'; painters and actors are monkeys and apes, on account of the imitative nature of their arts.[12] The stereotypes are reinforced by description: the 'whole figure' of a usurer is 'a just emblem of winter, famine, and avarice'; and Bowling is appropriately bandy-legged, weather-beaten, his identity as 'tar' marked by the pitch which stains his breeches.[13]

Those characters who are named are named largely according to the occupations they profess: thus, for example, Potion is an apothecary, Rifle a highwayman, the name drawing attention both to his being armed, and to his practice of 'rifling' the possessions of his victims; Rapine is a usurer, Strap a barber from a family of shoemakers, Rinser a footman, Cringer a Member of Parliament, Staytape a tailor, Vulture a bailiff, Whipcord a ship's chandler and Gripewell a pawnbroker; Syntax and Concordance are school-masters, Bellower and Marmozet are actors. Sailors have such names as Oakhum, Marlinspike, Bowling ('bowline') and Rattlin ('ratline').[14] Scots are given recognizably Scottish names, with the exception of Random himself, whose Christian name however extablishes his national identity; a Welshman is Morgan; Irishmen are called Odonnell, Oregan, and so on.

The characters in the novel are thus not only described primarily in terms of their occupational or national identities, they are named after them, so that those identities become the more fixed and all-determining; and those who have no occupations – aristocrats, squires, metropolitan men of fashion – are still named in such a way as to fix them in a character appropriate to their situation. We find squires called Bumpkin, Gawky, Gobble, Thicket and Top[e]hall; men and women of fashion are named after their habits of speaking, for their is a life not of action but of talk: Rattle, Chatter, Bragwell, Banter, Snapper; and Lords who imagine themselves to be on permanent exhibition, who move through the world conscious of their power and superiority, include Frizzle, Trippett, Stately, Shrug and Strutwell. The practice of naming characters in such a way as to confirm them in their occupational, social, or national identities is almost as old as comedy; what is unusual about *Roderick Random* is the profusion of such names implying the fixity of the characters in those identities: there are at least eighty such names, and every character represented or mentioned in the book who is named, is named after this fashion, with the single and significant exception of Random himself, whose name implies that only he eludes stereotypical definition.

We have seen that to be thus fixed in an occupational or other determining identity was understood in the writing of the mid eighteenth century to be a disability: the habit of concentration on one particular activity is inimical to the acquisition of that comprehensive view, to the attainment of that elevated viewpoint, from which society can be grasped in terms of relation, and not simply of difference; and the point is continually confirmed in this novel. Many of the characters in the book are represented as being entirely limited in their view of the world by the positions they occupy within it. The most notable of these is Roderick's uncle,

Tom Bowling, the first of a sequence of sailors in Smollett's novels who understand the land as an extension, sometimes a puzzling one, of life at sea. It is not simply that he speaks always in naval terms; he is 'so much a seaman' that he applies those terms to everthing he speaks of. On his first introduction, for example, he is attacked by some hounds and kills them, provoking the fury of their owner, Roderick's cousin 'the foxhunter':

Upon which my uncle stepped forwards with an undaunted air, at the sight of whose bloody weapon, his antagonists fell back with precipitation; when he accosted their leader thus: – 'Lookée, brother, your dogs having boarded me without provocation, what I did was in my own defence. – So you had best be civil, and let us shoot a-head, clear of you.' Whether the young 'squire misinterpreted my uncle's desire of peace, or was enraged at the fate of his hounds beyond his usual pitch of resolution, I know not; but he snatched a flail from one of his followers, and came up with a shew of assaulting the lieutenant, who putting himself into a posture of defence, proceeded thus: – 'Lookée, you lubberly son of a w__e, if you come athwart me, 'ware your gingerbread-work. – I'll be foul of your quarter, d__n me.'[15]

So he continues throughout the book, as much liable to be misinterpreted by those who do not understand his terms as they are by him; for he is, according to Roderick, 'unacquainted with the ways of men in general, to which his education on board had kept him an utter stranger'.[16] A few other examples (for perhaps now we can dispense with lists) will perhaps do to confirm the degree to which so many of Smollett's characters are similarly strangers to the ways of men in general, on account of their 'faculty habits': the recruiting sergeant who talks military terms in his sleep; the barrister Roderick meets on the stage to Bath, who discusses warfare, and an *amour de voyage* between two fellow passengers, 'in terms': 'although the English had drawn themselves into a premunire at first, the French had managed their cause so lamely in the course of the dispute, that they would have been utterly nonsuited, had they not obtained a noli-prosequi'; the physician with an interest in etymology who had convinced himself that *bibere* means to drink, not largely but moderately; 'this was only a conjecture of his own, which, however, seemed to be supported by the word *bibulous*, which is particularly applied to the pores of the skin, that can only drink a very small quantity of the circumambient moisture, by reason of the smallness of their diameters'.[17]

An uniform plan I have said more than enough to establish that the social world of *Roderick Random* is one of extreme differentiation and fragmentation; I now want to discuss how it is that the novel, and the society it creates, could nevertheless be understood by Smollett as coherent. For that a novel which does not 'deviate from nature', in its depiction of the variety of the social world as Smollett understood it, and that in achieving unity as a novel it could thereby reveal the usually invisible unity of the society it represented, were themes that engaged Smollett in two important theoretical comments on the form. In the dedication to his third novel, *Ferdinand Count Fathom* (1753), he writes:

A Novel is a large diffused picture, comprehending the characters of life, disposed in different groupes, and exhibited in various attitudes, for the purpose of an uniform plan, and general occurrence, to which every individual figure is subservient. But this plan cannot be executed with propriety, probability or success, without a principal personage to attract the attention, unite the incidents, unwind the clue of the labyrinth and at last close the scene by virtue of his own importance.[18]

The 'picture', then, which is the novel, is 'diffused'; in a review of 1763, attributed to Smollett, he uses the word again – the novel is 'a diffused comedy unrestrained by the rules of the drama, comprehending a great variety of incident and character'. [19] It exhibits the variety of society, and of a differentiated, fragmented society imagined as scattered across the picture surface; but the insistence on diffusion, on difference, is contained by an equal concern with uniformity, with 'general occurrence' (or 'coming-together'), 'to which every individual figure is subservient.' Indeed, when Smollett writes that the characters are disposed in groups 'for the purposes of an uniform plan', he seems to be flirting with the language of natural theology, as if 'order in variety' is the novelist's plan and purpose for the world of the novel as it is God's for the world he has created; for like the universe described in the *Essay on Man*, the picture is at once diffused and *composed*, and its diffusion, like that of the divinely ordered economic society sketched out in Pope's poem, is not the enemy but the basis of its composition. It is from the position of the observer, outside the picture, that the scattered groups form some sort of coherent pattern, but, in the novel at least, that pattern is by itself only rudimentary, and needs to be confirmed by the activity of the principal personage, who attracts our attention, so that we follow his movement, as it were, from group to group; and in that way he ensures that we grasp the picture as an orderly arrangement of different 'passages', and thus he 'unites' the incidents that the picture displays.

The metaphor of the picture is important not only in the notion it offers of composition, of an order visible to those who stand outside it, but in the tensions it creates – and has already created in my account of Smollett's theory – by presenting the novel as a static composition through which the principal character moves in time. It is in the eighteenth century that criticism in England begins to differentiate between the visual and the literary arts particularly in terms of an opposition between the possibilities available to synchronic and diachronic narrative; and this passage seems not only aware of that critical opposition, but to exploit it. The discussion of all characters but the principal is concerned to emphasize their immobility in a manner we can relate directly to the fixed quality of characterization we have already noticed. They are passive beneath the hand of the artist: they are 'disposed', and 'exhibited' – in the review already referred to, the argument again makes use of a pictorial metaphor, and the point that the lesser characters should be subservient to the principal is again reinforced by a passive verb: they should be 'kept from advancing forwards'. The whole sentence from this review is worth quoting, to reinforce the tension that arises from an attempt to describe the *process* of a novel in terms of the static *product* which a picture may in some sense be regarded as. Writing of the principal character, Smollett says:

He must still maintain his dignity, like the chief figure in the foreground in a picture; and the author, as the painter, must take care to preserve a 'keeping' in his performance; that is, all the other characters shall be in some measure, subservient to the principal, and kept from advancing forwards so far as to rival the chief of the drama, in the attention of the reader.

The movement from picture, through drama, to a work *read*, may be confused and yet is in another light entirely appropriate; for the lesser characters, 'exhibited in . . . *attitudes*' – the word calling attention to the fixed identities and positions attributed to characters defined by occupational or regional peculiarities – are discussed in terms of a picture, but the principal is referred to as the hero of a play, in which we can more plausibly imagine him moving around among various groups to whom fixed positions in the scene have been assigned. The whole work however, is a novel, which we encounter as 'readers', and create a visual equivalent of the characters described on the page according as we are encouraged to do so by the representational skill of the novelist.

The 'principal personage' is, then, mobile; he operates with active infinitives: 'to attract ... unite ... unwind ... close'; and as important as the word 'unite' is 'unwind' for it seems he unwinds the 'clue' to the labyrinth of a society made up of different 'groupes', not only for the benefit of the spectator, but as a process from which he also learns. The discovery that the society of the novel is at once diffused and composed is made by that character in his own progress through it; at the end, when he 'closes the scene' – when he has threaded his way through to the far distance – he must occupy, as he looks back to the groups disposed between his position and the spectator's, a similarly comprehensive viewpoint as the spectator occupies, so that both are enabled to grasp that the people they observe are disposed not simply in groups but in comprehensible relations. The novel thus 'comprehends' the characters of life in two senses of the word: it includes them, and it is a means of understanding them; in a review of *Peregrine Pickle*, John Cleland put particular stress on this function of contemporary 'realistic' novels, that 'they may serve as pilot's charts, or maps of those parts of the world, which every one may chance to travel through; and in this light they are public benefits'.[20] The novel offers us an image of society as a labyrinth, as uncharted country, and also the understanding to find our way through it, and so to grasp how it is constructed.

Roderick's education The lesser characters, then, as Smollet explains in the dedication to *Ferdinand Count Fathom* and in the review I have referred to, wait motionlessly to be brought into relation and connection by the mobility of the principal personage; and nothing makes that opposition clearer than the contrast between the names of those lesser characters, on the one hand, which fix them in their (mainly occupational) identities, and on the other the name of the hero himself, Roderick Random. In the first place, no doubt, the name is intended to draw attention simply to the fact that as Smollett says Roderick shares 'the disposition of the Scots', who are 'addicted to travelling';[21] for in the course of the novel

Roderick moves from his family estate somewhere in Scotland, to Glasgow, to Newcastle, to London, to the West Indies, to Sussex, to the continent, to London, to Bath, to London again, back to Sussex, to South America, back to the West Indies, to London again, and eventually, of course, back to the family estate. But the emphasis Smollett puts on the necessary mobility of the hero in those critical remarks we have just examined invites us to see the name Random as drawing attention equally to the fluid identity of Roderick, which cannot be contained by or fixed in the frozen 'attitudes' of the characters 'subservient' to him. I have said that in *Roderick Random* people are what they do; but Roderick himself is the exception that proves the rule, for he changes his occupation continually, without ever taking on the stereotypical characteristics of the 'normal' practitioners of the various occupations he enters.

On leaving school, he becomes a university student with a bent towards 'the *Belle Lettre*'; and when his uncle is no longer able to support him in that condition, he takes a post as assistant to a surgeon. He is soon obliged by circumstances to leave that employment and Scotland as well, and on coming to London he attempts to qualify as a surgeon's mate in the Navy; and though eventually he succeeds in this, no vacancy can be found for him, and he becomes instead assistant to an apothecary. He is dismissed by his master on being falsely suspected of theft, and is pressed on board a man-of-war as a common sailor; but his qualities and qualifications being recognized he achieves the rank of surgeon's mate. On returning to England, he is shipwrecked on the Sussex coast, and is found employment as a footman to a gentlewoman, whose niece Narcissa he will eventually marry. In this condition he rescues Narcissa from an attempted rape by a neighbouring squire who is also, unfortunately, a justice of the peace; so that he is forced to leave this employment too. He is carried to France by some smugglers, and enlists as a private soldier in the French army; but meeting again his former valet, Strap, who has found means to make himself comfortably off, the two of them return to London with the idea that Roderick can be fitted out as a gentleman; and he duly becomes a fortune-hunter. He is not successful in finding a rich heiress to marry, and becomes briefly a place-seeker, attaching himself to an Earl who happens to be a homosexual, and who uses his apparent interest at court (for in reality he has none) to attract potential lovers; and so Roderick turns to fortune-hunting again, but quickly exhausts his funds and

Strap's, falls into debt, and is carried to the Marshalsea. His debts are eventually paid by his uncle, who has made himself rich as a merchant adventurer, and who, about to set out on another voyage, employs Roderick as ship's surgeon, and lends him money to 'purchase an adventure' – goods for sale overseas – and thus to set up as a merchant adventurer himself. They carry a cargo of slaves to South America, where Roderick rediscovers his long-lost father, who had 'disappeared' when Roderick was still a baby. His father has also become rich by trade, and returns to Britain with his son, where he buys the family estate, and thereby Roderick becomes, finally, the gentleman he had always imagined himself to be.

The habit or necessity of moving from one position to another is of course a traditional feature of the picaresque novel: but it is treated quite differently by Smollett than it is by his available models in the genre. Thus Gil Blas, typically, changes masters on numerous occasions, but, typically again, he does not thereby change his *occupation* nearly as often; and though, like Roderick, he too becomes, briefly, a physician and a fortune-hunter, he ussually appears as a footman, *valet de chambre* and (as his fortunes look up) as a steward or secretary of increasing but fluctuating influence, before becoming, like Roderick, a gentleman farmer. Until he achieves that position of independence, however, he is almost always more or less of a servant in some quality or another, as is usually the case with the heroes of such novels. It is the greater openness, the greater occupational diversity, of Smollett's eighteenth-century Britain as against Le Sage's seventeenth-century Spain, that enables and obliges Roderick to be represented as repeatedly changing his *occupation* rather than, simply, his *master*, as he proceeds through the novel; as it also enables and obliges Smollett to specify much more precisely the general variety of occupations in society than Le Sage does.

Roderick's claim to be a gentleman is not, indeed, very well founded, though Roderick – for the narrative is in the first person throughout – does not draw attention to the fact: he is the only son of the youngest son of a 'gentleman of considerable fortune and influence' though his father has evidently been brought up to expect to be able to maintain his condition as a gentleman – he has 'made the grand tour', and at the start of the novel does not seem destined to the fate of many youngest sons, to put his status at risk in becoming, say, a merchant, or an impecunious army officer, until he marries against his own father's wishes and is disinherited.[22] But it is Roderick's belief in his own gentility that enables him to accept the various 'low' employments he is forced into, without ever feeling himself to be what he does. Between quitting his post as an apothecary's assistant in London, and being impressed into the Navy, he lives briefly with a prostitute. She tells him the story of her life, and he reflects upon the greater wretchedness of her situation; for

If one scheme of life should not succeed, I could have recourse to another, and so to a third, veering about to a thousand different shifts, according to the emergencies of my fate, without forfeiting the dignity of my character, beyond a power of retrieving it, or subjecting myself wholly to the caprice and barbarity of the world. [23]

'Without forfeiting the dignity of my character, beyond a power of retrieving it': Roderick is a 'gentleman-born'; whatever else he might have to become, as he veers about 'to a thousand different shifts', he is always that – the 'dignity of his character' is the dignity of his character as a *gentleman*, a character he wants only funds to support; so that whatever apparent occupational identity he may casually take on, whatever he may be forced to *do*, his true character is to do nothing, to be disengaged from the fixed identities assigned to those whose destiny it is to work for a living.

Throughout the novel he asserts his quality as a gentleman, even as it is questioned by other characters, and even though it is threatened continually by his need to earn his own bread. His uncle, who at first contemplated sending him to sea when he found himself charged with the responsibility of overseeing Roderick's future, agrees to send him to university only when he is persuaded by Syntax, the school usher, that Roderick's 'genius' would one day make his fortune on shore. It might then have followed that Roderick would have regarded his university education as a means of equipping himself to enter one of the learned professions; but though he has some interest in mathematics, natural and moral philosophy, and comes to understand Greek 'very well', 'above all things, I valued myself on my taste in *Belle Lettre*, and a talent for poetry, which had already produced some morceaus, that brought me a great deal of reputation'. Roderick uses his time at university, in fact, to become generally literate and polite, rather than to fit himself for any particular future occupation. On two occasions, the wisdom of a young man with his diminished prospects receiving an education at university at all is questioned: first by Mrs Potion, an apothecary's wife, who 'wished I had been bound to some substantial handicraft, such as a weaver or shoemaker, rather than loiter away my time in learning foolish nonsense that would never bring me in a penny'; and, second, by one of his examiners at Surgeon's Hall; 'my friends had done better if they had made me a weaver or shoemaker, but their pride would have me a gentleman (he supposed) at any rate'.[24]

Little as Roderick is able to 'support the character of a gentleman', this is his main concern throughout the novel: he asserts his gentility whenever it is questioned, and often when it is not. In a quarrel with his first employer, the surgeon Crab, he retorts that he is 'descended from a better family than any he could boast an alliance with'; challenged to a boxing match by a coachman, he replies that he 'would not descend so far below the dignity of a gentleman, as to fight like a porter' – and this when he is employed as a footman. Accused by a gascon soldier of having affronted, by his criticism of the ancien régime, the King of France, Roderick fights and loses a duel, but refuses to ask pardon, 'a mean condescension' which 'no gentleman … in my situation' should perform; and when confronted by the mother of Melinda Goosetrap, his first intended victim when he sets up as a fortune-hunter, he tries to compensate for having to acknowledge the smallness of his fortune, by pointing out that he is 'a gentleman by birth and education'. [25]

At every point in the novel when, for however brief a space, he appears to be comfortably settled and is not uncomfortably off, he makes a point of reassuming in public his true condition or something like it. Irritated that in the house of the London apothecary, Lavement, he is treated as 'a menial servant', he dresses himself in his best clothes, in which 'vanity apart', he made 'no contemptible figure', and manages to be mistaken by the daughter of the house for a man of far greater quality than his situation in the house suggests. He soon acquires the character of 'a polite journeyman apothecary' – the oxymoron directed ironically at his own vanity by the secure gentleman Roderick who, having recovered his father and estate at the end of the book, then sets out to write it, secure that his status will never again be called into question. Indeed, he soon comes to look upon himself as 'a gentleman in reality', and learned to dance of a Frenchman whom I had cured of a fashionable distemper; frequented plays during the holidays; became the oracle of an ale-house, where every dispute was referred to my decision; and at length contracted an acquaintance with a young lady, who found means to make a conquest of my heart, and upon whom I prevailed, after much attendance and solicitation, to give me a promise of marriage. [26]

That at this stage Roderick is far from being the 'gentleman in reality' he believes himself to be – one who not only is, but can support the condition of, a gentleman, is again clear to Roderick, the gentleman narrator: for gentlemen do not have to wait for holidays to go to the theatre, nor pride themselves on being deferred to in ale-houses, nor (it is to be hoped) mistake needy prostitutes, for that is what the young lady is, for rich heiresses, which is what she claims to be. But the point remains, that on all occasions Roderick is determined to cut the best figure he can – and so at once to appear to be as much of a gentleman as his means will allow, and as little attached as possible to the occupation he happens at one time or another to be following.

In the same spirit of naive vanity which his later self can afford to record with playful irony, when he happens to get hold of some money in the West Indies, he begins to look upon himself 'as a gentleman of some consequence', buys himself a laced waistcoat, and makes 'a swaggering figure for some days, among the taverns'. Employed as a footman by Narcissa's aunt, he cannot resist revealing to aunt and niece that he is a master of Italian, French, and the learned languages, as well as that he has a talent for making elegant verses – for which admission he is rewarded by being treated by them rather with more reserve, than with more respect. When he re-encounters Strap in France, who has been left a considerable wardrobe by his deceased employer, a nobleman, Roderick gives a loving and long inventory of his clothes and trinkets (for Strap gives them all to him), and is delighted to be able to 'put on the gentleman of figure'. On his release from the Marshalsea and before he leaves with his uncle for South America, he finds time to appear in his 'gayest suit' at a coffee-house, to 'confound' a former friend with the magnificence of his dress; and when finally he is able to make an unquestionable assertion of his gentility, at the end of the novel, he is still vain enough to record that

a certain set of persons, fond of scandal, began to enquire into the particulars of my fortune, which they no sooner understood to be independent, than the tables were turned, and our acquaintance was courted ....[27]

It is important that throughout these continual assertions that he is of gentle birth, and these continual attempts to appear as the gentleman he believes himself to be, Roderick does not really know how a gentleman should behave, and how he should appear; and this is true in spite of the fact that a number of the 'good' characters in the book acknowledge his 'true' status often enough. His schoolfriend Strap accompanies him everywhere as his humble valet, and does his best to keep him supplied with funds – and this in spite of Roderick's attempt to drop his acquaintance as an embarrassment, when he first believes himself to be 'a gentleman in reality', and in spite of his angrily describing his own extravagance as gentlemanly, and Strap's thrift as 'vulgar'; for Strap is Scotsman enough to accept his duty to serve a gentleman of his own locality, as unquestionably as ever an eighteenth-century highlander accepted the authority of his clan chief. Mrs Sagely, who first befriends him when he is shipwrecked in Sussex, immediately accepts Roderick as the gentleman he claims to be, in spite of his appearing at her house in nothing but 'a seaman's old jacket'; Narcissa, even before he has demonstrated to her his polite accomplishments, regards him as one 'who had so much of the gentleman in my appearance and discourse, that she could not for her soul treat me as a common lacquey' – and even her domestics come to refer to him as 'Gentleman John'. [28] Such people are ready enough to acknowledge that Roderick escapes being defined by the apparent identities – as vagrant, seaman, footman – that he is obliged to affect; but it is one thing for him to be recognized as being 'better' than what he appears to be, and another to be accepted as a gentleman when it is as a gentleman that he is trying to appear.

Thus, when he is able, after his period in France, to dress as a gentleman and to go to work, so to speak, as a fortune-hunter, he finds his gentility questioned as it never had been before. The fashionable physician Dr Wagtail introduces him to a group of gentlemen in London, as 'a mighty pretty sort of gentleman' who has 'made the grand tour – and seen the best company in Europe'; to which one of the group, Banter, replies that he takes Roderick to be 'neither more nor less than a French *valet de chambre*'; and though he later explains that this was a joke at Wagtail's expense,

Roderick is 'extremely nettled' at the remark. As Roderick becomes known in London, Banter informs him that the 'town' has no high opinion of his pretensions to be a gentleman, and believes him to be nothing more than 'an Irish fortune-hunter' – a guess sufficiently close to the truth to discompose Roderick still more. Melinda Goosetrap circulates a rumour, again not far from the truth, that he is a fortune-hunter 'who supported himself in the character of a gentleman by sharping'; and Lord Quiverwit, a rival suitor to Narcissa, challenges Roderick to a duel, but questions whether he has 'spirit enough to support the character' he 'assumes'.[29] The opinions are largely the product of malice, but still serve to make us wary of accepting Roderick's status at his own estimate: for to achieve the character of a gentleman that Smollett finally establishes for Roderick at the end of the book, it is not enough to be of gentle birth; nor is it enough (though it is indispensable) to have the means to support oneself without any need to follow an employment; it is also necessary to behave, and to think like a gentleman, and this is something Roderick has to learn.

On his first appearance in London, dressed in the finery that Strap has made over to him, he goes to the theatre, and, to show himself off to proper effect, he sits in a front box,

where I saw a good deal of company, and had vanity enough to make me believe, that I was observed with an uncommon degree of attention and applause. This silly conceit intoxicated me so much, that I was guilty of a thousand silly coquetries; and I dare say, how favourable soever the thoughts of the company might be at my first appearance, they were soon changed by my absurd behaviour, into pity or contempt. [30]

It is the very vanity that forces Roderick to claim to be, and to try to appear as, a gentleman on every occasion, that prevents him from behaving as the gentleman he is nevertheless always conscious of being. One obligation the plot must necessarily fulfil, if Roderick is to be established as a 'gentleman in reality', is of course to provide him with a fortune, not only that he may support himself in the condition to which he believes himself entitled, but so that he can put aside the lack of gentlemanly candour, of openness and frankness of dealing, involved in the attempt to support himself in that condition without the funds necessary to do so; but another and equally important obligation, though it is fulfilled rather perfunctorily, is to establish that by the end of the book Roderick has learned to be the gentleman that he will be accepted as without question in his future life. To some extent, of course, these obligations are one and the same, for his vanity and lack of candour were forced upon him by his poverty, and when that disappears, so, we may expect, will they. But as the various portraits of proud noblemen and fox-hunting squires make clear, there is more to being a gentleman than birth, money or even good manners: one must acquire that comprehensive view of society which is an exclusive but not invariable attribute of the true gentleman, and which brings with it that sureness and correctness of judgement in the affairs of society, so evident in the ironic tone of Roderick's narrative, and so lacking in his earlier behaviour which that irony is concerned to satirize.

Whatever vices have been cultivated in Roderick by the contrast between his birth and his fortune, it is pointed out by two characters, whose opinions we have every reason to trust, that his indigence and his sufferings have qualified him better to be a gentleman, than a youth and early manhood spent in affluence would have done. Miss Williams, the prostitute whom Roderick had earlier intended to marry, and who turns up towards the end of the novel as Narcissa's loyal maid and confidante, reassures him that

altho' some situations of my life had been low, yet none of them had been infamous; that my indigence had been the crime not of me, but of fortune; and that the miseries I had undergone, by improving the faculties both of mind and body, qualified me the more for any dignified station.

The same point is made by Roderick's father, when he has heard the story of Roderick's life; he

blessed God for the adversity I had undergone, which, he said, enlarged the understanding, improved the heart, steeled the constitution, and qualified a young man for all the duties and enjoyments of life, much better than any education which affluence could bestow.

That the life Roderick has led has 'improved' the 'faculties' of his body, has 'steeled' his 'constitution' as to have lived the life of such a squire as, for example, Narcissa's brother, hunting by day and drinking port by the bumper at night, would not have done, may be acknowledged without further comment. And that his sufferings have 'improved' his heart does not require much more: an essential qualification for being a gentleman as Smollett envisages the condition, is to be benevolent; benevolence is a quality notably lacking in the noblemen and gentlemen whom Roderick encounters in the book, from his grandfather who is described in the first paragraph of the novel as having a 'singular aversion' for beggars, to Narcissa's brother, again, who in the last paragraph of the book is still trying to appropriate her fortune by fraud. As is clear, for example, by his reaction on hearing Miss Williams's account of her life, and particularly by his treatment of the sick and the impoverished on board ship and in the Marshalsea, Roderick's own experience of hardship has taught him to do his best to alleviate the hardship of others; so that just as his father, before he disappeared, had been 'the darling of the tenants' on the family estate, so Roderick, on his return there, promises to be the same. [31]

What is for our purposes more in need of comment, is that Roderick's experiences have improved the faculties of his mind, have 'enlarged the understanding'; for if this argument of Miss Williams and Roderick's father can be made good, it must be by showing that his experiences, and particularly his experience of the numerous occupations he enters, has given him a more comprehensive grasp of the society he lives in, than a gentleman brought up in more fortunate circumstances could have acquired; and this is, perhaps, the crucial theme of the book. For in the course of Roderick's 'thousand shifts' – his employment for example in the various branches of medicine, on board ship, and as a soldier in the French army – he adds to the polite education he had attained at university, a practical knowledge of the procedures, and the language, of various professions and occupations, which is represented as being often more accurate than the knowledge which the various practitioners of those individual occupations have acquired. When he first goes to the surgeon Crab for employment, he reveals that in addition to having cultivated his interest in *belles-lettres*, he understands

a little pharmacy, having employed some of my leisure hours in the practice of that art, while I lived with Mr. Potion: neither am I altogether ignorant of surgery, which I have studied with great pleasure and application.

The knowledge Roderick has acquired, he has acquired as a gentleman amateur, in his 'leisure hours', with application, but also with pleasure; and he adds to this knowledge during the period of his employment with Crab, to a point where he is evidently more qualified in the various branches of medicine than anyone in the novel who has received a professional training in the art, with the possible exception of Morgan, who also has a claim to be a gentleman. On a number of occasions he reveals a wide knowledge of the 'dialect', as Johnson calls it 'of navigation': and in his discussion of the conduct of the seige of Cartagena, and of the battle of Dettingen, he reveals a full knowledge of the language of military strategy and fortification, a knowledge fuller, indeed, than that of an old general whom he meets, and who shows himself ignorant of what Roderick describes as 'one of the most simple terms of fortification'. [32] As we have seen, he also understands, and as narrator can represent phonetically, a number of regional pronunciations of English and the dialect words associated with them; and has a full knowledge of two modern and two ancient languages.

We can see, of course, Roderick's ability to reproduce this variety of languages simply as an exigency of the first-person narrative, which if it is to include such a variety, has to attribute a knowledge of them to the teller of the tale; but that is certainly to miss the point, that Roderick acquires that knowledge in the course of his life, and that it is in large measure his acquisition of them which enables him to appear at the end of the book as a complete gentleman of 'enlarged understanding' who is qualified therefore to write the account of British society that he is writing, and to 'unite the incidents' of the novel, and to 'unwind the clue of the labyrinth' made by the apparently 'diffused' panorama of characters 'disposed in different groupes, and exhibited in various attitudes'. The act of writing the book is, as we have seen, an act of looking back on that panorama from a viewpoint in the background of the picture which 'closes the scene', a viewpoint made as comprehensive as the reader's by virtue of the knowledge Roderick has acquired in threading his way among the various characters, and learning the procedures and languages of their various occupations, without, however, ever making the mistake of imagining that any one of those languages is in itself adequate to making a comprehensive description of the contents of the picture.

To show himself qualified to write the novel, therefore, Roderick must understand all the languages it must include, and must use them, also, only as each is appropriate, and not as, according to Johnson, the members of occupational fraternities do, who make their knowledge 'ridiculous' by the 'injudicious obtrusion' of terms into conversations on general topics.[33] Thus, he does not, as Bowling does, apply the language of the sea to anything but the sea; or the language of law to warfare, as the barrister does; or the language of warfare to anything but its proper object, as does the soldier; nor must he allow his knowledge of words used in a technical sense in medicine to obliterate his knowledge of their use in common conversation, which is the offence of the physician Dr Wagtail. To use the terms of an art as if they can describe anything other than the objects of that art, is to show oneself lacking in that comprehensive knowledge, that enlarged understanding, which must grasp the diversity of the world if it is also to grasp its unity.

But to describe that unity, another language is required, a language poised impartially between all the occupational and regional dialects the novel exhibits; and this must be, of course, that 'common' language 'without which', according to Dr Concordance, Roderick will be 'unfit for business' in England,[34] and which is common only in the sense that it is free equally of all the vices of idiosyncrasy that characterize the other languages in the novel. This is the language of the narrative itself, which acts as a permanent and continual corrective on the various different dialects it encloses, so that each time that it appears, after a passage of occupational or regional dialect, it pulls us back to the central position that we must occupy, as we inspect the picture, if we are to understand the 'uniformity' it is concerned to elicit out of apparent diffusion. And this is also a language which Roderick, it seems, must learn; his education at a village school in Scotland left him speaking in a Scottish accent which identifies him as a Scot on a number of occasions in the early part of the novel – by Strap in Newcastle, by a confidence-trickster and by a justice of the peace in London. It seems to be only by about the time that he believes himself (however erroneously) to be a 'gentleman in reality' that he ceases to be identifiable by his accent; and it is only from about then – though Smollett's practice is not entirely consistent – that his own voice can enter the passages of dialogue in the novel; for had it done so earlier, Roderick the narrator would perhaps have had to record himself speaking a dialect which could be represented phonetically, as only the language of the centre, of the gentleman of metropolitan experience, whose language cannot be identified as 'a' language, cannot be. Roderick does of course speak, in some sense, before this point; but his early speeches are in various ways contained as a part of the narrative, and therefore appear as spoken in the language of the gentleman that he acquires only later. His speech may be marked by inverted commas, but in that case it will take the forms and tenses of reported speech; or it may take the form of direct speech, but without inverted commas, and this when the utterances of other characters are being framed and marked according to the usual practice of representing dialogue.

Roderick then must learn the language of the centre as he must learn the language of the circumference; and that he has acquired it with success is first evident when in the final paragraph of the final chapter, the tense changes to the present, and Roderick, at last in a position to offer a comprehensive account of his progress through the society of the novel, writes the first paragraph of Chapter I:

I was born in the northern part of this united kingdom in the house of my grandfather, a gentleman of considerable fortune and influence, who had on many occasions signalized himself in behalf of his country; and was remarkable for his abilities in the law, which he exercised with great success, in quality of a judge, particularly against beggars, for whom he had a singular aversion.

This paragraph tells us almost as clearly as anything could of Roderick's success in supporting, now, the character of a gentleman, in that he has acquired the tone and the attitude appropriate to one. There is the 'genteel irony' [35] directed either against the judge's own opinion of himself, or against his reputation among those who, with equal lack of benevolence, unquestioningly believe that the interests of one's country are automatically served by an aversion for the indigent. There is Roderick's own implied benevolence, not only towards the beggars themselves, but towards his grandfather, whose 'aversion' he is content to criticize by that irony. And there is a confident, gentlemanly comprehensiveness of vision, evident in the word 'singular' – for a gentleman avoids singularity in language and behaviour, which (as Chesterfield warns) may 'give a handle to ridicule'[36] – and in his describing the place of his birth not as 'Scotland', as if it is disjoined from England, but as the 'northern part' of this 'united kingdom', as one portion of what he has come to understand as one unified society – and this less than two years after Culloden, for the victims of which Smollett had written an elegy, 'The Tears of Scotland' (1746), which expressed a courageous degree of resentment at the cruelty of the English.

Smollett and Chesterfield Of Smollett's later novels, all but one describe the education of a gentleman who becomes eventually worthy of the station assigned to him. The exception is *Ferdinand Count Fathom* (1753), a novel whose name suggests that it should be regarded, in Cleland's terms, as a 'pilot's chart' of the progress through the 'ocean of life' of that other principal character in fiction who can be at once everything and nothing, the confidence-man. Of the others, *The Adventures of Peregrine Pickle* (1751) is probably the least interesting, and describes the youth and early manhood of a wandering hero, and the extremely lengthy process by which he learns the behaviour appropriate to a member of the substantial country gentry. *The Adventures of Sir Launcelot Greaves* (1760–1), a novel in the manner of *Don Quixote*, has as its central character a baronet who, before the opening of the novel, had been the ideal of the benevoient paternalist landowner but who, apparently unhinged by love, has taken to wearing armour and travelling the country 'to act as coadjutator to the law, and even to remedy evils which the law cannot reach'. The problem of the novel is whether Greaves is to be regarded by us, as he is by almost all the characters he meets, as a 'lunatic knight-errant';[37] for it is clear that he has a more complete grasp of the condition of England and of the virtues necessary to its government that anyone else in the book.

This is how Greaves describes the qualities necessary to a knight-errant:

> ...towards the practice of chivalry, there is something more required than the virtues of courage and generosity. A knight-errant ought to understand the sciences, to be master of ethics or morality, to be well versed in theology, a complete casuist, and minutely acquainted with the laws of his country. He should not only be patient of cold, hunger, and fatigue, righteous, just, and valiant, but also chaste, religious, temperate, polite, and conversable, and have all the passions under the rein, except love, whose empire he should submissively acknowledge.

There is not much here, except that the knight be patient of cold and hunger, and that he submit to the empire of love, which we have not seen attributed throughout this book to the ideal of the eighteenth-century gentleman, who is certainly better described by this account than is the knight of romance; so that a part of the problem of determining whether Greaves is mad or not, is the question of whether anyone who seriously attempted, not simply to exhibit, but to employ the virtues of the gentleman in a society as corrupt as that described in the novel, would not appear to be an anachronism as ludicrous as Sir Launcelot, 'armed cap-à-pie'.[38] At the end of the novel, Greaves lays aside his armour and, if he had lost his senses earlier, may now be assumed to have recovered them; he marries and settles down again to the benevolent management of his estate. But the change seems to be handled more as a necessity for the conclusion of the novel than as an indication that earlier it had been Greaves himself, and not the other characters, whose understanding of virtue and corruption had been impaired.

Smollett's only epistolary novel, *The Expedition of Humphry Clinker* (1771) is also his last. The epistolary form is one which, from the point of view of one of the questions considered in this book – whether it was still possible in the mid eighteenth century to have a comprehensive view of society – must appear to propose a reply in the negative; for the form will normally attribute only a small portion of knowledge to each of the correspondents, and, in leaving the possibility of a complete knowledge only to the author and reader, implies that this completeness is available to them only *as* author and reader, who will have as fragmented a perception of the world they live in as do the correspondents of theirs. The novel describes a journey undertaken by a valetudinarian, a prickly Welsh gentleman called Matthew Bramble, who is seeking to recover his health. Accompanied by his sister, nephew, niece, a maid, and by Humphry Clinker whom he engages on the road as a manservant, Bramble goes to various spas, to London, Edinburgh, Glasgow and thus down the western side of England until, at the end of the novel, he is about to return to his estate. The chief symptom of Bramble's illness, or hypochondria, is a testy impatience with everything he encounters until, in the course of his travels, and by the education they provide, he 'has laid in a considerable stock of health', and has recovered the balanced and tolerant view of the world as it should be seen from the secluded, independent estate of a country landowner.[39] In recovering that view, he recovers the form also from the diffusion and fragmentation it threatens, and at the end of the book is in a position to offer apparently authoritative judgments on the action of the novel and the society it represents.

But of all the gentlemen whom Smollett thus brings to a clearer understanding of the world, it is Roderick whose experience is the most comprehensive, and whose education is the most remarkably unlike what has appeared, elsewhere in this book, to be appropriate to a man of his position. Indeed, if we compare Roderick with the 'fine gentleman' defined by Steele (see above, p. 37), he will seem almost a parody of that universal man. The gentleman, according to Steele, must have been 'led through the whole Course of the polite Arts and Sciences': well, Roderick had done his best to study the polite arts as an impecunious student at a Scottish university; as for the polite sciences, he can offer at least a competent knowledge of pharmacy and physic. 'He should be no Stranger to Courts and Camps' – Roderick has enlisted as the client of a nobleman without influence, has had some acquaintance with the less polite end of polite society in Bath and London, and has served as a private soldier in a foreign army. 'He must travel to open his Mind, and enlarge his Views' – Roderick has managed, as a mercenary, some sort of tour of Europe, and as a surgeon's assistant and merchant-adventurer has even been to the new world. 'He must not forget to add ... the Languages and bodily Exercises most in vogue' – Roderick does well here, for in addition to the classical languages and French and Italian, he has acquired an understanding of a host of regional and faculty dialects, and as for bodily exercises, he has a great propensity to get into fights, and knows the jargon of pugilism.[40]

The gentleman that Smollett has defined, in Roderick and in his father, whose life has also not been without its vicissitudes of fortune, is strikingly unlike the gentleman Steele describes, or the one whom Chesterfield attempts to define in his letters to Philip Stanhope; or whom Dyer or Thomson had imagined surveying the varied landscape of English society, or whose language was being determined by eighteenth-century writers of grammars. For Smollett, it seems, birth, affluence, polite learning, and a freedom from occupational determination, are necessary but are not sufficient conditions for the nurture of a gentleman whose 'enlarged understanding' can grasp the pattern of connection and relation in the society he observes. As I have said, the notions and the language of the gentleman as they have been defined earlier in this book have been defined primarily by negation: they are not the notions and the languages of anyone whose occupational or regional affiliations we can recognize, and in this view a gentleman is in, so to speak, a condition of empty potential, one who is imagined as being able to comprehend everything, and yet who may give no evidence of having comprehended anything. The other gentlemen or aristocrats who appear in *Roderick Random* clearly fail to measure up to his ideal: the squires are certainly without the politeness that comes with education, or the benevolence that comes with understanding, and the noblemen are so locked within a world of courtly intrigue, patronage, and interest, that they have lost any sight of the true interests of the society they pretend to serve: both are without the benevolence, the sympathy, so important to Shaftesbury's notion of the gentleman: the ability to know how you would feel in someone else's shoes; and that Roderick has it is due to the fact that he has been in almost everyone else's shoes. Smollett's gentleman looks, by contrast with squire or nobleman, to be a very bourgeois ideal: though he must be well born, well off and well educated, he acquires his understanding, he earns it, by a practical acquaintance with the vicissitudes and varieties of social life, and comes to understand society as a whole because he comes to understand its parts, and not simply because, understanding nothing in particular, he is assumed therefore to understand everything in general.

From 1739 to the early 1750s Chesterfield was writing a long series of letters to Philip Stanhope, his illegitimate son, advising him on how to acquire a 'gentlemanlike manner', that 'je ne sçais quoi qui plait'; [41] and though Chesterfield, of whose gentlemanly civility Smollett had no high opinion, has a good deal in common with Smollett in his estimation of the character and function of a gentleman, he differs from him on that subject in ways which point not only to what we could think of as the difference between an aristocratic, and Smollett's more bourgeois ideal of gentility, but also to what was becoming a new sense, in the middle and second half of the eighteenth century, of who it was who could understand the social and economic relations by which society coheres. Chesterfield is as certain as Roderick that 'sottish drinking' and 'rustic sports' will 'degrade' a gentleman; as convinced, if not more so, of the need for a gentleman to speak the language of 'good company', which is usually to be learned only from those 'of considerable birth, rank and character'; [42] and he is equally concerned to establish that a gentleman has to acquire a knowledge of the world which cannot be acquired by, for example, the 'learned parson, rusting in his cell at Oxford or Cambridge', who

knows nothing of man, for he has not lived with him, and is ignorant of all the various modes, habits, prejudices and tastes, that always influence and often determine him.

For Chesterfield no less than for Smollett, the knowledge of the world which is to be acquired by, and which distinguishes a gentleman, is to be learned not only from books but practically, by intercourse with 'the world'. It is inimical to any singularity whether of character or occupation; for just as 'Whoever *is had* (as it is called) in company for the sake of any one thing singly, is singly that thing,' so to be a 'gentleman in reality' one must be as near as possible 'the *omnis homo, l'homme universel*',[43] whose faculties are developed in harmonious balance with one another, so that one is, ideally, no one thing in particular, but an epitome of all men in general.

But on what precisely constitutes the knowledge of '*l'homme universel*', and on how he acquires it, Chesterfield and Smollett are far apart. For example, one of Chesterfield's most repeated and most urgent injunctions to Stanhope is that he should at all costs avoid 'low company': 'people of very low condition, whatever their parts or merits may be', and especially that which 'in every sense of the word, is low indeed – low in rank, low in parts, low in manners, and low in merit'. Such company will communicate to Stanhope, however careful he is to avoid the taint, 'a vulgar, ordinary way of thinking, acting, or speaking', which 'young people contract' among servants; and for Chesterfield the keeping of low company is not to be justified, as it certainly is in the case of Roderick, on the grounds that it helps develop a full knowledge of the world. The 'world' is, in fact, a quite different place, a quite different notion, for Chesterfield and for Smollett: for Chesterfield, it is often best rendered as '*le monde*'; a gentleman is one '*qui a du monde*';[44] and a knowledge of the world, though it is not, as the habit of referring to it in French suggests, exclusively a knowledge of the fashionable world, is largely that, and when it is more than that, can still to a surprising extent be learned in the fashionable world. Chesterfield intended Stanhope for a career in diplomacy and statesmanship, and is continually urging him to acquire, as he makes the grand tour, a knowledge of the laws, constitutions, customs, even the commerce of the countries he visits, as well as their languages; such knowledge is to be found, where not in books, by enquiry among the polite.[45] To it is to be added a diligent attention not only to the manners and address, but also to the weaknesses of men of fashion, of the '*monde*'. It is such people that govern the world, and so who are, in a sense, the 'world' that Stanhope must learn to understand and manipulate.[46]

The knowledge of the world which Chesterfield, the Whig magnate, is trying to define is the knowledge appropriate to a far more considerable gentleman than Roderick would ever become or would ever wish to be: one who will 'contribute to the good of the society in which he lives' in a more dazzling manner than the retired country landowner. It is certainly not that minute knowledge that Roderick acquires, and could only acquire, from those who know their own business well, and nothing much besides. Thus Stanhope has no need to know anything of 'algebra, chymistry, or anatomy', which 'are never, that I have heard of, the objects of eloquence', and which, if introduced into private conversation, would indicate a man anxious to make an undignified display of his learning. Stanhope should learn perhaps 'a little geometry and astronomy; not enough to absorb your attention, and puzzle your intellects, but only enough, not to be grossly ignorant of either'. In general, 'those arts or sciences, which are peculiar to certain professions, need not be deeply known by those who are not intended for those professions',

as for instance; fortification and navigation; of both which, a superficial and general knowledge, such as the common course of conversation, with a very little enquiry on your part, will give you, is sufficient[47]

To become '*l'homme universel*' Roderick entered a series of different occupations or professions, and learned the arts, the sciences, the terms 'peculiar' to each – which, if they come to be satirized when used inappropriately, were still to be *understood* – so that his understanding of the world in general was based on his knowledge in detail of its component elements. To become the universal man as Chesterfield understands him to be, Stanhope need become only learned and polite: 'if you will but ... exert your whole attention to your studies in the morning, and to your address, manners, air and *tournure* in the evenings, you will be the man I wish you',[48] The theoretical knowledge of the world he requires will come to him from books; the practical knowledge will come to him in the assemblies of those '*qui ont du monde*', from studying to imitate their manners, and to understand their characters.

The comparison of the gentleman as represented by *Roderick Random* and by Chesterfield provokes two related observations. The first is that however successful the novel may be in persuading us that only a gentleman like Roderick can seriously be imagined as able to perform the task of comprehensive observation, a gentleman like Roderick cannot seriously be imagined at all. 'Princes', writes the Rambler, 'when they would know the opinions or grievances of their subjects, find it necessary to steal away from guards and attendants, and mingle on equal terms among the people'.[49] But that dream of a temporary and informative descent, of a Prince Hal or a Peter the Great, is a dream of the folk-tale or the novel, and *Roderick Random* is a fiction of the comprehensive vision which announces that vision as capable now of being acquired only by the jack-of-all-trades, servant of none, that Thomson had been obliged to represent in the mythical exploits of Peter or the allegorical figure of the Knight of Industry, and that Smollett represents in a hero whose 'adventures', however much verisimilitude may attach to each of them individually, cannot possibly be imagined as occurring to any individual except in a work of fiction. We may read the novel either as a criticism, a parody even, of the idea of the gentleman and his ability to see and understand the variety of social identities and the relations between them, or we may read it as an extreme, a rather desperate attempt to vindicate them; but it does not matter much which reading we choose, for in either case the novel suggests only the impossibility of the gentleman in the real world doing what Roderick does, or what Thomson claimed Talbot or Lyttelton could do.

We are left, however, with another possible observation, as we are by Johnson, by Dyer, by Ferguson, by Smith: that the claim to a comprehensive knowledge may now be made instead by the writer – for of course Smollett, to write the novel, must know all that Roderick knows. And such a knowledge may pausibly be thought to have been the possession of a writer such as Smollett was, or was to become, who published, in addition to his novels, poems, plays and polite essays, a medical treatise, a volume of travels, a *Complete History of England*, and an eight volume work entitled (if you please) *The Present State of All Nations*, as well as editing the *Critical Review*, a periodical concerned to digest and criticize the current state of knowledge across as many arts, professions, and sciences as possible. It is the knowledge such writers as Hume, or Goldsmith, or Johnson or Smith strove to acquire; which aimed to grasp the relations of a multitude of social activities and practices by paying a detailed attention to as many of them as possible; so that a comprehensive knowledge of society may certainly, by the third quarter of the century, be more easily imagined in the man of letters than in the gentleman of fashion.

This certainly seems to be the claim made by Fielding in *Tom Jones*, a novel not much less remarkable than *Roderick Random* for the variety of occupations and faculty languages included in its representation of 'the mazes, the winding labyrinths' of human nature and society. To these mazes, it seems, the gentleman, one who has set himself up in 'the business that requires no apprentice-ship', is a far less sure guide than the author. Squire Allworthy is apparently the paragon of the retired and independent country gentleman: a man of 'solid understanding', 'a benevolent heart', 'vast natural abilities', a considerable share of learning, and a large estate;[50] and yet the plot of the novel is dependent upon his making, in its first seven books, a catastrophic series of misjudge-ments on the characters and actions of those over whom he exerts authority as relative, employer, benefactor or magistrate: misjudgements which are represented by Fielding as arising not only from the determination of others to deceive him, but from his own detachment from the society over which he presides, and with which – the term will be defined in a moment – he has no 'conversation'. The narrator, however, is careful to excuse rather than condemn Allworthy for these failures of judgement, for to do so is an opportunity for him to display an insight into Allworthy's character as well as into the characters of whom Allworthy, by virtue of his position and responsibilities, might have been expected to judge more competently.

That the writer of such histories as *Tom Jones* is, or should be, more knowing than the 'gentleman' is a point which Fielding does not leave to rest upon the mere fact of his being the *author* of the characters, the society, and the plot he creates: the author of such books requires qualifications not to be looked for in 'gentlemen' authors, however 'considerable' a figure they may make 'in the republic of letters'. For a historian, even in the sense of a novelist, in addition to learning and 'humanity', requires, according to Fielding, two qualifications without which a comprehensive view of the society he recreates in his writings is impossible: 'genius', and a 'conversation' which is 'universal'.[51]

'Genius' he defines as 'that power or rather those powers of the mind which are capable of penetrating into all things within our reach and knowledge, and of distinguishing their essential differences'; one aspect of genius is 'invention', by which 'is really meant no more (and so the word signifies) than discovery, or finding out; or to explain it at large, a quick and sagacious penetration into the true essence of all the objects of our contemplation'. It is genius that teaches an author 'to know mankind better than they know themselves', and can guide him through the 'labyrinths' of the world. A universal conversation – Fielding uses the term in the sense given by Johnson, of 'commerce', 'intercourse' or 'familiarity' – is one which involves a knowledge of 'all ranks and degrees of men';

for the knowledge of what is called high life will not instruct him in low; nor, *è converso*, will his being acquainted with the inferior part of mankind teach him the manners of the superior.[52]

'A true knowledge of the world', he insists, 'is gained only by conversation, and the manners of every rank must be seen in order to be known'; only thus can an author discover those 'certain characteristics in which individuals of every profession and occupation agree', and 'one talent of a good writer' is 'to be able to preserve these characteristics, and at the same time to diversify their operations', which he is able to do only if conversant with, not only the 'wise, the learned, the good, and the polite', but with 'every kind of character from the minister at his levee, to the bailiff in his spunging-house; from the dutchess at her drum, to the landlady behind her bar'.[53]

But evidently the kind of knowledge acquired by such a writer as Smollett, Fielding, or Johnson, as much obliged by the exigencies of his trade to develop a wide understanding of society as stimulated thereto by a disinterested curiosity, is not the knowledge of Roderick. The range of Fielding's writing is no less wide than Smollett's, and includes numerous plays and periodical essays, some verse, a history, a journal, political and legal pamphlets, and essays on practical social administration; and no doubt he based much of his claim to a 'universal conversation' on his experience as a magistrate in London. Smollett's experience of other occupations

than writing was unusually wide: he was a physician, and sometime
a ship's surgeon; he had some specialist knowledge of pharmacy,
and arguably of warfare; but much else of what he represents
Roderick as discovering by practice, he had discovered himself in
the course of his career as an author, whose trade is to find out by
inquiry what others learn by experience; and the same of course
was true of Fielding. It is the knowledge of men who, as novelists,
can without undue difficulty display a knowledge adequate to the
comprehension of the world they have constructed, because they
have constructed it; and the condition of its construction was of
course precisely that they could show it to be comprehensible. As
we have seen, writers such as Johnson or Ferguson, attempting to
describe a world they thought of themselves as observing, not as
inventing, were not over-convinced that the professional writer
was much more adequate to that task than the detached and
independent gentleman had been: and as much as anything else it
was this crisis of social knowledge that the writers we have been
studying bequeathed to the Romantics.

Notes and references

Introduction: artificers and gentlemen

1   Patrick Colquhoun, *A Treatise on Indigence* (London 1806). King's statistics, which appear in his 'Natural and Political Observations and Conclusions upon the State and Condition of England 1696', were first published in the edition of George Chalmers (London 1804), and were recently reprinted in an edition by Peter Laslett (Farnborough, Hants. 1973).
2   Colquhoun, *A Treatise*, pp. 25–6.
3   *The Spectator*, no. 2, 2 March 1711.
4   Bernard Mandeville, *The Fable of the Bees*, ed. Phillip Harth (Harmondsworth 1970), p. 358.
5   Adam Smith, *An Enquiry into the Nature and Causes of the Wealth of Nations,* eds. R. H. Campbell, A. S. Skinner, and W. B. Todd (Oxford 1976), vol. i, pp. 15–16, 22–23.
6   Mandeville, *The Fable of the Bees*, pp. 68, 360.
7   Pope, *An Essay on Man*, ed. Maynard Mack (London 1950), Epistle II, l. 237; Pope's note to ll. 231ff; ll. 249–254; Epistle IV, section vi.
8   Shaftesbury, *Characteristics,* ed. John M. Robertson (London 1900), vol. i, p. 84.
9   Hume, 'Of Moral Prejudices', in *Essays Moral, Political and Literary*, (London 1741–2); reprinted (Oxford 1963), p. 573.
10 Hume, *A Treatise of Human Nature* (London 1739–40), vol. ii, p. 73; (Book II, part 1, section xi).
11 For a valuable account of the meanings of 'society', and one which touches particularly on Hume's uses of the word, see Raymond Williams, *Keywords: A Vocabulary of Culture and Society* (London 1976), pp. 243–7.
12 Hume, *A Treatise,* vol. iii, pp. 137–40 (Book III, part 2, section vii).
13 Ferguson, *An Essay on the History of Civil Society*, ed. Duncan Forbes (Edinburgh 1978), p. 182.
14 Smith, *The Wealth of Nations*, vol. ii, pp. 782–4.
15 Smith, *The Wealth of Nations*, vol. ii, pp. 781, 788.
16 Ferguson, *An Essay*, pp. 181–2.
17 Ferguson, *An Essay*, p. 182.

18   Pope, *Essay on Man*, Epistle I, 1. 59.
19   Hume, 'The Stoic', *Essays*, p. 150
20   Hume, 'Of Refinement in the Arts,' *Essays*, p. 277; 'Of Commerce', *Essays*, p. 269.
21   Hazlitt, 'The New School of Reform', in *The Plain Speaker* (London 1826), reprinted in *Works*, vol, xii, ed. P. P. Howe (London and Toronto 1931), p. 182.
22   Shaftesbury, *Characteristics*, p. 77; Mandeville, *The Fable of the Bees*, p. 54.
23   Defoe, *The Compleat English Gentleman*, ed. Karl Bullbring (London 1890), p. 216.
24   Fielding, *The History of Tom Jones* (1749), Book VIII, ch. viii.
25   Johnson, *The Rambler*, no. 173, 12 November 1751; no. 99, 26 February 1751.
26   Thomas Sprat, *The History of the Royal-society of London* (London 1667), p. 113.
27   *The Guardian*, no. 34, 20 April 1713.
28   Mandeville, *The Fable of the Bees*, pp. 342–3. For the meanings of 'Conversation', see below, pp. 208.
29   Defoe, *The Compleat English Gentleman*, p. 8.
30   Mandeville, *The Fable of the Bees*, p. 337.
31   *The Tatler*, no. 207, 5 August 1710.
32   Defoe, *The Compleat English Gentleman*, p. 256 ff. For a discussion of the involvement of landed property in a credit-economy, see J. G. A. Pocock, *The Machiavellian Moment: Florentine Political Thought and the Atlantic Republican Tradition*, (Princeton, N. J. 1975), ch. xiii.
33   'Of the middle Station of Life', *Essays*, pp. 579–84.
34   *The Rambler*, no. 137, 9 July 1751.
35   *The Adventurer*, no. 107, 13 November 1753.
36   *The Rambler*, no 105, 19 March 1751.
37   *The Rambler*, no. 208, 14 March 1752; *The Adventurer* no. 131, 5 February 1754.
38   *The Rambler*, no. 19, 22 May 1750; no. 43, 14 August 1750.
39   *The Rambler*, no. 43, 14 August 1750; 'Preface' to *A Dictionary of the English Language*, (London 1755), pages unnumbered; the quotation appears on the final page of the 'Preface'; *The Adventurer*, no. 137, 26 February 1754.
40   *The Rambler*, no. 151, 27 August 1751; no. 9, 17 April 1750.
41   Defoe, *The Compleat English Gentleman*, p. 98.
42   Ferguson, *An Essay*, pp. 219, 218, 187.
43   Ferguson, *An Essay*, pp. 185, 186, 237.
44   Ferguson, *An Essay*, pp. 183, 189.
45   Ferguson, *An Essay*, pp. 179, 178, 183.
46   Ferguson, *An Essay*, pp. 183, 179, 203.

47 Ferguson, *An Essay*, p. 183.
48 Smith, *The Wealth of Nations*, vol. i, p. 21.
49 Burke, *Reflections on the Revolution in France*, 2nd edn (London 1790), p. 65.

Chapter 1 An unerring gaze: the prospect of society in the poetry of James Thomson and John Dyer

1 James Thomson, *A Poem to the Memory of the Right Honourable the Lord Talbot, Late Chancellor of Great Britain* (London 1737), ll. 148–9, 25–6, 35–8, 50–6, 66–7, 21–4, 27–9.
2 Thomson, *Talbot*, ll. 92, 39–41, 56–61.
3 'The Happy Man' first appeared in *Miscellaneous Poems by several Hands, Publish'd by Mr Ralph* (London 1729), pp. 345–6; I quote ll. 1–7, 19–26.
4 A version of 'Winter' appeared in 1726, followed by versions of 'Summer' (1727) and 'Spring' (1728). A version of 'Autumn' first appeared in 1730 in the first collected edition of *The Seasons;* expanded and much revised versions of the whole poem were published in 1744 and 1746. The quotations in this essay follow the edition of James Sambrook (Oxford 1981).
5 'Autumn', 1. 46.
6 'Spring', ll. 242–304.
7 'Spring', ll. 832–48, 248–301.
8 The phrase is used of *The Seasons* by Ralph Cohen in his invaluable analysis of the poem, *The Unfolding of 'The Seasons', a Study of James Thomson's Poem* (London 1970), *passim*; see below, p. 73.
9 'Summer', ll. 1381–4, 1384–91; 'Spring', 1. 290.
10 'Summer', ll. 1398–1437.
11 'Summer', ll. 1438–45.
12 'Spring', ll. 868–76, 878–80, 900–3.
13 'Spring', ll. 909–26, 928–31, 951, 954–6.
14 George Crabbe, 'Letter I, General Description', *The Borough* (London 1810), p. 7.
15 'Spring', ll. 101–13
16 'Spring', 1. 1161.
17 'Summer', ll. 1604–19.
18 'Summer', ll. 326–8.
19 'Spring', ll. 556–72, 857–60, 883–6; *James Thomson 1700–1748; Letters and Documents*, ed. Lawrence McKillop (Kansas, 1958), p. 26; quoted by Sambrook (ed.), *The Seasons*, p. 336.
20 'Summer', 1. 1595; *Liberty* (London 1736), IV, ll. 1175–6.
21 For a discussion of this problem, see Pocock, *The Machiavellian Moment*, especially ch. xii.
22 *Liberty*, IV, ll. 528–39.

23   'Summer', ll. 1446–66; 'Autumn', ll. 43–133.

24   'Summer', ll. 21–8; 'Autumn', ll. 11–18; 'Winter', ll. 30–9.

25   *A Letter on the Spirit of Patriotism*, written in 1736, was first printed in 1749; I quote from Bolingbroke's *Works* (London 1754), vol. iii, pp. 4, 6. By 1744 the relationship between Bolingbroke and Lyttelton had soured: Lyttelton accepted office under Pelham, whom Bolingbroke did not trust to abandon Walpole's methods for securing parliamentary majorities. The rupture between Bolingbroke and Lyttelton perhaps explains why the former, who, as interpreted by Lyttelton, may have had considerable influence on the content of the later editions of *The Seasons*, is accorded no honourable mention in the poem. For Bolingbroke and patriotism, and for an account of his influence on Lyttelton, see Isaac Kramnick, *Bolingbroke and his Circle* (Cambridge, Mass. 1968), especially chs. 1, 8.

26   'Winter', ll. 656–8, 684–8.

27   See Sir Joshua Reynolds, *Discourses on Art*, ed. R. Wark (New Haven, Conn. 1975), p. 72.

28   'Winter, ll. 950, 964–71, 984–5.

29   Defoe, *The Compleat English Gentleman*, pp. 36–7.

30   'Winter', ll. 952–62.

31   See Pocock, *The Machiavellian Moment*, ch. i, and part 3, *passim*.

32   Cohen, *The Unfolding*, p. 95.

33   'Winter', ll. 583–7, 1046–69.

34   'Summer', ll. 329–30; Thomson, *Talbot*, ll. 27–9.

35   'Winter', ll. 1053–9.

36   Goldsmith, *The Traveller, or, The Prospect of Society*, 2nd edn (London 1765) l. 372.

37   Thomson, *The Castle of Indolence. An Allegorical Poem Written in Imitation of Spenser* (London 1748; hereafter *TCOI*). All quotations from the poem are taken from the second edition, also published in 1748, reprinted in facsimile, with an introduction by George Parfitt, by the Scolar Press, (Menston 1973). This phrase is from Canto I, stanza xxii.

38   *TCOI*, I, ix–xix.

39   *TCOI*, I, lvi.

40   *TCOI*, I, iv; I, ix.

41   *TCOI*, I, x. This stanza should be compared with lines 219–25 of Wordsworth's poem in the stanza of Spenser, 'The Female Vagrant' (*Lyrical Ballads*, 1798), where the speaker also describes a life of pastoral idleness, where 'all belonged to all', also to reject it.

42   *TCOI*, I. x; I, xvi.

43   *TCOI*, I, xxxiv; I, xxxvi–xxxviii; I, xxxiii.

44   *TCOI*, I, lxxi–lxxii.

45   *TCOI*, I, xi–xvii.
46   *TCOI*, I, xiii; I, xiv.
47   *TCOI*, I, xlix; I, li–liv; *The Spectator*, no. 2, 2 March 1711.
48   *TCOI*, II, ix; II, xi–xiv.
49   *TCOI*, II, xxx.
50   *TCOI*, II, xlix; II, l; II, liv.
51   *TCOI*, II, lv; II, lvi.
52   *TCOI*, II, lx; II, lvii.
53   Addison, 'An Essay on the Georgics', in Dryden's *The Works of Virgil* (London 1697).
54   Samuel Johnson, *Prefaces, Biographical and Critical, to the Works of the English Poets*, vol. x (London 1781), p. 7 of 'The Life of Dyer'. For some well-informed discussion of *The Fleece*, see John Chalker, *The English Georgic: A Study in the Development of A Form* (London 1969) and Richard Feingold, *Nature and Society: Later Eighteenth-Century Uses of the Pastoral and Georgic* (Hassocks, Sussex 1978).
55   John Dyer, *The Fleece* (London 1757); all quotations in this essay are taken from the revised version of the poem, in *Poems by John Dyer*, LL B (London 1761); reprinted in facsimile by the Scolar Press (Menston 1971). These lines are from p. 51.
56   *Poems*, pp. 118, 169, 55, 128, 51; for Ferguson, see above, pp. 45–8.
57   *Poems*, pp. 52, 54n., 58.
58   *Poems*, pp. 60–2.
59   *Georgics*, III, ll. 72–88; Tickell, 'A Fragment of a Poem on HUNTING', ll. 69ff., *The Works of Thomas Tickell*, in *Minor Poets* (Dublin 1751), vol. ii; Somervile, *The Chace* (London 1735), I, ll. 238–55; Grainger, *The Sugar–Cane* London (1764), IV, ll. 72–7.
60   *Poems*, p. 69.
61   *Poems*, pp. 79, 80.
62   *Poems*, pp. 59–60.
63   *Poems*, pp. 84–5.
64   *Poems*, p. 128; for Mandeville, see above, p. 20.
65   *Poems*, pp. 91–2.
66   *Poems*, p. 131.
67   *Monthly Review* I, (1757), p. 340; *Poems*, pp. 165–6.
68   *Poems*, pp. 187–8; Pope, *Windsor Forest* (London 1713) ll. 385–6, 400–1, 427–31.
69   John Philips, *Cyder* (London 1708), II, ll. 656–61, 652.
70   *Poems*, pp. 51–2, 82
71   *Poems*, p. 54.
72   *Poems*, p. 138.
73   *Poems*, pp. 112–13.

74   See above, p. 43, and below p. 158.

Chapter 2   The language properly so-called: the authority of common usage

1   *The Castle of Indolence,* Canto II, stanza xxiv.
2   Thomas Sheridan, *British Education* (London 1756), pp. 212–13, 213–14; Sheridan, *A Rhetorical Grammar of the English Language* (Dublin 1781), p. xv; 'A Dissertation of the Causes of the Difficulties, which occur, in learning the English Tongue', in *A Course of Lectures on Elocution* (London 1781 edn), p. 300.
3   *The Letters of John Clare,* ed. J. W. Tibble and Anne Tibble (London 1951), p. 133.
4   Most of the texts referred to in this essay have been reprinted by the Scolar Press (Menston), in a collection of facsimile reprints, R. C. Alston (ed.), *English Linguistics 1500–1800.*
5   See for example James Beattie's appeal to the 'common rule of equity' in his discussion of regional accents, *The Theory of Language* (London 1788); reprinted in facsimile with an introduction by Kenneth Morris (New York 1974), p. 91.
6   James Nelson, *An Essay on the Government of Children* (London 1756), p. 329.
7   *The Spectator,* no. 165, 8 September 1711; Samuel Johnson, *A Dictionary of the English Language* (London 1755; hereafter Johnson, *Dictionary*), p. 10 of 'Preface' (pages unnumbered); Thomas Paine *The Rights of Man* (1791–2), ed. Henry Collins (Harmondsworth 1969), p. 117.
8   See Plato's *Cratylus,* and James H. Stam's discussion of the *Cratylus* in *Inquiries into the Origin of Language: The Fate of a Question* (New York 1976), pp. 83–8; Bacon, *Offer to King James, of a Digest to be made of the Laws of England* (London 1629); William Blackstone, *Commentaries on the Laws of England* (Oxford 1765–9), vol. I, p. 64.
9   Horace, *De arte poetica,* 1. 72.
10   Blackstone, I *Comm.,* 76.
11   John Locke, *Two Treatises of Civil Government* (1689–90), ed. Peter Laslett (Cambridge 1963), II, p. 15; II, pp. 4–14; II, pp. 87–9; II, pp. 199ff.; II, p. 220; 'Preface'.
12   Locke, *An Essay Concerning Human Understanding* (London 1689), Book III, ch. 1, i–ii; ch. 2, i; ch. 2, viii.
13   See James Knowlson, *Universal Language Schemes in England and France, 1600–1800* (Toronto and Buffalo 1975), ch. 3.
14   Locke, *Essay,* III, 2, viii; III, 6, li.
15   Locke, *Essay,* II, 9, viii.

16 Locke, *Civil Government*, II, 87, 119; Blackstone, I *Comm.*, 205.

17 Locke, *Conduct of the Understanding* (London 1706), section 19, in J. W. Adamson (ed.), *The Educational Writings of John Locke* (Cambridge 1922), p. 215.

18 Blackstone, I *Comm.*, 123; James Thomson and David Mallet, *Alfred, A Masque* (London 1740), Act II, Scene V.

19 Sir Edward Coke, quoted by Christopher Hill, *Intellectual Origins of the English Revolution* (Oxford 1965), p. 250.

20 Blackstone, I *Comm.*, 63; Sir John Davies, *Report des Cases* (Dublin 1615), 'Preface Dedicatory', p. 4 (pages unnumbered); William Prynne, *Demophilus, or the Assertor of the People's Liberty* (London 1658), p. 48.

21 Blackstone, I *Comm.*, 17; Hill, 'The Norman yoke', in *Puritanism and Revolution* (London 1958), ch. 3.

22 Hill, 'The Norman yoke', section ii; Blackstone, III *Comm.*, 317.

23 For Bacon, see above, p. 216, note 8; Watts, *The Art of Reading and Writing English* (London 1721), p. xix.

24 Swift, *A Proposal for Correcting, Improving, and Ascertaining the English Tongue* (London 1712), p. 8; Lowth, *A Short Introduction to English Grammar* (London 1761), pp. ii–iii, vi.

25 Swift, *A Proposal*, p. 27; Lowth, *A Short Introduction*, p. 125n.

26 Buchanan, *The British Grammar* (London 1762), p. 73n. and 'Dedication'.

27 Blackstone, I. *Comm.*, 5ff.; Locke, *Thoughts Concerning Education*, section 164 (Adamson edn, pp. 125–6); *The Tatler*, no. 234, 7 October 1710; Anon., *A Grammar of the English Tongue*, 2nd edn (London 1712), p. 6.

28 *A Grammar of the English Tongue*, 2nd edn, 'Preface', p. A3; the point appears to have been first made by John Wallis, *Grammatica Linguae Anglicanae* (Oxford 1653), p. xxv.

29 Maittaire, *The English Grammar: or, an Essay on the Art of Grammar* (London 1712), p. v; *A Grammar of the English Tongue* 2nd edn, 'Preface', p. A3; pp. 4–6 of unnumbered pages in 'Preface'.

30 *A Grammar of the English Tongue*, pp. 5–6.

31 For a brief account of such proposals, see Albert C. Baugh, *A History of the English Language*, 2nd edn revised (London 1959), pp. 317–26.

32 *The Spectator*, no. 135, 4 August 1711.

33 Swift, *A Proposal*, pp. 8, 9, 26–7, 21–2, 17.

34 Swift, *A Proposal*, pp. 30–1.

35 Swift, *A Proposal*, pp. 29, 41; there is a discussion of this issue in Louis A. Landa's introduction to Oldmixon's *Reflections on Dr Swift's Letter* (London 1712), Augustan Reprint Society series 6, i, (Ann Arbor 1948).

36   Oldmixon, *Reflections*, pp. 2, 6–7, 18, 25, 30; *Eikon Basilike* was a volume of supposed meditations by Charles I, published about the date of his execution – 30 January 1649; thereafter, sermons preached on that day were often highly monarchist in content – see Henry Fielding, *The Adventures of Joseph Andrews* (London 1741), Book I, ch. xvii; for Johnson, see below, p. 160. The stereotypical notion, frequently to be met with in eighteenth-century England, of the French language as more regular than the English language, and kept so by order of the Academy, should be compared with Peter Rickard's account of the discussion of usage and idiom in eighteenth-century France, in *The Embarrassments of Irregularity: The French Language in the Eighteenth Century* (Cambridge 1981).

37   *A Grammar of the English Tongue*, 1st edn (London 1711), p. 67; Anon., *Bellum Grammaticale, or the Grammatical Battel Royal* (London 1712), p. 48; Lowth, *A Short Introduction*, p. 7.

38   Blackstone, I *Comm.*, 74; Buchanan, *Linguae Britannicae Vera Pronunciatio* (London 1757), p. 1; Rice, *An Introduction to the Art of Reading* (London 1765), p. 354 (pages wrongly numbered – this page should be p. 254).

39   Buchanan, *British Grammar*, pp. 129, 132; for other, similar examples, see Ian Michael, *English Grammatical Categories and the Tradition to 1800* (Cambridge 1970), ch. 2.

40   Ash, *Grammatical Institutes; an Easy Introduction to Dr Lowth's English Grammar* (London 1763), p. 141; Ash, *The New and Complete Dictionary of the English Language* (London 1775); vol. i, p. 6; Blackstone, I *Comm.*, 76; John Fell, *An Essay towards an English Grammar* (London 1784), p. xii; Blackstone, III *Comm.*, 327.

41   Quoted by Hill, *Intellectual Origins*, p. 250.

42   Quintilian, *Institutio Oratoria*, Book I, c. vi, sections 43–5; Greenwood, *An Essay towards a Practical English Grammar* (London 1711), pp. 36–7.

43   George Campbell, *The Philosophy of Rhetoric* (London 1776), vol. i, pp. 358, 347–8; for Coke, see Hill, *Intellectual Origins*, ch. 3; Blackstone, I *Comm.*, 77.

44   Rice, *An Introduction*, pp. 195, 313; William Kenrick, *A Rhetorical Grammar of the English Language* (London 1784), 'Advertisement'; George Neville Ussher, *The Elements of English Grammar* (Gloucester 1785), p. 1; John Jones, *Practical Phonography* (London 1701), p. 1; *Bellum Grammaticale*, p. 22.

45   Campbell, *Rhetoric*, vol. i, pp. 345, 353–4.

46   Campbell, *Rhetoric*, vol. i, pp. 345–6.

47   Johnson, *The Idler*, no. 70, 18 August 1759; *The Rambler*, no. 99, 26 February 1751.

48   Campbell, *Rhetoric*, vol. i, pp. 348–51; Johnson, *The Rambler*, no. 194, 25 January 1752.
49   Blackstone, I *Comm.*, 63, 74; Abraham Tucker, *Vocal Sounds* (London 1773), p. 3.
50   Johnson, *Dictionary*, 'Preface' (p. 7, pages unnumbered); Campbell, *Rhetoric*, vol. i, p. 359.
51   Robert W. Malcolmson, 'A set of ungovernable people', in John Brewer and John Styles (eds.), *An Ungovernable People: The English and their Law in the Seventeenth and Eighteenth Centuries*, (London 1980), pp. 85, 126, 127.
52   Sheridan, *A Course of Lectures*, pp. 319–20; Campbell, *Rhetoric*, vol. i, pp. 345, 354; Joseph Priestley, *Rudiments of Grammar* (London 1761).
53   Watts, *The Art of Reading and Writing English*, p. 30; R. Brinsley Johnson (ed.), *The Letters of Hannah More*, (London 1925), p. 183.
54   Loughton, *A Practical Grammar of the English Tongue* (London 1734), 'Advertisement'; Collyer, *The General Principles of English Grammar* (Northampton 1735), pp. v–vi; Ash, *Grammatical Institutes* 'Preface'; Burke, *Reflections on the Revolution in France*, 2nd edn (London 1790), pp. 63, 72.
55   *A Grammar of the English Tongue*, 1st edn, 'Preface' (p. 7, pages unnumbered).
56   Murray Cohen, *Sensible Words: Linguistic Practice in England 1640–1785* (Baltimore, Md 1977), ch. 2; Cohen's excellent study is an indispensable guide to much of the material examined in this essay.
57   Buchanan, *The British Grammar*, p. 7.
58   Lowth, *A Short Introduction*, p. xiv.
59   Loughton, *A Practical Grammar*, p. ix; Wiseman, *Complete Grammar*, 1764 – quoted by Cohen, *Sensible Words*, p. 88.
60   Blackstone, IV *Comm.*, 432.
61   Campbell, *Rhetoric*, vol. i, p. 366; Tucker, *Vocal Sounds*, p. 55; Rice, *An Introduction*, p. 51; Buchanan, *The British Grammar*, p. 6n., Campbell, *Rhetoric*, vol. i, p. 379.
62   Blackstone, I *Comm.*, 165; Burke, *Reflections*, p. 64.
63   Johnson, *The Plan of a Dictionary of the English Language* (London 1747), p. 17; *The False Alarm* (1770), in J. P. Hardy (ed.), *The Political Writings of Samuel Johnson* (London 1968), p. 47. All quotations from Johnson's political writings are taken from this volume.
64   Hardy (ed.), *Political Writings*, pp. 51, 92.
65   Hardy, *Political Writings*, p. 112.
66   Blackstone, I *Comm.*, 64.
67   Johnson, *Plan*, p. 33; *Dictionary*, 'Preface' (p. 2:, page numbers in brackets refer to unnumbered pages in the *Dictionary*).

68   Johnson, *Plan*, pp. 25, 19; *Dictionary*, 'Preface' (p. 1).
69   'Advertisement' to *A Dictionary of the English Tongue* . . . *Abstracted from the Folio Edition by the Author, the seventh edition, corrected by the author* (London 1783): *Dictionary*, 'Preface' (p. 2); *Dictionary*, 'Grammar' (p. 6 of 'Grammar').
70   Johnson, *Dictionary*, 'Grammar' (p. 4); *Plan*, p. 10; *Dictionary*, 'Preface' (p. 2).
71   Blackstone, I *Comm.*, 70; and see Burke, *Reflections*, p. 292.
72   Johnson, *Plan*, p. 10; *Dictionary*, 'Preface' (p. 2).
73   Johnson, *Dictionary*, 'Preface' (p. 2); 'Grammar' (p. 1).
74   Johnson, *Plan*, pp. 4, 11, 28–9, 18.
75   William Cowper, 'Table Talk', in *Poems* (London 1782), pp. 17–18.
76   Johnson, *Dictionary*, 'Preface' (p. 7); *Plan*, p. 4.
77   For a discussion of the word list in the *Dictionary*, see W. K. Wimsatt, *Philosophic Words: A Study of Style and Meaning in the . . . 'Dictionary' of Samuel Johnson* (New Haven, Conn. 1948), from which these examples are taken.
78   Johnson, *A Dictionary* . . . *abstracted from the Folio Edition*, 'Grammar' (p. 9 of 'Grammar').
79   Buchanan, *An Essay towards establishing a Standard for an Elegant and Uniform Pronunciation of the English Language* (London 1764), pp. v, vi; *The British Grammar*, pp. 40–1; see also Hugh Jones, *An Accidence to the English Tongue* (London 1724); reprinted (Menston 1967), p. 13, where it is argued that of the five principal dialects of English – the Northern, or Yorkshire; the Southern, or Sussex; the Eastern, or Suffolk; the Western, or Bristol – the fifth is 'the *Proper*, or *London Language*'.
80   Rice, *An Introduction*, p. 195; Johnson, *Dictionary*, 'Grammar' (p. 4).
81   Johnson, *Dictionary*, 'Preface' (p. 8).
82   Johnson, *Dictionary*, 'Preface' (p. 8); *The False Alarm*, in Hardy (ed.), *Political Writings*, p. 55.
83   Johnson, *Dictionary*, 'Preface' (pp. 4, 9–10).
84   Johnson, *Dictionary*, 'Preface' (pp. 9–10); Horace, *De arte poetica*, ll. 60–2.
85   *The Bravery of the English Common Soldiers* was first printed in *The Idler* . . . *the third edition, with Additional Essays* (London 1767), vol. ii, pp. 325–30; Johnson, *Prefaces, Biographical and Critical, to the Works of the English Poets*, vol. iv (London 1779), pp. 11–12 of 'Roscommon'; *Dictionary*, 'Preface' (p. 10).
86   Rice, *An Introduction*, p. 45.
87   Priestley, *A Course of Lectures on the Theory of Language and Universal Grammar* (Warrington 1762), pp. 132–3: Priestley, *Rudiments*, pp. iv, v, 28n.

88 Priestley, *Rudiments*, pp. vi, vii, x; Priestley, *A Course of Lectures*, pp. 136–7.
89 For the teaching of English in Dissenting Academies, see H. McLachlan, *English Education Under the Test Acts* (Manchester 1931), *passim*.
90 Rupert E. Davies, *Methodism* (Harmondsworth 1963), p. 26.
91 Priestley, *Rudiments*, pp. vi, vii, 15n., 20n.
92 Priestley, *Rudiments*, pp. 46, 47–8, vi; Priestley, *A Course of Lectures*, pp. 3–8, 301.
93 Priestley, *A Course of Lectures*, pp. 184–5.
94 Priestley, *A Course of Lectures*, pp. 115–6, 184–5.
95 Campbell, *Rhetoric*, vol. i, pp. 345–66, 374ff.; Blackstone, I *Comm.*, 76ff. For an extended discussion of Campbell's 'canons', see Sterling Leonard, *The Doctrine of Correctness in English Usage* (Madison 1929), ch. ix.
96 Campbell, *A Sermon on the Nature, Extent, and Importance of the Duty of Allegiance*, preached at Aberdeen, 12 December 1776, (Aberdeen 1778); see Stephen's essay on Campbell in *DNB*; see *DNB* also for John Fell; for the Society for Constitutional Information, see Albert Goodwin, *The Friends of Liberty* (London 1979).
97 Sharp, in Fell's *Essay*, p. xii; Campbell, *Rhetoric*, vol. i, pp. 340–1, 344.
98 Fell, *Essay*, p. xi; Campbell, *Rhetoric*, vol. i. p. 387.
99 Campbell, *Rhetoric*, vol. i, p. 366; Blackstone, IV, *Comm.*, 51, and see the introduction to Gareth Jones (ed.), *The Sovereignty of the Law: Selections from Blackstone's Commentaries* (London 1973), pp. xxixn.
100 Fell, *Essay*, 'Advertisement'; *DNB*; McLachlan, *English Education*, p. 180.
101 Fell, *Essay*, pp. x, 61, 114; Johnson, 'Life of Roscommon', p. 12.
102 See Tucker's *The Country Gentleman's Advice to his Son* (London 1761), pp. 26–7; Tucker, *Vocal Sounds*, pp. 114, 116.
103 David Abercrombie, *Studies in Phonetics and Linguistics* (London 1965), p. 68; quoted from Sheridan, 'A Dissertation' (see above, p. 216, note 2), in Spence, *The Grand Repository of the English Language* (Newcastle-upon-Tyne 1775) (p. 4 of 'Preface', pages unnumbered); Spence, *Dhĕ Ĭmpŏrtănt Triăl ŏv Tŏmŭs Spĕns* (London 1808), p. 70.
104 Quoted in Abercrombie, *Studies*, p. 74.
105 Nares, *Elements of Orthoepy* (London 1784), pp. xviii–xix, xx; Cohen, *Sensible Words*, p. 96
106 Nares, *Elements*, pp. iii–v.
107 *A Letter from Mr Burke to a Member of the National Assembly*, 4th edn (London 1791), p. 5; Nares, *Elements*, pp. v, vi, xv, viii–ix.

108   Nares, *Elements,* pp. xxii, v, 268, 270; Burke, *Reflections,* pp. 31, 35, 80, 84, 90.
109   Burke, *Reflections*, p. 292.
110   Paine, *Rights of Man*, p. 219; William Godwin, *The Enquirer* (Dublin 1797), Part II, Essay 12, 'Of English Style'.
111   Blackstone, I *Comm.*, 141.
112   For a full discussion of notions of 'correctness' in the eighteenth century, see Leonard, *The Doctrine of Correctness, passim.*

Chapter 3   A diffused picture, an uniform plan: Roderick Random in the labyrinth of Britain

1   Smollett, *The Adventures of Roderick Random* (London 1748); edited with an introduction by Paul-Gabriel Boucé (Oxford 1979; hereafter *RR*), p. 62. Among critical studies of Smollett, I have found these the most useful: Ronald Paulson, *Satire and the Novel in Eighteenth-Century England* (New Haven, Conn. 1967), ch. v; P. G. Boucé, *The Novels of Tobias Smollett* (London 1976); Damian Grant, *Tobias Smollett: A Study in Style* (Manchester 1977); and John Sekora, *Luxury: The Concept in Western Thought, Eden to Smollett* (Baltimore, Md 1977); and G. S. Rouseau, *Tobias Smollett, Essays of Two Decades* (Edinburgh 1982).
2   *RR*, pp. 78, 176, 291.
3   *RR*, pp. 212, 343, 348.
4   *RR*, pp. 233, 223, 317.
5   *RR*, pp. 325, 332, 147, 267, 273, 22–3, 14, 43, 263.
6   *RR*, pp. 66–7.
7   *RR*, pp. 81, 96, 196, 259–60, 313, 22–3.
8   *RR*, p. 286.
9   James Beattie, *The Theory of Language* (1788); reprinted with an introduction by Kenneth Morris (New York 1974), p. 93; see also Hugh Jones, *An Accidence to the English Tongue* (London 1724); reprinted (Menston 1967), pp. 11–13. Jones makes similar points about the mutual unintelligibility of speakers from different regions of England, 'so would it be a good Diversion to a polite *Londoner* to hear a *Dialogue*'between 'a *Yorkshire* and a *Somersetshire* downright *Countryman'.*
10   The translation appeared several months after the publication of *RR*, also in 1748.
11   *RR*, pp. 10, 11, 22, 323, 5, 47, 116.
12   *RR*, pp. 7, 9, 10, xlvii, 277, 391.
13   *RR*, pp. 50, 8.
14   Changes in pronunciation since the mid eighteenth century have concealed the relation of these nautical terms and the names derived

from them. 'Bowline' would have been pronounced 'bowlin', and 'Bowling', also 'Bowlin'; 'ratline' and 'Rattlin' would similarly have been homophones.

15 *RR*, pp. 15, 9.
16 *RR*, p. 8.
17 *RR*, pp. 43, 327, 325, 268.
18 Smollett, *The Adventures of Ferdinand Count Fathom* (1753); edited with an introduction by Damian Grant (Oxford 1978), pp. 2–3.
19 *Critical Review,* XV (1763), p. 532. This review is attributed to Smollett by P. J. Klukoff, *Notes and Queries* (December 1966), p. 466; see also Klukoff's essay, 'Smollett and the *Critical Review*: criticism of the novel 1756–63', *Studies in Scottish Literature*, vol. iv, no. 2 (1966).
20 *Monthly Review*, IV (1751), p. 356.
21 *RR*, p. xlv.
22 *RR*, pp. 1–2.
23 *RR*, p. 136.
24 *RR*, pp. 15, 20, 22, 86.
25 *RR*, pp. 28, 227, 247, 295.
26 *RR*, pp. 99, 104, 108.
27 *RR*, pp. 206, 224, 256, 401, 431.
28 *RR*, pp. 315, 216, 223, 227.
29 *RR*, pp. 270, 278, 284, 359, 364.
30 *RR*, p. 257.
31 *RR*, pp. 342, 415, 5.
32 *RR*, pp. 27, 264; for the quotation from Johnson, see above, p. 158, and p. 220, note 81.
33 See above, p. 134.
34 *RR*, p. 96.
35 Lord Chesterfield, *Letters to his Son and Others,* Everyman edn (London 1929; hereafter Chesterfield); letter of 26 July 1748. Except where noted, all letters cited are to Philip Stanhope, Chesterfield's illegitimate son, and all dates of letters are old style.
36 Chesterfield, letter to Philip Stanhope (his godson), 31 October NS (1765).
37 Smollett, *The Adventures of Sir Launcelot Greaves* (London 1760–1), chs. ii, xix.
38 Smollett, *Greaves*, chs. vii, ii.
39 Smollett, *The Expedition of Humphry Clinker* (London 1771), Bramble to Dr Lewis, 20 November.
40 *RR*, p. 155.
41 Chesterfield, p. 8; 22 October 1750; 1 November 1750; 12 November 1750.

42   Chesterfield, 4 October 1746; 19 April 1749; 12 October 1748.
43   Chesterfield, 30 April 1752; 5 September 1748; 22 September 1749.
44   Chesterfield, 12 October 1748; 27 September 1749; 30 April 1752.
45   Chesterfield, 9 December 1746; 30 June 1747; 15 January 1748; 16 February 1748; 9 March 1748; 26 July 1748; 5 September 1748; 29 March 1750; 19 November 1750; 3 January 1751; 18 March 1751.
46   Chesterfield, 4 October 1746.
47   Chesterfield, 16 August 1741; 9 December 1749, 28 February 1751, 26 July 1748.
48   Chesterfield, 22 September 1749.
49   *The Rambler*, no. 150, 24 August 1751.
50   Fielding, *The History of Tom Jones* (London 1749), Book XIII, ch. i; Book X, ch. vii; Book I, ch. ii; Book I, ch. x.
51   Fielding, *Tom Jones*, Book XIV, ch. i; Book XIII, ch. i.
52   Fielding, *Tom Jones*, Book IX, ch. i; Book XIII, ch. ix.
53   Fielding, *Tom Jones*, Book XIV, ch. i; Book X, ch. i; Book XIII, ch. i.

Index

The abbreviation 'qu.' refers to
occasions where the attribution
of a quotation is not given in the
text, but will be found in the
notes.